Mutual Life, Limited

Mutual Life, Limited

ISLAMIC BANKING,
ALTERNATIVE CURRENCIES,
LATERAL REASON

Bill Maurer

PRINCETON UNIVERSITY PRESS

PRINCETON AND OXFORD

Library of Congress Cataloging-in-Publication Data
Maurer, Bill, 1968–
Mutual life, limited : Islamic banking, alternative currencies,
lateral reason / Bill Maurer.
p. cm.
Includes bibliographical references and index.

ISBN 0-691-12196-6 (alk. paper) — ISBN 0-691-12197-4 (alk. paper)
1. Banks and banking—Religious aspects—Islam. 2. Banks and banking—
Islamic countries. 3. Finance—Religious aspects—Islam. 4. Finance—
Islamic countries. 5. Money. 6. Currency question. I. Title.

HG3368.A6M378 2005
332.1′0917′67—dc22   2004019757

British Library Cataloging-in-Publication Data is available

This book has been composed in Janson
Printed on acid-free paper. ∞
pup.princeton.edu
Printed in the United States of America
10 9 8 7 6 5 4
ISBN-13: 978-0-691-12197-0 (pbk.)
ISBN-13: 978-0-691-12196-3 (cloth)

For Tom, side by side.

And for S., B., G., and G., in that order.

Fragment of an Ancient Mythologist

"In an island near the Orcades, a child was born whose father was Aeolus, the god of the winds, and his mother a nymph of Caledonia. They tell of him that he learned unaided to count with his fingers; and that from his fourth year he distinguished metals so well, that his mother having given him a ring of tin in exchange for one of gold, he perceived the deceit, and threw it away.

"When he had grown up, his father taught him the secret of enclosing the winds in skins, which he afterwards sold to all the travelers: but as the trade in winds was not very brisk in his country, he left it, and went up and down the world, accompanied by the blind god of chance.

"During his travels he learned that gold glittered in every part of Betica; and he hurried thither at once. He was very badly received by Saturn, who reigned then: but that god having quitted the earth, he judged it wise to go into all the cross-roads and cry continually in a hoarse voice, 'People of Betica, you think yourselves rich, because you have silver and gold! I pity your error. Be ruled by me: leave the land of the base metals; come into the empire of the imagination, and I promise you riches which astonish even you.' He immediately opened a great number of the skins which he had brought with him, and dealt out his merchandise to all who wished it.

"Next morning he returned to the same cross-roads, and cried, 'People of Betica, would you be rich? Imagine that I am very rich, and that you are very rich: get yourselves into the belief every morning that your fortune has been doubled during the night: rise, then, and if you have any creditors, go and pay them with what you have imagined, and tell them to imagine in their turn.'

"A few days after he appeared again, and spoke as follows: 'People of Betica, I perceive that your imagination is weaker than it was a day or two ago; try to bring it up to the strength of mine: I will place before you every morning a bill, which will be the source of wealth for you: you will see only four words, but they will be of the highest significance, as they will settle the portions of your wives, the fortunes of your children, and the number of your domestics. And, as for you'—addressing those of the crowd who were nearest him—'as for you, my dear children (I may call you by that name, since you have received from me a second birth), my bill shall decide as to the magnificence of your equipages, the splendour of your feasts, and the number and pensions of your mistresses.'

"Some days later he came into the street, quite out of breath, and cried out in a violent passion, 'People of Betica, I counseled you to imagine,

but you have not done so: well then, I now command you to imagine.'
With that he left them abruptly; but on second thoughts retraced his
steps. 'I understand that some of you are odious enough to keep your gold
and silver. For the silver, let it go: but the gold . . . the gold . . . Ah! That stirs
my anger! . . . I swear, by my sacred windbags, that if you do not bring it
to me, I will inflict dire punishment upon you.' Then he added, in the
most seductive manner imaginable, 'Do you think it is to keep these
wretched metals that I ask them from you? A proof of my good faith is,
that when you brought me them some days ago, I gave you back at once
one half.'

"Next day, he kept at some distance, and endeavored with soft and flat-
tering voice to worm himself into their favor. 'People of Betica, I learn
that a portion of your wealth is in foreign countries: I beg you to have it
sent to me; it will oblige me very much, and I will never forget your kindness.'

"The son of Aeolus was addressing people who were in no mood to be
amused, yet they could not restrain their laughter; which caused him to
slink away in a shame-faced manner. But, his courage having returned, he
risked another little petition. 'I know that you have precious stones: in
the name of Jupiter, get rid of them; nothing will so impoverish you as
things of that kind; get rid of them, I tell you. Should you be unable to
do so yourselves, I can provide excellent agents. What wealth will pour in
upon you, if you follow my advice! Yes, I promise you the very best my
windbags contain.'

"Then he got up on a platform, and, in a more resolute tone, said, 'People of Betica, I have compared the happy condition in which you now are
with that in which I found you when I first came here; I behold you the
richest people in the world: but, in order to crown your good fortune,
allow me to deprive you of the half of your wealth.' With these words, the
son of Aeolus soared away on rapid wings, and left his audience dumb
with amazement, a result which brought him back next day, when he spoke
as follows: 'I perceived yesterday that my speech displeased you very
much. Very well! suppose that I have said nothing at all as yet. It is quite
true; one half is too much. We must find some other expedient to arrive
at the result which I have proposed. Let us gather all our wealth into one
place; we can do so easily, because it does not occupy much space.' Immediately three-quarters of their wealth had disappeared."

—Montesquieu, 1899. *Persian Letters*. Translated by John Davidson
London: Gibbings and Co. Letter 142.

Contents

List of Illustrations and Tables

Preface

THIS BOOK may at first seem abstract, yet abstraction is that which it most seeks to unseat. It documents on-the-ground, everyday understandings of money among people who are forging their own modes of finance through Islamic banking and non-state-based alternative currencies. But it also queries the documentary impulse that would demand a holistic account of the grounds of the everyday. Contemporary efforts to redefine money and finance bring to the fore the questions of value, substance, and standardization that inform money's creation and acceptability across a range of transactions. Value, substance, and standardization involve a series of abstractions from a supposedly prior, messy reality, and abstraction begs the question of money's adequacy to that reality. The book places problems of abstraction and adequation at the center of modern monetary formations and their alternatives. As it does so, it finds analogous problems in the practice of social thought. It tries to loosen the hold of the problematic of abstraction and adequation on the critical analysis of money and finance, and on social inquiry generally.

I use the term "adequation" in this book with reference to the Latin phrase, *adequatio intellectus et res*, the action of bringing one's concepts in accord with reality, words with things, mind with matter. As Marc Shell (1978, 1982, 1995) has argued, money materializes the problem of adequation. Money has been the source of endless philosophical interest, and has informed Western metaphysical debates about being and knowing. Can a coin, as material substance, ever be adequate to its value in exchange? And where does such value reside—in the metallic substance itself, or in the ideas inscribed on the die and impressed in the metal? Nietzsche's assault on metaphysics remained stamped with metaphysics' *charakter* (the *charakter* is the die used to produce the obverse impression on a coin):[1] "Truths are . . . metaphors worn out and without sensuous power; coins which have lost their impressions and now matter only as metal, no longer as coins" (quoted in Shell 1978:154). And Heidegger, even in his arguments against the notion of truth as the adequation of *intellectus* and *res* and in favor of a notion of truth as "unconcealment" (*aletheia*) still depended on the monetary metaphor and "propositions about coins" that neglect the coin's own status as a proposition (p. 154; see Shell 1982:162–77).[2]

The idea that knowledge of truth comes from the adequation of thought to world has a contorted chain of authority. Kant defined truth as "the agreement of knowledge with its object," adopting St. Thomas Aquinas's conception from the *Summa Theologica* (I, q.16, a.2) and *Quaestiones Disputatae de Veritate* (q.1, a.1). Kant took the object not to be a real, sensuous thing in the world but an object of knowledge.[3] It is unclear where Thomas acquired his conception: either the ninth-century Jewish philosopher Isaac Israeli (ca. 832–ca. 932; Shell 1982:135) or the tenth-century Muslim Ibn Sina (Avicenna) via the latter's reflections on Aristotle.[4]

In *Meaning and Change of Meaning*, Gustav Stern used the term adequation to refer to a specific linguistic process whereby a word shifts in meaning due to a "shift in attention from one characteristic of the referent to another" (Stern 1931:318). His example was the English word *horn*. Originally referring to an animal's horn, the word's primary meaning shifted over time to mean a musical instrument. This occurred, Stern argued, because people's use of animal horns for making music caused the notion of "animal horn" to become "subsidiary" and the notion "musical instrument" to become "predominant" (p. 317). The word thus gradually became adequate to the new reality, a reality transformed by changing social conditions—the use of animal horns as musical instruments.

It would be easy to dismiss the formula *adequatio intellectus et res* as a modern metanarrative, and Stern's theory of meaning change as rooted in a preperformative conception of language. Yet, when it comes to money, scholars across the disciplines are continually surprised to discover that money is "just" meaning, or that finance is fiction. When faced with the question of money's being adequate to anything at all, people often stop in wonder, and the reflection leaves their practical activity at a momentary impasse. If they think about it awhile, they realize that they knew all along that money is backed by "nothing." Still, they are often struck when they encounter new financial forms the backing of which by anything "real" is an open question.

Islamic banking and alternative currency proponents are not so surprised, although they are given to wonderment. Their very endeavor seeks to exploit the gap between representation and reality presumed in the formula of *adequatio intellectus et res* that infuses money and finance. In place of the impasse, they substitute a species of casuistry, a moral practical reason that replicates some of the implicit forms of social inquiry, but that also runs parallel to them. I draw from this some lessons about the value of laterality, of to-one-sideness, for knowledge of financial forms, seeking a language next to my objects that replicates their movements and shape.[5] Loosening the grip of adequation may also help to turn around the implicit assessments of abstraction in many discussions of money. It also has implications for social inquiry generally, a practice that defines itself in relation to the adequacy of its representations, its abstractions, to a reality that supposedly precedes it.

My argument is that anthropology, like Islamic banking and alternative currencies, is a series of experiments—explicit or not—with the social significance and constitution of transactions. Not simply exchanges, which often presume stable subjects and objects and a metric of commensurability, but also substitutions where nothing appears to move; accelerations, which seem to speed things up even as they may in fact slow to a halt; or asymptotic approaches toward some ideal truth; passages through and across rather than removals, expellings, or alienations.[6] The book demonstrates how parties to transactions who cast their activity as "other" to dominant capitalist forms are, like anthropologists, fellow travelers along the routes of social abstraction and analysis. Anthropology lies alongside the worlds of those I studied, not adjudicating theory and practice but transacting the parallel knowledges, the paralanguages (languages lying to one side, as opposed to metalanguages hovering above), the dense lateralizations that obtain between the subjects and objects of my inquiry, and their lateralizations, their interconnections with each other, and with "me," "anthropology," and "critique." This is an ethnographic discovery, not only a theoretical point.

Acknowledgments

MANY PEOPLE and institutions have contributed to the development of this project, lying alongside it and me as we have forged each other over the years. Hugh Raffles and Stefan Helmreich saw the shape of the project before I did, and the book is the better for their careful eyes and critical pens. I owe a very special debt to Annelise Riles, Hirokazu Miyazaki, Tony Crook, Adam Reed, and Iris Jean-Klein, who read the manuscript in its entirety and offered generous feedback at a crucial stage and intellectual inspiration throughout. Saba Mahmood and Charles Hirschkind had faith in the project from the beginning and provided checks on my sometimes undisciplined exuberance toward the end. Jane Fishburne Collier and George Allen Collier have offered steadfast support and continue to exemplify the intellectual collegiality and personal comraderie that make the anthropological life worth living.

I have been exceedingly fortunate to be a member of the Department of Anthropology at the University of California at Irvine during a time of great intellectual ferment. I will single out Karen Leonard for particular thanks first. At the start of my interest in Islamic banking, Karen began e-mailing me odds and ends and surreptitiously placing items in my mailbox—newspaper clippings marked with highlighter pen, advertisements, stray bits of data, off-color jokes. That material formed the basis of an archive, and Karen's support forms the backbone of this book. Susan Greenhalgh, Kaushik Sunder Rajan, and Mei Zhan read parts of the book and offered cunning commentary; they will likely recognize their handiwork here. Victoria Bernal, Mike Burton, Teresa Caldeira, Frank Cancian, Leo Chavez, Jim Ferguson, Inderpal Grewal, Cecelia Lynch, and Liisa Malkki contributed to the project with a citation here, a conference there, and general scholarly collegiality all around. I thank Susan Coutin and Barbara Yngvesson for letting me participate in their co-taught course on theory and law and for conversations as the book took form. Several graduate students assisted in the development of this project: Alexandru Balasescu, Megan Crowley-Matoka, Thomas J. Douglas, Tina Gehrig, Kyriaki Papageorgiou, and David McKee through research assistance, and Maurizio Albahari, Caroline Melly, and Neha Vora through a reading of the entire manuscript. A competition with Kimberley Coles (which I lost) spurred on the writing; and Amy Levine and Jason Ettlinger at Cornell get mention for not having mentioned anything at all (to my relief!).

Two other institutions provided homes during the writing of parts of this book—the Research School of Pacific and Asian Studies and the Center for

Women's Studies at the Australian National University, and the Department of Anthropology at Duke University. At the former, I thank especially Katherine Gibson, Margaret Jolly, Rosanne Kennedy, Nelly Lahoud, Gregory Rawlings, and Kathyrn Robinson. At the latter, I thank especially Katherine Ewing, Diane Nelson, and Robyn Wiegman. I also thank audiences at Cornell, New York University (especially Julia Elyachar and Timothy Mitchell), Yale, Duke, the University of North Carolina at Chapel Hill (especially Don Nonini and Judith Farquhar), UCLA, UC Irvine, UC Berkeley, UC Santa Cruz, UC Davis (especially Suzana Sawyer), the University of Kentucky (especially Susan Roberts), and the American Studies Institute at Dartmouth (especially Don Pease). I am also grateful for conversations with John Borneman, John Bowen, Mariane Ferme, Julie Graham, Carol Greenhouse, Susan Hirsch, Roger Lee, George Marcus, Gregory Starrett, Marilyn Strathern, Katherine Verdery, Caitlin Zaloom and to others, too numerous to mention, who have given time to this effort since I began this project. No one mentioned here should be blamed for this book's shortcomings, which are my responsibility alone.

The research was supported by a grant from the National Science Foundation, Law and Social Sciences Program (SES-9818258) and partially by a grant from the Russell Sage Foundation. The University of California at Irvine provided leave time and other support, as did the University of California Humanities Research Institute. I also thank Mary Murrell at Princeton University Press, and two reviewers (Nigel Thrift, and one who preferred anonymity) for clear and helpful commentary that helped me bring this book to completion. Hanne Winarsky, Jennifer Nippins, and Linny Schenck at Princeton University Press answered a constant stream of questions during the final stages. I would also like to express my thanks to Cindy Crumrine for her copyediting skills, and J. Naomi Linzer for preparing the index.

I would like to thank Danielle Mann and the Wadsworth Atheneum for permission to reproduce the painting, *Time Is Money*, on the cover of the paperback edition of this book. The artist, Ferdinand Danton, Jr. (ca. 1877–ca. 1939), was an art forger who traveled under a number of assumed names and specialized in trompe l'oeil paintings of money. Of this piece, Bruce W. Chambers writes, "The wide frame is 'made of' the same rough wood as the painting, even to the point of continuing the cracks that separate the planks. While the frame, which projects forward from the picture plane, casts a real shadow, Danton has painted a recessed square in the frame's lower right corner with its own illusionistic shadows. Both the painting and the frame are punctured with nail holes: some are real holes in the wood, while others are trompe l'oeil illusions. Some of the real holes have painted splinters" (Chambers 1988:82). Danton's work and his biography, both "symphon[ies] of contrasts between reality and illusion" (p. 82), appropriately highlight the process of abstraction, adequation, and reference that are the concern of this book and the money-forms it describes.

People in Ithaca, New York, and in the global circuits of Islamic banking and finance unselfishly gave me their time and their insights. I thank especially Lisa Maurer, Maureen Kelly, Melissa Pollack, and Patrice Jennings in Ithaca; the staff of Yayasan Gaya Celebes in Makassar; and Yahia Abdul-Rahman in California. My hope is that even where they disagree with my characterization of their alternative financial and monetary activities, those who have allowed me to share in their conversations and activities will at least see something recognizable enough to allow the debates we have begun to continue. For debate is the essence of the thing.

My greatest debt is to Tom Boellstorff, who has provided constant support and encouragement as well as complaints (generally necessary if not always appreciated) and criticism (always well deserved). He introduced me to Indonesia, and much, much more, and he has patiently if bemusedly sat beside me during my attempts to speak and write as if languages could ever be adequate to anything. I dedicate this book to him . . . and his dastardly accomplices.

A Note on Transliteration

"ARABIC" TERMS are transliterated according to the most common practices of those Islamic bankers whose primary language of dissemination and argument is English. As diacritical marks are rarely used in their forums, they are omitted here. Indeed, the terms should not necessarily be thought of as Arabic, but as supplements to the emerging global English of Islamic banking and finance. Sometimes, of course, the terms are Indonesian, too. Even the English ones.

Lateral Reasons for a Post-reflexive Anthropology

ON JULY 11, 1998, before I had imagined this book, at a time when the research that would comprise it was only beginning to take form, I found myself walking in on a screening of the Frank Capra film, *It's a Wonderful Life*.[1] Prodded by a colleague, I arrived, slightly late, at a conference about Islamic banking. I do not remember what I expected, but I certainly did not expect what I saw.

The founder of a southern California Islamic investment firm was standing next to a television in front of an audience of about three hundred in a large darkened conference room. On the screen, George Bailey, played by Jimmy Stewart, had just hung up the telephone on Henry F. Potter, the richest man in the county. Potter had gained control of the bus lines and the department stores, and had just taken over the local bank. His sights have been set on the Bailey Building and Loan Association for some time. After all, he explained earlier in the film, what is a Building and Loan good for when all it does is lend to people without collateral at low interest rates? "What does that get us? A discontented, lazy rabble instead of a thrifty working class." Sensing opportunity after bailing out the bank, he is eager to take over the Building and Loan, buy up the town's real estate, and sell it back to the good people of Bedford Falls at a profit. At Potter's instigation, the bank has called in the Building and Loan's debt. George's Uncle Billy, without thinking, has handed over all the cash, "every cent of it." And the people of Bedford Falls have rushed to the Building and Loan, passbooks in hand, desperate to get their money and worried that their savings have been wiped out.

George Bailey lingers before a photograph of his father, the founder of the Building and Loan, hung above a plaque with the motto, "All That You Can Take with You Is That Which You Have Given Away." He leaves his office and addresses the nervous people, who are pressed against the tellers' counter. "Now, just remember that this thing isn't as black as it appears." Sirens blare outside, and the people turn away from George for a moment to look out the window, then turn back to him. He explains that Potter has guaranteed the bank's deposits and that the bank will reopen in a week. "But George, I got my money *here*," one replies. "Did he guarantee *this* place?" another demands. George explains that, no, Potter is not guaranteeing the Building and Loan. One of the townspeople, Charlie, says he wants to cash out his shares, and take his money now. George replies, "No, but you . . . you . . . you're thinking of this place all wrong. As if I had the money back in a safe. The money's not here, why, your money's in Joe's house, that's right next to yours, and in the Kennedy house, and Mrs. Macklin's house and in a hundred others. You're lending them the money to build and then they're gonna pay it back to you as best they can. Now what are you gonna do, foreclose on them?" Charlie insists on getting his money now. Reluctantly, George has him sign some papers and says he'll get it back in sixty days, per their agreement for the original share purchase. Just then, another man runs in and tells the crowd that Potter is offering fifty cents on the dollar, cash, for shares of the Building and Loan, redeemable immediately. "Better to get half than nothing!" someone shouts. A commotion ensues as people clamor for the exit.

George leaps over the counter and puts himself between the people and the door. "I beg of you not to do this thing. If Potter gets hold of this Building and Loan there'll never be another decent house built in this town. . . . Now, we can get through this thing all right. We've got to stick together, though. We've got to have faith in each other." The people respond, "I've got doctor's bills to pay"; "Can't feed my kids on faith!" Just then Mary, George's newlywed bride, shouts from behind the counter, "I've got two thousand dollars!" and holds up a wad of bills. It is the money for their honeymoon. George joins her behind the counter and says, "This'll tide us over until the bank reopens." He proceeds to disburse money, the payments based on people's stated needs ("Could I have seventeen-fifty?" one woman meekly asks) and guaranteed only by George's faith in them.

Six seconds to six o'clock and George has two dollars left. He, Mary, his Uncle Billy, and Cousins Tilly and Eustace count down the seconds and then lock the doors. They have managed to stay in business for one more day. They place the two remaining dollars in a tray, and George offers a toast: "To mama dollar and to papa dollar, and if you want this old Building and Loan to stay in business you better have a family real quick." "I wish they were rabbits," says Cousin Tilly. Holding the tray aloft, they skip and sing, back into the safe.

At this point in the film, the host of the Islamic banking conference paused the videotape player. He pointed to the screen, the images of Jimmy Stewart and company frozen in the middle of their conga-line dance through the office, and said, "This is the first *lariba* movie." There was a murmur in the crowd, a few giggles, some whispering. *Lariba*, Arabic for "no increase," is a term that has been popularized in Islamic banking to refer to the industry's attempts to avoid interest. "You've probably seen it at Christmas," he continued. People laughed at the irony of the statement, myself included. At the time, I did not notice another irony: the juxtaposition of Cousin Tilly's wish for rabbit-like fecundity of the inert bills in the tray, and the proclamation that the film exhibited a *lariba* sensibility. Much later in my study, however, I would be led to a provisional and contested understanding that the form of increase (*riba*) prohibited in Islamic banking is not always identical to animal-like fecundity, and that the moral discourse on *riba* is not simply the same as the Aristotelian objection to the reproduction of nonliving things recoded as a prohibition of "interest." At least, that was the case for some. As I would also find, the form of the argument about *riba* itself anticipated all the positions one could take on the question of such fecundity. The effect was to feel stranded, without unequivocal closure.

The host explained further that trust in others and faith in the community is the foundation of Islamic banking, and he echoed the words of George's father on the plaque in the Building and Loan office by repeating his own firm's slogan, "The Best of People Are the Most Useful to Others."[2] "This is what made America," he continued, the screenimage still frozen on the television monitor as he spoke, "and these are the values that have been lost in America, and we're trying to bring them back to America. Our children will be the foundation of Islamic banking in the United States."

The rest of the evening was devoted to formal talks and presentations. One in particular stuck with me. The notable Pakistani economist Khurshid Ahmed mentioned William Greider's (1997) book, *One World, Ready or Not*. He then outlined his own view of global financialization:

> Now, instead of money being used for production of physical assets, we have created a monetary world where we are creating claims on claims on claims of assets; options; the financial world has no physical reality. It benefits the rich. In the last few years, how many billionaires have been created? The concentration of wealth and power is taking place. The twentieth century, while a century of growth, prosperity, affluence, is also a century in which the United States has emerged as a world power. In the twenty-first century, we will have to re-discover the role of money for the creation of physical assets—even Mr. Soros sees this now.[3] Prosperity must go together with equity, toward a redistribution of wealth and income, and a rediscovery of the productive process. Islamic banking can make a singular contribution to this twenty-first century. (Khurshid Ahmed, American Finance House-Lariba, 5th Annual International Achievement Award Symposium in Islamic Banking, Pasadena, Calif., July 11, 1998)

The events of that evening captured my imagination, from Jimmy Stewart to Depression-era community savings organizations, the critique of the imaginary character of modern money and even the invocation of Greider. I began to form ideas for a research proposal that would explore contemporary alternatives to modern money and finance. This proposal imagined comparisons between offshore finance, which I had previously studied in the Caribbean (e.g., Maurer 1995, 1997, 2000), Islamic banking, and the alternative currency movement. I was interested in efforts to remake money in the image of community. I knew of the Ithaca, New York, alternative currency experiment because my sister lived there and because an old high school friend now worked for a credit union in town that accepted deposits in Ithaca HOURS, the local currency. I was beginning to read about Islamic banking's efforts to create financial forms and institutions that avoided interest, efforts that sometimes included proposals to remake the money-form itself, since contemporary state-based currencies are bound up with government debt. And I had already been surprised in my Caribbean work by the way financial globalization there often fostered new understandings of identity and community. The research would eventually take me from California to London, Ithaca, St. Lucia in the Caribbean, and Makassar, formerly Ujung Panjang, on the island of Sulawesi, Indonesia. It would also result in my becoming credentialized in Islamic banking, and being invited to speak at an Islamic banking conference by the man who had first introduced me to Jimmy Stewart.

In my research proposal, I was concerned with "comparisons" among Islamic banking, alternative currencies, and offshore finance (bracketed, for the most part, for the purposes of this book). How did participants in alternative financial systems imagine the boundaries of community? How were these boundaries morally charged? What kinds of exclusions did they create? My work in the British Virgin Islands had shown how offshore finance depended upon and sustained deep divisions between citizens and the children of immigrants, divisions that got naturalized and racialized, even as it created new forms of community for British Virgin Islanders. While broadly sympathetic to the alternative financial communities I set out to study, I wanted to remain attentive to the way finance set some people apart as it brought others together. Still, the main thrust of the proposal was an emancipatory one (not least because I was applying for funding from agencies concerned with law and rights): attending to alternative forms of money might provide survival strategies for everyone in the era of financial globalization.

One might be tempted to say that a lot has happened in the domain of money since I began this research. Those happenings include: the Asian and Argentine financial crises; the collapse of Long Term Capital Management; the dissolution and reformation of the major international accountancy firms in the wake of scandal; the Euro; the Enron affair; the introduction of not one, but two new designs for U.S. dollars; the debacle of the U.S. presidential election of 2000; the bursting of the stock market bubble; unprecedented low interest rates and the ballooning of the real estate bubble; the events of September 11, 2001; the wars on Afghanistan and Iraq;

Total Information Awareness. Some of these events impacted the research and writing of this project, although not in ways I might have predicted had I known they were coming. I do not want to engage in any speculative retrospection, however, because these events are all part of the world I am writing within and not sidetracks away from some clearly defined path that I, and others, set out on beginning July 11, 1998.

Of greater concern to me than the effect of these events on this project is the implicit analytical framework that presumes guaranteed trajectories impacted by "external" events. That implicit framework reveals itself in the empirics of any research endeavor and the analyses built "after" them. The charter of field research and the empirical data warranting social analysis became an object of this study almost from the start, as the possibilities of empirical observation and the referencing of an external world through language were made problematic by the money-forms I was trying to study. They were not especially unique or peculiar in this regard. After all, modern money has been the archetype of the problem of the adequation of sign to referent, word to world, *intellectus et res*: how can a piece of paper truly stand for abstract value? Other moneys similarly staged the problem of the adequation of value and object, back as far as the minting of the first coins whose value was "politically authorized" rather than based on their weights or purities (Shell 1982:1). The problem of adequation and reference is also central to analytical abstraction, which generates intellectual interest, and the empirical project, which makes of "raw data" conceptual tender.

In the inductive method of social inquiry, for example, first comes data, then comes analysis. The data preexist and are not contingent on the analysis. Analysis provides the measure of data and the means of its circulation in a community of minds. While it should be second nature since Max Weber to recognize the implication of the questions asked in the facts found, the naively empirical impulse specifying much of what passes for social research remains troublingly central to contemporary inquiry, not least because any inquiry named "social" automatically invests in that moniker a reality, however circumscribed, that is supposedly external to the inquiry itself, despite all protestations to the contrary (slogans like, "What distinguishes the social from the natural sciences is that in the former the researcher is part of the reality researched"). No matter how implicated we are in the worlds we analyze, no matter what the objective limits of objectivism or the complicity between ourselves and our subjects, the empirical impulse absorbs the reflexive one by means of a perspectivalism that is additive to, not transformative of, the empirical project.[4] We add new views to the subject, or listen to other voices; in this modality of reflection, reflexivity thus facilitates the discovery of more and more data. It does not fundamentally refigure the practices delineating the interior and exterior of inquiry—the observer and the observed, the sensorium and the sensed—

Cultural studies of finance hark back to the writings of George Simmel (1907), who postulated that money in capitalist society can provide both a bedrock for social relationships and an acid eroding all vestiges of community. As Turner summarizes, "[B]y making interpersonal relations more abstract, money . . . undermine[d] the traditional world in which power was manifest in terms of overt interpersonal dependency" (1986:99). Simmel's vision was of a world that had undergone a shift from *gemeinschaft* to *gesellschaft*, from communities based on face-to-face relationships, mechanical solidarity, and interpersonal trust to a society based on organic solidarity, the division of labor, and the impersonal relationships of monetary transactions. In such a world, Simmel proposed, social cohesion would be possible only if money, the cornerstone of social relationships in capitalist society, were fixed, stable, rational, and objective. Simmel proposed a dialectical relationship between money and social stability: only in "stable" societies where interpersonal trust was valued and enforced by law would money acquire stability; money's stability would then work like a cement to maintain social stability, and solidify the rule of law over the rule of "men."

Building on Simmel, Susan Strange (1986) has taken the end of Bretton Woods and the rise of floating and uncertain exchange rates as causal for the end of social and economic stability, giving rise to what she terms, following Keynes, "casino capitalism" (Keynes 1935). Like Strange, other contemporary commentators on the end of Bretton Woods and the apparent disorganization of international finance have argued that along with these changes has come a breakdown of "trust," a decline in interpersonal interaction in a financial sphere dominated by new information technologies and computer software that the *New York Times* calls, in its own gee-whizzy spin on Keynes's metaphor, "Nintendo capitalism" (Hershey 1996; see Harvey 1989).

not even by "participation," which also presumes a subsequent extraction of the researcher from the researched and a retreat to the study, and denies the contorted chronometric of memory and the mutual spatiotemporal intrusions of field and study (Strathern 1999).

The text above comes from the grant proposal that inaugurated my inquiry into alternative financial forms. The proposal centered on the possibilities afforded by alternative finance for a new "ground" to contemporary money, and was written in dialogue with the political economy of the post–Bretton Woods era (e.g., Helleiner 1994; Strange 1986). At the time, I viewed these alternatives as effects of or responses to the end of fixed exchange rates, and the apparently novel hyperreality of contemporary monetary instruments. There was an explicit temporal and developmental trajectory, too: from money made by fixed rates ($f1$) and a stable society (s) to money made by floating rates ($f2$) and a nervous condition, a nonsociety ($\not{s}$). The social stood for order. Casino capitalism eroded trust and brought disorder. The people I had decided to "study," "my informants," would be people who tried to settle that nervousness by regrounding money in an x:

faith, community, jurisdiction. My work proceeded from the causal assumptions that $f1$ generated s and $f2$ eroded it into s, the temporal assumption that $f2$ followed $f1$, and that therefore s followed s. (Whether s could be located just before Simmel's time or during the Bretton Woods regime was left as ambiguous as it was in the work of international political economy scholars.) The first question the research would answer was whether alternative financial forms effected a reverse transformation, from $s \rightarrow s$, via a third form of money (call it $f3$) at least locally or in some circumscribed sense for the participants, if only in their fantasies. And the second was whether the xs people used to reground money ($f3$) in the social would create new inequalities or instabilities, or in fact would "work," and create a new social world (call it u, for utopia) that exceeded the first with its emancipatory potential. One or the other. The research endeavor would proceed, thus: First, solve for x; then, see if x makes a u; finally, measure the liberatory potential of u: does it make more or fewer people more or less "free?"

If, after all, anthropology is not a quest for an accurate description of a social reality, but a "scale model of all the mistakes to be made in figuring [it] out," and if those mistakes are already anticipated by the social reality "under" investigation (Wagner 2001:xiii), the temporal and causal assumptions in the grant proposal would be made to run backward from the answers they presuppose. Another way of putting this is to say that the proposal would be made to wait for some missing term to complete it in a contingent future.[5] Anthropology would then be a practice of lateral reading and writing, neither descriptive nor explanatory but repetitive, multiplicative, and/or accelerative.[6] Not only do the assumptions already run in both directions in Simmel, of course (nervous moneys make nervous societies and nervous societies make nervous moneys); this very operation was already perceived by people in the social worlds I chose to study (some of whom, it turns out, chose to study anthropology in advance of our encounter). The grant proposal started from Simmel's theories of money and community; Islamic bankers and local currency proponents started from some very Simmel-sounding theories of money and community, too. Study and field intruded into each other when, in interview situations, I was repeatedly presented with reading lists to work through "before" the "real" interview would take place. My assignments included Marcel Mauss, William Greider, Lewis Solomon, Margrit Kennedy, Janet Fitchen, and Simmel himself, among others. They are all to be found in the bibliography of this book. The bibliography could be said to be an expanded interview transcript, "raw data."

My anthropological training also became a resource for many of the people I talked to. I had expertise in "primitive" or "natural" economies; I knew about "gift exchange"; I understood "barter." In Indonesia, my knowledge of Islamic banking in the United States was taken as knowledge of Islamic banking in the abstract, although Indonesia was often the presumed universal standard for everything else in these conversations (as one interlocutor asked me, "What's the English word for *fleksibel*?" and another, "Do they have horses in America?"). My knowledge was useful, too, as it provided points of comparison with contemporary practices as well as, possibly, new techniques or new ideas to try out in other contexts. At the same time, however, people often imagined those contexts as in the past, a past to which they wanted to effect a return. This would be a return to a world before the modern separation of fact and value, economy and society. For some, living in the world of Islamic banking and alternative currency was *already* life in a world "before." In proposing and living in a world before the modern settlement (Latour 1999) that has separated off domains like nature and culture, religion and economy, even as hybrids of these domains continually proliferate, they also objectified this prior world as such, denying its intercalation with the present world. They did so even as they made new hybrids that folded past and present together in the projects they were attempting to live now: the Islamic economy, and the natural barter economy. And they did so even as they waited for an uncertain future to provide whatever might be necessary to complete their project and make it truly universal.

For example, people I met thought they were living in a natural barter economy, and at the same time objectified it as an "economy," if only when they contrasted it to a commodity economy. Yet actively living the barter economy—"before" it could even be conceptualized as "an economy" or as "barter"—should lie in the way of or prevent any idea or enactment of a commodity economy or, indeed, an economy as such. One could "invest in" or "believe in" barter, as one could in Islamic banking. "I believe pretty strongly in barter," a woman in Ithaca told me, "because barter relationships historically have been direct." Another Ithacan mused, "That connection between the economy and community, yeah, we were early [on] saying that, anthropologically, you cannot separate the two." The sundering of economic value and human values is supposed to be overcome in direct, unmediated barter exchange; yet the negation of the separation between value and values underwrites the very separation it aims to unsettle, and the aim itself obviates the actual life within whatever commodity economies imagine true barter to be.

Now, one critical response might be simply to state that people who think they are living in a natural barter economy today are participating in an identity project, one legible in only capitalist imaginaries, and little else. Less charitably, one might dismiss them as naïve. Yet taken as a knowledge project, their intellectual move is reminiscent of the operations of an anthropology that tried to enframe other ways of being only after the fact of having specified the division between worlds that can produce anthropologies of other worlds, and those other worlds, which by definition cannot produce anthropologies. The aim of producing a "total" description of another cultural world obviates actual life within whatever the world that spawned anthropology imagines those other worlds to be. The Ithaca HOUR, the local alternative currency in Ithaca, New York, is supposed to facilitate barter by providing a means of exchange tied to labor time. It "helps people with something to trade find each other," I was told. Yet its very form—as paper money—interrupts that aim. A resident of Ithaca who had gradually stopped using HOURS explained that the currency experiment should have been like "disappearing task forces," which "come together, are formulated and . . . then they just disband when they've served their purpose." If you were really living in "barter," your mode of being would be the end in itself, and would exist in relation only to itself rather than some external good.

There was a temporal incongruity, a present living in a past-contingent tense, a past that did not "happen" not least because it was, for some, "still" present but also and at/in the same time it was a potential not realized in "the" past. Islamic banking emanated from scriptural sources and medieval contractual forms that were not necessarily realized or revealed in the past in the manner in which they had been "recuperated" in the present. Alternative currencies engage Marcel Mauss or Paul Bohannan more than they do the Trobrianders or the Tiv, or, rather, the Trobrianders and the Tiv whose precontact ontologies are legible only after their anthropological textualization (that is, only after "contact" and its subsequent erasure). From some people, these past contingencies provoked charges of fakeness or insincerity against those who would attempt to live them: they represented an inauthentic Islam, they approached counterfeiting, they were self-serving not community-serving, or they produced false societies with an unclarity at their core. Indeed, in Indonesia, an expression used to describe Islamic banking was *tidak jelas*, not clear.

The grant proposal assumed that the financialized world economy and its alters were separate and separable entities; it presumed the same of the researcher and the social. Yet, as discussed in chapter 1, Islamic banking, alternative currencies, and "the economy" are densely intertwined. Which was the precondition for the others? The end of Bretton Woods and the oil price rises that flooded the world with petrodollars, for example, co-occurred with a new quest for purity on the part of wealthy Middle Eastern Muslims seeking a means to clear consciences, give alms, and spiritually renew themselves. Muslims suddenly with lots of spare cash. To the extent that petrodollars and Islamic finance sustained one another, the global financialization that has preoccupied political economists in many disciplines can be said to have been Islamic from the start. Meanwhile, floating exchange and floating interest contain within themselves fixed exchange and no interest: the float can remain constant, and the rate can fall to zero. Indeed, in the course of my research, the latter occurred, at the point where the interest rate crossed the inflation rate and the United States's economy became interest-free, for some interbank lending, at least. Whether or not it was thus *lariba* became a matter of intense debate, a debate that hinged on whether *riba* is equivalent to "interest," and whether this kind of equivalence as an operation of abstraction is even permissible in Islamic banking. To the extent that Islamic finance is constituted by these kinds of debates, what has been called the financialization of the world economy after the end of Bretton Woods is thus always-already "Islamic banking and finance."

And Islamic banking and Ithaca HOURS were also always in advance the internal ground of comparison for each other, but not always and not without contention, remainder, or confusion. Midway through the research I became fascinated with small gold coins circulating in in the city of Makassar on the island of Sulawesi in Indonesia. These coins occupy chapter 5. Tracing their origins, as a good anthropologist would, I found them to sit at the intersection of an ongoing conversation among a set of Islamic bankers interested in creating a global Islamic alternative currency, who had visited Ithaca, New York, to sit at the feet of the master architect of Ithaca HOURS in order to learn how to make a money. The World Gold Council, an international trade organization, got wind of their efforts and copied them, marketing gold coins to people in majority Muslim countries as a means of "interest-free" saving for the purposes of making the pilgrimage to Mecca. In Indonesia, the coins were distributed by the state-run national pawnshop. And, at the time of my research, counterfeits were beginning to circulate, as well.

Islamic banking and Ithaca HOURS became necessary to one another in my own efforts to restage what I saw them doing. They do not "represent" each other or "shed light" on each other so much as they draw on each other—but only sometimes, contingently and laterally. They metastasize into one another, but that metastasis is not essential to either of them, nor is it causal. For each overlaps and interconnects with other things, too. People in the worlds this book attempts to restage are sometimes racked with doubt about their endeavors in the domain of money and finance, but not always. The two "cases" do not automatically suggest each other, either. At every step my effort to "compare" got interrupted by the form of that which I was "comparing." For example, the obvious comparisons with which I started held that one of the cases was explicitly religious and Islamic, one secular or perhaps implicitly religious and Christian; one was global, one extremely local; one is very serious and important, the other is basically a joke. But as those gold coins made explicit, at every move my efforts to describe or to explain the worlds I was participating in felt false.

Where the comparison was concerned, which was serious and which the joke? Which religious and which secular? The comparative coordinate system folded back into itself. The descriptions unraveled as their words slipped away from any referents and instead revealed the tropes of Islamic banking, alternative currencies, and my inquiry as open and unsteady. This is a familiar enough experience in anthropology and has to do with the work of translation. But it was all the more troubling because the operations of Islamic banking, alternative currencies, and my analysis leaned heavily on even as they cut across the formula of *adequatio intellectus et res*, the bringing-into-relation of words and things and the problem of referentiality that has supposedly structured the money-form, the work of translation, and the analytical enterprise itself. If "the concepts we have settle for us the form of the experience we have of the world," as Peter Winch (1958:15) famously wrote, here was a profoundly *unsettling* set of cases.

ISNAD: OR, ANALYTICAL MESHES

From Clifford Geertz's reading of Wittgenstein, anthropology learned to look for publicly enacted meanings and their uses rather than remain bound to certain cognitivist fallacies concerning the nature of mind and symbol. As Geertz wrote, "culture consists of socially established structures of meaning in terms of which people do such things as signal conspiracies and join them or perceive insults and answer them" (1973:12–13). The task of anthropology is to help "find our feet" when the understanding of such structures of meaning fails, and to "formulate the basis on which one imagines ... one has found them" (p.13). Fieldwork in this mode of inquiry "existed inside another form of life" and metaphors of boundary crossing or culture brokering dominated the disciplinary endeavor (Marcus 1999:97), as did the literary and epistemological device of "thick description," which conjured a relation between anthropological inquiry and a "real" ground and texture of social life captured by anthropologists' use of anecdotes, rendered "raw" data, "a note in a bottle" (Geertz 1973:9).

Criticisms of Geertz focused mainly on the question of totality or wholeness performed by those textual devices, yet often have been framed in terms of getting down to a more "real" ground of social life—to conflicts, for example, that put into question shared, public meanings (a move that is ironic given Geertz's own emphasis on conflict)—or to something called "political economy." After the disciplinary critiques of the 1980s, many anthropologists, tired of the demands of textual reflexivity for anthropological practice, have either absorbed the critique by proffering move "voices," or negated the critique by getting "back to business," collecting empirical facts and documenting daily realities, eschewing the "wholes" of systems of meanings embodied in symbols perhaps but proffering ever more promissory bottle-bound notes. The reflexive turn tended to query the "I" but not the "there" in the old textual formulas establishing the ethnographer's presence in the field. Even the critique of the spatial formations of anthropological knowledge left relatively untouched the empirical ground of the discipline, the kinds of data that would be brought to bear on its reformulated questions (Gupta and Ferguson 1997).

Lingering over the contorted temporalities of alternative money and finance, and the hybrid forms that instituted them, led me to question the empiricist impulses of my initial inquiry. For an anthropology only recently recovered from the self-criticisms of the 1980s, the impulse to get back to the empirical is strong indeed. Recognizing the practical difficulty of delineating "cultures" has not obviated the attempt to listen in on "other voices in other rooms" (Geertz 2000:247). Difference is still the stock in trade of the discipline, and difference is still locked into the local and the empirically accessible. The traditional view of difference—of "alternative" currencies, for example—posits a sort of numerical multiplicity in the objective world. For example: There are many "different" currencies. The anthropological record is full of money-forms (brass rods, shells, stones, letters of credit). Yet "alternative" in this sense is difference of one *kind*: infinite multiplicity of the same: many cultures, many moneys, but still "culture" and "money." Many voices, many views, no closure implied by their anthropological entextualization—but still "voices," and "views." The perspective is quantitative and enumerative (bourgeois, even). Data exist in the world to be counted, classified and sorted, and every factum is a datum; yet they are still "facts" and "data."[7]

Another view of difference—which unsettles even the difference between "views" specified in this manner, not to mention the very distinction between difference and sameness—places it not within the realm of the empirical but that of the potential. Here, difference has a temporal character; it "appears in pure duration" as an "internal multiplicity of succession, of fusion, or organization, of heterogeneity, of qualitative discrimination, or of *difference in kind*: it is a *virtual and continuous* multiplicity that cannot be reduced to numbers" (Deleuze 1988:38, original emphases). Gilles Deleuze borrowed Henri Bergson's examples from the experience of consciousness, where "a complex multiplicity such as a feeling may contain a number of elements imperfectly perceived, but once these elements are distinctly perceived by consciousness, the feeling inevitably changes its nature as a result" (Patton 2000:36). Multiplicity or difference arises from "changes in nature at each moment of the division, without any one of these moments entering into the composition of the other" (Deleuze and Guattari 1987:483). What Deleuze calls "virtual" realities are thus "actualized by being differentiated" (Deleuze 1988:97). Virtual reality is to be distinguished from possible reality, the latter always taking the form of the real while the former's actualization puts into question that prefiguration as it continually multiplies. This would be alternative not in the sense of numerical multiplicity, then, but alternative in another sense of the word's Latin root, *alternāre*, oscillating in time, like alternating current in an electric wire.

Alternāre changes the charge of the anthropological form of difference as incommensurability or irreducibility; it stops its circulation as coin of the anthropological realm only to accelerate it, such that difference/sameness circulates all over, but not as one would predict in advance without those missing terms from the future that may arrive, or may not. This is not difference and repetition, then, but difference and substitution, where substitution trucks in homologies, samenesses whose difference the act of substitution re-stages. This book, then, is an effort to create a form that will elicit debates homologous to those that accelerate/alternate in the worlds it "de-scribes," it unwrites. It connects the electric wire to you, the reader. It runs those currencies through you, only to demonstrate that you were always-already laterally connected. This meanwhile opens up the circuit itself. Thus, the electicism of this text is not of a piece with 1990s experiments in ethnographic writing: the point is not just juxtaposition for the sake of unsettling the narrative flow, but that *as well as* an unsettling of the very familiarity of that device. My eclecticism in this text—from the pattern of citation to the use of inset text boxes and the like—parallels that of those whom I "studied" but also is intertwined with their use of similar textual devices and patterns of citing authority. The point here is the achievement of a homology of form, and, at the same time, a ramping up of the kinds of textual achievements of my interlocutors. It is not strictly parallel or homologous, then, but also densely laterally enmeshed and accelerated, speeded up, so that the enmeshments encountered in the field can be replicated and heightened in the space-time of a reading of this book.

Bergson's engagement with questions of the possible was directed toward placing intuition alongside (and probably above) speculative inquiry. "*Objects* and *facts* have been carved out of reality. Philosophy must get back to reality itself," he wrote (1911: 239, original emphasis). Yet philosophy had sought to reintegrate those objects and facts, arranging experience for the "facility of action and of language" (p. 240) rather than of true experience itself. That arrangement permitted philosophy to reserve for itself the privileged position of the arbitrator of means of accessing truth and at the same time the privileged position of recognizing its own fragility. "If metaphysic is only a construction, there are several systems of metaphysic equally plausible, which consequently refute each other, and the last word must remain with a *critical* philosophy, which holds all knowledge to be relative and the ultimate nature of things to be inaccessible to the mind"

(p. 24, original emphasis). Anthropology, of course, has held the position of just such a critical philosophy for some time, as critiques of anthropological relativism have made clear. I am interested in a double move: First, what would it mean for anthropology to become intuitive in Bergson's sense, or to truck in the differences of Deleuze's virtual realities?[8] Then, what would it mean for anthropology to *question* the familiarity with and stabilizing effect of presently unfamiliar notions like becoming, intuition, and the virtual that might result from such trade?

This book proposes answers by means of its own performance. It has diverse affinities, each of which continually undercuts the others. One key affinity is with the seductions of Actor Network Theory and the work of figures like Bruno Latour and Michel Callon, who provide a freedom to trace networks that contingently concatenate subjects, objects, natures, cultures, words and worlds. The analytical difficulty of such entanglements, however, is that they can take on verbs, and once they do, they can become subjects. They can then be specified in grant proposals and identified in the world as empirical facts, possibilities that prefigure a real that is given in advance. Latour's realism is problematic for the same reason that it is so useful: refusing the separation of ontology from epistemology opens up the innumerable black boxes that warrant "reality," but it does so in terms of that refusal's own agnosticism. When entanglement, networks, and the like are employed to name a phenomenon in the world, they assume an externality to the nominator and reinstitute knowledge as empirical and instrumental, aiming at something—a more complete picture—for a community of knowers. This picture includes as agentive the natural, the non-human, and the material rather than taking them as that which "the work of social construction works upon" (Mitchell 2002:2); but by expanding the field of reference and action to infinite horizons it has the potential to augur the untangled human observer and the now infinitely vaster field of empirical data ready to be explored.[9] In this respect, any inquiry that would employ Actor Network Theory as a theory would do well to heed Latour's own admonition that the data are not given, but rather achieved (Latour 1999:42). In other words, the point is not to identify entanglements and name them when you see them, but to obviate that very move as the analysis proceeds and to remain very much *within* that procession. Tentatively, then, I am supplementing Wittgenstein's aphorism, "not empiricism yet realism" (1983:325) thus: "not empiricism, not realism yet virtualism."

For Latour, reference is not a problem of the adequation of word and thing, because human and nonhuman practices link form and matter in an infinite series of transformations and recursions. The "gap" between language and the world is reconfigured by the circulations of momentarily stabilized words and things, mediations that generate other words and things, naming and becoming new, effective, realities. Thus, for Latour,

"There is truth and there is reality, but there is neither correspondence nor *adequatio*. To attest to and guarantee what we say, there is a much more reliable movement—indirect, crosswise, crablike—through successive layers of transformations" (Latour 1999:64), redistributing words and things along a reversible chain "transport[ing] truth:" "*The word 'reference' designates the quality of the chain in its entirety,* and no longer *adequatio rei et intellectus.* Truth-value *circulates* here like electricity through a wire, so long as this circuit is not interrupted" (Latour 1999:69, original emphasis).[10]

The chain of reference extends infinitely in either direction and presumably wraps around again (to eat its own tail?) in order for the circuit to be complete. Latour's electric current metaphor is of course richly evocative, not least because ancient coins derived their value wholly from the *electrum* of which they were made, and not from any inscriptions the coins carried: *adequatio* was not the issue there, either, until the Lydians, according to Herodotus, simultaneously instituted coinage backed by political authority and the tyranny that accompanied it (Shell 1978:12).

It is, rather, the circuit that is the problem. The chain's infinite expanses seem to close in on themselves, less "indirect, crosswise, crablike" than other spatiotemporal or faunal formations, like the radiality of, say, starfish or sand dollars. The last are particularly important, for their pentamerous homological form is belied by their radical underdetermination: unlike their echinodermatic brethren, their five sections are not perfectly homologous but are often irregular[11]—radiality without any center, pentamery without any universal cover of law (Cartwright 1999:6).[12] Crabs move crosswise, while echinoderms' movements challenge even linearity's others.

Circulating reference's reference to circulation allows the abstraction and stabilization of circulation itself as a new social problematic. Latour's goal is a realism that is perhaps too real for comfort, and can become of a piece with new social imaginaries of circulation that recapitulate old teleologies and dialectics. "Economics owes its present appeal," we are told, "partly to the sense that it, as a discipline, has grasped that it is dynamics of circulation that are driving globalization" (Lee and LiPuma 2002:191). And social analysis had better catch up. "[C]irculation is a cultural process with its own forms of abstraction, evaluation, and constraint, which are created by the interactions between specific types of circulating forms and the interpretive communities built around them" (p. 192). This is a setup: the form of the argument leads to the quest for comparisons (with "non-capitalist circulations" for example, or the sorts of "alternatives" explored in this book) and the specification of those forms of abstraction, evaluation, and constraint. This is useful as far as it goes, but it reinstitutes narratives of transition (from production-centered to circulation-centered . . .) and leaves unquestioned the most tantalizing aspect of its unconscious desire: finding a representation *adequate to* a reality for *another* interpretive community—the intellectual or analytical one. If, as Nigel Thrift has argued, "there is no intellectual community which can be separated off from other communities, in which the intellectual community has the power to decode the world, whilst all the other communities just slope ignorantly about" (Thrift 1996:22), these interpretive communities must include the analysts and their objects, intercalated, networked together, who are circulating reference and circulated by it, each performing the others in a dance of multitudes where *adequatio* is not the only step in town.

This book attempts to take "the enmeshed condition as the starting point" (Sykes 2003:163). It takes seriously "the complexity of what we name in order to escape complexity" (Thrift 1996:16). In addition to Actor Network Theory, this book thus has affinities with Nigel Thrift's "nonrepresentationalist style" of inquiry. By "style," Thrift stresses he is not trying to build a new overarching theory that will provide the critical metalanguage adequate to the world. Rather, he is after "a means of *valuing* and *working with* everyday practical *activities* as they occur" (Thrift 2000:216, original emphasis). This is a style "after words," in both senses: subsequent to the failed quest for that metalanguage, and at the point where language fails because its formula of adequation has no longer got the monopoly in the market for truth.

Webb Keane has asked, "Have we even now escaped the ontological division of the world into 'spirit' and 'matter'" (Keane 2003a:409)? The difficulty of escape has to do with the very imperative. Why escape at all? My strategy in this book is to follow the movements of Ithaca HOURS and Islamic banking, which sometimes attempt the escape into another realm of signification and value without a universal cover of law, yet other times are fundamentally bound up with the logic of value brought about by the operations of adequation and abstraction to and from a "material" reality. They alternate between one and the other, never settling on a stable resting point, never fully closing off the conversation, the circulation, or the analysis, and certainly never resolving into a new synthesis. For Islamic banking, this motion without endpoint itself can constitute virtue: the point is not to mirror the divine or try to come up with a practice adequate to it, but rather to continually engage in the work of doing and being and becoming, work that itself is virtuous practice. Judgment comes not from where you are in the end, but from what you're doing along the way. Trying is good enough.[13]

The problem is the pull of modes of inquiry that rightly eschew but then take the form of description, which, under the sign of the operations of *adequatio*, already prefigures explanation and explanadum—the facts in the world and the description after it. I am after something else (I follow in time something else, too, as that which I am after has already preceded me in the field's encounter with the study and the study's encounter with the field):[14] neither description as such, nor explanation as such, but dense lateralizations with objects and subjects that are already densely lateralized with each other and with the thing I call me and my work. By taking the space of this text to enact these lateralizations in the time of your reading, I am not intending to claim that a new analytical category—the lateral—is adequate to a new or recently discovered lateralized reality. The point is rather an extension and acceleration of the lateralizations and their durative potentialities, enacted in the mutual yet limited engagement between the writing and the reading.[15]

So, for example, from time to time I lean on a series of anthropological and other interlocutors in order to build an argument. Figures like Bruno Latour, Roy Wagner, Marilyn Strathern, Gilles Deleuze, Marc Shell, John Locke, and C. S. Peirce constitute a series of chains of narration underlying the claims of my current venture, my *isnad* (pl. *asanid*), an Islamic banker might say: the chain of authority warranting my text back to some imagined ultimate source. At the same time, I am wary of the fact that the multiple and sometimes intertwining *asanid* are not always mutually reinforcing. They sometimes cavort promiscuously with one another; the results are sometimes barren, sometimes fertile, sometimes to one side of the logic of the relation warranting kinship, knowledge and chains of proof. The Arabic word *isnad* has other metaphorical possibilities: a mesh, a network; leaning, dependence; and trust. Never really secure in the knowledge that a story from the life of the Prophet is "authentic," practitioners must rely on the science of judgment to weigh *asanid* while trusting the safety net subtending the activity itself.

LATERAL ASSEMBLAGES FOR A POST-REFLEXIVE ANTHROPOLOGY

This book is not after descriptive adequacy or a new "theory" of signs and their relation to or constitution of worlds. Rather, it restages others' attempts to make words adequate to worlds as they also conduct other activities very much to one side of those efforts in the meantime. The effect is an oscillation (*alternāre*) between adequation and other modes of praxis. This book tries to replicate and accelerate that oscillation.[16] It does not seek to "describe cultures" so much as to place the effort to so do in the same frame as that which takes for granted cultural difference and the knowledge apparatuses that it warrants.

Marilyn Strathern's rereading of Maurice Leenhardt's ethnography, *Do Kamo* (1979) is suggestive in this regard. Leenhardt addressed his reader directly:

To understand what I am writing here, it is necessary to visualize the Melanesian social landscape [Il faut, pour comprendre ce que j'écris ici, avoir sous les yeux

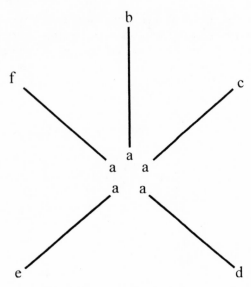

Figure 1. "The personage located by means of his relationships" (After Leenhardt 1979, fig. 12, p. 154)

le paysage social mélanésien; Leenhardt 1947:249]. A young man is never encountered alone but always in a united group of 'brothers' maintaining the same relationships as a unit with other groups. Even in their amorous adventures, they dread being alone. . . . In fact, all adopt the same personage in these groups; they *are* the same personage. If we look at nouns designating individuals in present-day languages, we find collective terms. *Pamara*, the uterine nephew, is in fact a plural. (Leenhardt 1979:154, emphasis added)

Leenhardt here introduced a diagram (figure 1).

He wrote, then, inserting his own perceptual apparatus into the text, that "it is apparent that we can put several *a*'s on our sketch and call them replicas of the body of one personage. . . . And I see that *a* does not correspond to a unique human body but to *all* the bodies of brothers and sisters in the same social positions. . . . Their social reality is not *in* their body but in this empty place where they have their names and which corresponds to a relationship" (p.154, emphasis added).

Taking Leenhardt seriously and truly attempting to see with him the "social landscape," one could multiply the *a*'s and the web of lines, except that doing so would suggest that each letter represents one individual human body, which is not what there is to be seen. Each *a* is a replica of the body of one personage, and at the same time a group of similar people. The *a* thus cannot be captured by the logic of empirical observability and specification. It could never properly be "*sous les yeux.*" It is a virtual object, its duration and becoming are what generate interest, and what cannot be seen or represented on the page. It is interesting that Leenhardt introduces this discussion by addressing the reader in the same temporal frame as his writing, in the present continuous tense, stressing the act of his writing in a present time with the reader, and replicating the durative sense of Melanesian becomings in his very book. As Strathern writes, his only "mistake" (her word) had to do with that "empty place," his only error "was to conceive of a center at all" (Strathern 1988:269). Refusing the structure of error, I would simply add that his language lies alongside others, where mistakes can be made and where the very idea of a mistake can be obviated by multiple and polyvalent emergences.

One could see these Melanesian worlds as analogous to the lateralizations I am proposing here: radiality without a center, and so forth. The analogic, however, sets up its own series of relations and divisions to worlds "out there" and presumes the ends it supposedly seeks to find. If "relations are not the object of a representation, but the means of an activity" (Deleuze 1991:120), the practical unfolding of the activity takes precedence over the specification and stabilization of relations. Not empiricism, not realism, yet virtualism. The effort of this book is not, however, to resist analytical moves that would draw analogies or identify homologies, but rather to allow such moves to lie alongside others without any synthetic or absorptive metatheoretical rubric to bring them under one sign of law. As with Deleuze, the effort is to displace the dialectic modality of reason or adequation, which is difficult because "breaking with" dialectics is at the same time a "central tenet" of the dialectic (Butler 1987:184). Difference and repetition in the Deleuzean sense replaces "hypotactic subsumptions" with "paratactic conjunctions" (Boundas 1991:8), or, the relation of opposition and dialectical tension and synthesis with the unspecified and open-ended "relation" of mere conjunction—the "and," the principle of seriation that neither supposes nor denies relations of opposition, causality, analogy, homology, resemblance, or any other among its terms, "making possible convergence and compossibility as well as . . . divergence and resonance" (p. 184). For Deleuze, this *is* empiricism, of the sort Bergson sought through intuitionism, but I am not willing to stake a claim for it as any more or less accessible to the senses or more or less reflective of a real reality than other forms of empiricism. Revising Wittgenstein's formula further, then: from "not empiricism yet realism," to "not empiricism, not realism, yet virtualism," I would add, "empiricism . . . realism . . . virtualism . . .," the ellipses standing in for the paratactic conjunction of practical activity. The question is not of the relationalities subtending such an activity, but of lying alongside and proceeding in time with formations with which such activity is impossibly linked. Hence the title of this book, Mutual Life, Limited. It is the mutual yet limited nature of living together, alongside, humans and sand dollars and things and words and living and nonliving objects and everything in between—like money—that this book sets out to perform.

"To understand what I am writing here . . .," Leenhardt began. Perhaps his only problem, his generative nonerror, was his verb tense, present continuous and thus really in the world, not past contingent continuous and thus virtually there. Going through the motions, we just might discover what anthropology would have been becoming all along.

The Point Is to Exchange It

Chapter 1 enacts the difficulties in attempting to specify the subjects of Islamic banking and alternative currencies, and documents my ethnographic voyages through various means of doing so.[17] One strategy would be to argue that there are many "Islamic bankings" and "alternative currencies," and that my work is concerned with only a particular slice or certain species. That move, however, denies the universal reach these phenomena sometimes claim for themselves, and it also freezes in time the unfolding of these experiments in a way that closes off their own analytical potential. Scholars of Islamic banking and alternative currencies who differentiate themselves from participants will no doubt be frustrated and annoyed with this chapter, as it continually undercuts explanations of the "origins" of these phenomena and wanders widely over their topographically complex terrain rather than cutting one path. Participants in Islamic banking and alternative currencies may be frustrated by my undisciplined lateralizations and the interrelationships I sketch. Yet they will probably be familiar with the picture that emerges, even if in their own work they continually attempt to purify or prune the branches of the bush that currently comprises their movements. The chapter concludes with a reflection on the possibility of alternative economies.

Chapter 2 turns to matters of law and belief, documenting the case law warranting Ithaca HOURS and describing, after a fashion, the jurisprudential practices of Islamic economics and Islamic banking. It does so in order to address the charge that alternative currencies and Islamic banking are "fake," somehow not really real, a joke, an ideological smoke screen, or whatnot. These charges pivot around the question of meaning: do Ithaca HOURS and Islamic banking really mean anything at all? Writing against utilitarian approaches to meaning, I argue that the continual emergence of such questions obviates the definition of truth as adequation of reference to reality and thereby sits in the way of conventional descriptive and analytical trajectories. This obviation allows other work to trundle along, in the meantime.

Chapter 3 is concerned with the temporalities of Ithaca HOURS and Islamic banking, and the promise of a perfect market that each offers. It looks at the logics of economic maximization proffered in some circles and queries the possibility of alternative values "under" capitalism. It also traces people's use of figures like Mauss to imagine alternative exchange, and, by placing Melville's short story, "Bartleby, the Scrivener," alongside some Indonesian texts, queries the impossible temporalities of the gift: past contingents, and future conditionals on which current practices depend.

Chapter 4 places Islamic mutual fund purification techniques alongside farmers' market transactions in Ithaca HOURS in order to open up the quantification procedures going on in each, and to point toward the relationship between abstraction, commodification, and number that these currencies restage. It attempts to suspend the logic of adequation and quantification by introducing that of substitution and another kind of numerology, one that rotates around substitutable units rather than the algebraic operation of setting sums to zero in order to "solve for x." Accepting money to pose the problem of abstraction, the chapter argues, is a roadblock to inquiry that nonetheless is necessary for other work to take place—the work of exchange itself.

Chapter 5 and chapter 6 are more firmly located in Indonesia than the others, and I worry that they will be read as documenting "instantiations" or "examples" of what has been written in the earlier chapters. It should be borne in mind that the dense entanglements that occupy their pages could instead be viewed as the "theory" that demanded the "data" provided in the preceding chapters. Chapter 5 traces the small gold coins used as a means of saving for the pilgrimage to Mecca, and chapter 6 looks at the open-ended yet stable constructs of Islamic insurance and cooperative societies.

The conclusion returns to the work of adequation and abstraction, and restages it via some of C. S. Peirce's and John Locke's writings on precious metals, language, and ethics. It revisits the monetary information of thought that has occupied writers like Marc Shell (1978, 1982, 1995) and attempts another cut through that information by opening up its moral character. The conclusion remains open-ended, however, a series of unanswered questions whose form sometimes escapes the materiality of the page, not least because the monetary sign trumps the matter/spirit division itself.

THE WORK OF THIS BOOK is thus not to find a new Archimedean point for critical analysis, nor to present a new logic of the social, but rather to query the conditions under which the social becomes legible. This book is also not after a theory of value either, for the mutual entanglements of value and values obviate such a quest. Indeed, the very search for a theory of value is a symptom of the supposed sundering of value and values. This sundering is exactly what, post-reflexively, Islamic banking and alternative currencies and this book challenge.[18]

Post-reflexively, because the work here is not toward a reflexive anthropology in the sense of letting others' voices tell their tales and being attentive to the authority of my own in structuring this book. In fact, I am perfectly content with my authorial power; I only wish I had more of it, as I watch my own analysis and my ownership of it disappearing into the text or undermined by my own reportage of events "from the field." What I am after is a mode of ethnography that undermines its empiric. I would be tempted to call this a nonempirical modality of ethnographic inquiry: for the stuff in the field presses on the study and often inhabits it, as when people "in the field" tell me to go to the library; and the stuff in the field challenges the sensorium's privilege by pointing up the networked complexity of fact and value, observation and analysis, and so forth. I resist the urge to name the modality of inquiry, however, because of some futures I can imagine were I to give it any name.

Indeed, I worry lest I be taken as too metatheoretical, as presenting no new data, nothing important, and having no politics, besides. I have already gestured toward some of the things that have happened since I began this project. I am writing in a world in which oil companies are awarded lucrative contracts after a war in Iraq over weapons that simply did not exist, and where these oil companies are domiciled in the same offshore financial centers as other entities labeled "terrorist," and have had—and may still have—dense yet opaque interconnections with those very entities. Yet that information seems not to generate interest, not least because it can never be "verified." When the empirics fail, other modes of reflection might become important. But there is no way of knowing in advance. As Elizabeth Grosz writes,

> life and duration, and thus history and politics, are never either a matter of unfolding an already worked out blueprint, or the gradual accretion of qualities which progress stage by stage or piecemeal over time. Duration proceeds not through the accumulation of information and the growing acquisition of knowledge, but through division, bifurcation, dissociation—by difference, through sudden and unpredictable change, which overtakes us with its surprise. (Grosz 2000:230)

"You're lending them the money to build, and they're gonna pay it back to you as best they can. . . . We've got to have faith in each other," George Bailey said. Alternative currencies and Islamic banking always face the charge: will they "work," will they effect "change," or, even, are they really

real or just fake? Do they have a use? The demand for an instrumentaliza-
tion of knowledge is levied against us all in terms of knowable futures and
clear emplottments.[19] This book rejects such a demand, in favor of allowing
knowledges to lie alongside each other in their entanglements and durative
becomings, as they continually divide, recombine, and exchange, in the
meantime.[20] Mutual life, open-ended yet limited.

CHAPTER 1

In the Matter of Islamic Banking
and Local Currencies

ONE OF THE MOST DIFFICULT aspects of this book's project is specifying its subject of study. First, the material is hopelessly intertwined with "other" material; the work of delineation and separation is confounded by the material's own work of networking, hybridization, and interconnection. Second, the very idea of the materiality of data, of those notes in bottles of which Geertz wrote, is undercut by the analytical work of the material itself: currency forms that put into question the relationship of adequation between word and thing presupposed by modern moneys and philosophies. People's creation, discussion and use of these currency forms are continually interrupted by their querying of the forms' veracity, reality, and sometimes very existence. Thus it was that I was repeatedly told that Ithaca HOURS are a "game," that they are "novelty items or souvenirs," and that Islamic banking is "just word-play." The activity of Islamic banking or local currencies is backed by "nothing," people said, or, is really just state money or conventional banking in disguise, and, so, "nothing" out of the ordinary. In making these statements, participants preempted analysts. "This is all very interesting but really rather banal," a sociologist told me.

My response: "Yes, indeed." The sociologist's statement, after all, was directly related to my third quandary in specie-fying this material—that is, rendering my data into specie, legal tender for the currency of contemporary social theory. Participants in these alternative money projects often resolved the first two problems, for the time being, by focusing on the technical aspects of their effort. They would reduce Islamic banking to a set of contractual forms and the capacities and efficacies they enlisted and enabled. They would reduce Ithaca HOURS to the mathematical operations of currency, time, and labor conversions. Time and again people familiar with my research have asked me questions like "But what *is* Islamic banking, *really*? What *are* local currencies? How do they *work*? What do they *do*?" and my answers repeated the technical specifications of participants themselves. My doing so affirmed their banality; the technical details are fun to get caught up in, to a point, but once you see how the apparatus works it ceases to be interesting because the problem with which you began is solved. As in a mystery novel, once the murderer is known, the mystery dissolves into the banalities of jealousy, betrayal, or greed. Focusing on the technical also left aside the real import of these questions and the explicit ontologies—the genera and species of money or finance—that they sought as answers.

The problem of specifying the material is interwoven with the analytical problem of how to represent these alternatives, both "within" and "outside" their worlds. Local currency proponents, at least since the 1980s, have debated the use of the terms "local," "alternative," "community," or "complementary" to describe their moneys, the adjectives often marking subtle ideological differences, regional variations, and the political-economic intention of the currency. Those who prefer "alternative," for example, tend to view their activities in terms of creating a wholly new "economy" that is separate from national economies. Those who prefer "complementary" imagine the money they are creating as supplementing the use of the national currency, especially for those people who rely on their activities in an informal economy to meet their needs.[1] Those who prefer "local" sometimes imagine a world of localities, each circulating wealth internally while occasionally reaching beyond them to form loose, interconnected networks. These preferences do not name hard and fast rules, of course, and often the same person will tack back and forth between them or use different names to describe them.

For Islamic banking, names are a central preoccupation. Although most in the business use Arabic terms for the various contractual forms they employ, some see these terms as obfuscation, or worry that they provide an Islamic veneer over practices whose status in *shari'a*, or Islamic law, is uncertain. At worst, some maintain, the use of such terms is merely a marketing ploy. For the most part, the lingua franca of Islamic finance is English; Arabic terms supplement it, and most if not all of those supplementary terms are nouns naming contracts or concepts. The field has settled on the terms, "Islamic banking" or "Islamic finance" or most often "Islamic banking and finance," sometimes abbreviated IBF, to name itself. But there are vocal and influential individuals within the field who insist that the term *lariba* better captures what it is that makes its activities unique—the avoidance of *riba*—and better exposes the field to the widest possible potential audience. "Islamic" may have negative connotations, for one thing, and furthermore one does not have to be Muslim to appreciate or participate in *lariba* banking. Along similar lines, especially after September 11, 2001, some began using the expression "faith-based" to describe their activities, a term popularized by President George W. Bush's "faith-based initiatives" to direct federal funds to religious social service institutions.

Naming becomes vexed as well when issues of permissibility seem to hinge on very finely tuned definitions. It sometimes marks the boundaries between different factions within the field. Said one Islamic banking professional:

There's two faces [or] aspects of Islamic banking, one which was doing it for the rich and affluent, the people from the Gulf countries that came to invest in big real estate projects and so on. . . . They spent all this money trying to change the word "interest" to the word "profit" or whatever. . . . I called it Mickey Mouse Islamic banking. And then [there is] the work that *we* are doing, which is the grassroots work, which calls things by their names.

The invocation of correct names tracks Qur'anic verses that relate how God taught the angels and Adam the names of all things and then made each perform before the others so that they might each know the truth of each other, as well as of God's infinite knowledge. Upon seeing Adam's demonstration of his knowledge of the names of things, all the angels except Satan then bowed down before him as God's vice-regent on earth (2:30–34). The paradox of calling things by their names is that we can never with our names capture all the qualities of the essence of the thing. The "Islamic" in the Islamic banking that is not Mickey Mouse Islamic banking, as the product of human activity, must be translated anew each time. On the other hand, Islamic bankers and their clients sometimes use the term "I-banking," capturing the newness and the nicheness of the field, rendering Islam a sort of placeholder for the practical activity bundled under the name. Here, the "I" could never bring under itself all the qualities of the object, and is thus always already hopelessly inadequate—or both adequate and inadequate, oscillating back and forth in the time of the discussion and the exchange.

The issue of naming also preoccupies those who take the time to "study" alternative currencies or Islamic banking as if from a position outside. This includes people like me, who believe they have no link with such phenomena apart from their research interest, an interest even the language of *lariba* does not escape, and the vast numbers of people who believe they are generally "inside" these phenomena and who author books and articles about them. There is a tendency to want to specify these phenomena in terms of other projects or movements, an impulse to categorize or classify. This extends, of course, to the incorporation of Ithaca HOURS and Islamic banking under the rubric of "alternative currencies" or "alternative economies," found not just in the book before you but in texts written "within" these socialities, such as Richard Douthwaite's (1996) *Short Circuit: Strengthening Local Economies for Security in an Unstable World* and Margrit Kennedy's (1995) *Interest and Inflation Free Money*—both of which were recommended to me on separate occasions by one of the founders of the Ithaca HOURS system as well as one of the founders of an American Islamic investment company. It is these entanglements between the inside and the outside of these alternatives, entanglements that obviate the very notion of the alternative, that trouble the matter of Islamic banking, local currencies, and their analysis. This chapter takes up Islamic banking and

Ithaca HOURS in turn, sketching out the symmetries and divergencies between these two alternatives as well as providing a basic road map of the territories each attempts to traverse. The concluding section takes up the question of the alternative itself, and asks whether the analytical impulse to name "alternative" economies, and alternative "economies," can be sustained in light of the networks the chapter replicates.[2]

ENTANGLED ORIGINS OF ISLAMIC BANKING

> *Question*: Are we allowed to claim tax deductions on our Zakat contributions?
>
> *Answer*: Surely, you must report all your Zakat contributions as your charitable contributions and take all legal exemptions and deductions. Any money that may come back to you from the federal or state taxes, you should apply that to your next year's income and pay the Zakat on it next year. There is great reward in giving money for Zakat, but there is no blessing in giving extra money to IRS.[3]

The Qur'an invokes *riba*, literally "increase," often translated as usury or interest, twenty times. Five verses in particular stand out:

Those that live on usury [*riba*] shall rise up before God like men whom Satan has demented by his touch; for they claim that trading is no different from usury. But God has permitted trading and made usury unlawful. He that has received an admonition from his Lord and minded his ways may keep his previous gains; God will be his judge. Those that turn back shall be the inmates of the Fire, wherein they shall abide for ever. (2:275)

God has laid His curse on usury and blessed almsgiving with increase. God bears no love for the impious and the sinful. (2:276)

Believers, have fear of God and waive what is still due to you from usury, if your faith be true, or war shall be declared against you by God and his apostle. (2:278)

Believers, do not live on usury, doubling your wealth many times over. Have fear of God, that you may prosper. (3:130)

That which you seek to increase by usury will not be blessed by God; but the alms you give for His sake shall be repaid to you many times over. (30:39)

The last is particularly intriguing, for it brings together *riba* and alms, *zakat* (also, literally, "increase") like two sides of a ledger that cancel each other out. It was also one of the earliest verses to have been revealed to Muhammad (Saeed 1999:20).

As I am using it here, and as those in the field use the phrase, Islamic banking and finance (IBF) refers to a worldwide phenomenon taking place in Malaysia, Indonesia, the United States, the United Kingdom, the Arabian peninsula, the Indian subcontinent, and, to a lesser extent, west and east Africa, and not simply the financial systems of those nation-states that have officially at one time or another "Islamized" their economies, such as the Sudan, Brunei, Iran, and Pakistan. The broadest definition of IBF would include all those activities understood to be financial or economic that seek to avoid *riba*—itself a term of considerable definitional anxiety— generally through profit-and-loss sharing, leasing, or other forms of equity- or asset-based financing. Global Islamic banking today owes much to the immigration of Middle Eastern and South Asian students and professionals to the United States and United Kingdom during the 1970s and 1980s, and the consolidation of large U.S. Muslim organizations such as the Islamic Society of North America and the Islamic Circle of North America. The oil boom in the Middle East during the 1970s, which sparked renewed interest in Islamic banking in many Muslim-majority countries (see, e.g., Warde 2000:92–93; Wilson 1990), also encouraged the development of a loosely knit interconnected international network of Muslim members of the business community, who, working for oil and chemical companies as well as financial firms, gained experience in Western regulatory and business environments. The main nodes of this network, however, were the financial and industrial centers of Europe and the United States, and not the Middle East or South Asia. Thus, although at present Saudi royals and entrepreneurs bankroll many Islamic finance conferences, journals, and academic institutions around the world, the main sites for intellectual production in Islamic economics are places like the Islamic Foundation in Leicester, England; the Institute of Islamic Banking and Insurance in London; and the Harvard Islamic Finance Information Program in Cambridge, Massachusetts.

Much like anthropologists debating their disciplinary projects and identities, people involved in Islamic banking and finance are continually engaged in an effort to define precisely what their field is. The foregoing description is a just-so story, and variations of it can be found in most of the books, articles, and encyclopedias of Islamic banking that have been published since the 1980s.[4] Indeed, a publishing boom has been taking place at least since the mid-1980s, following on the heels of a number of international conferences that took place from the mid-1970s to early 1980s. With the establishment in the late 1990s of two important Web sites (that of the Institute of Islamic Banking and Insurance in London, and the IBF Net site started by Mohammed Obaidullah in Bhubaneswar, India, in 1998) information proliferated about Islamic banking on the Internet, and many more people and companies posted many more Web sites.

With so much text out there, from so many different kinds of people, it is easy to understand why debates within Islamic banking so frequently go back to first principles, from the very possibility of human interpretation of the Qur'an, to the prohibition of *riba*, different styles of reasoning in jurisprudence, and so forth.[5] The constant tacking back and forth between heady philosophical and theological issues can be disorienting at times, both for participants and the participant-observer ("What is the efficient cause or *'illa* of gold?" "How should one weigh *shari'a* derived from the *hadith* versus the Qur'an?"), practical ones ("Where do you enter returns from *mudarabah* on a ledger?" "What is the best instrument for short-term project financing?"). Indeed, the very distinction between participant and participant-observer breaks down here, since everyone involved in Islamic banking at one time or another is compelled to take a step back and reflexively examine what it is he or she has been doing, and why.

Nonetheless, despite the avalanche of prose in the past twenty years, some distinct patterns do emerge, especially when one looks at the transnational dissemination of ideas about Islamic banking to places like Indonesia. Most writers, within and outside Islamic banking, cite a handful of key texts responsible for the early formation of the field, namely, the writings of Sayyid Abul al-A'la Maulana Maududi (1903–79) and Sayyid Qutb (1906–66), founders of the Jama'at-i Islami in India and the Muslim Brotherhood in Egypt, respectively. Interestingly, however, it is Maududi who gets more play, primarily because of the citation practices of other South Asian writers who tend to rely more heavily on his English and Urdu texts rather than the Arabic works of Qutb or his disciples.

Another pattern traceable to citation practices is the divergence between those texts that seek to outline an entire "Islamic economic system" and those that focus on techniques and contractual forms. The latter are dominant in the field today in citational terms, although the two sets of texts often converge, and sometimes appear side by side in anthologies (or, in the bodies of their authors, at conferences). The former often begin with an understanding of *riba* as contrasted to *zakat*. The latter begin with an understanding of *riba* in contrast to legitimate forms of profit making, hanging much of their argument on the verse "God has permitted trading and made usury unlawful" (2.275), which seems to imply that the prohibition of *riba* was meant to direct people toward lawful profit making through trade. This is the interpretation of Muhammad Nejatullah Siddiqi (1931–), born in Gorakhpur, India, and currently professor emeritus of economics at King Abdulaziz University, Jeddah, Saudi Arabia, where he helped establish the International Center for Research in Islamic Economics. It is also the interpretation of Muhammad Abdul Mannan (1938–), born in Bangladesh, educated at Michigan State University, and professor at the Center for Research in Islamic Economics in Jeddah. Of "first generation" scholars in the field, that is, those who took up the mantle of Maududi and were instrumental in the field's initial formation as a scholarly endeavor, Siddiqi and Mannan are perhaps the most widely cited Islamic economics scholars in the world—Siddiqi more so because of his sheer output. Both have published almost exclusively in English.

Mannan conceives of Islamic economics as a social science founded on principles that do not differ much from conventional economics, except for the understanding that Islamic economic activity is/should be guided by a set of behavioral norms and ethics deriving from the moral precepts of Islam. His methodology is "eclectic" (Haneef 1995:21), a blend of neo-classical economics, Keynesianism, and even some Marxism, leading some to criticize Maanan's writings as "internally inconsistent" (p. 21; Kuran 1986). Where Mannan attempts to theorize a broadly conceived "Islamic economy," Siddiqi is more concerned with implementation and execution. Siddiqi's analytical approach is "a 'modified' neoclassical one" (Haneef 1995:44). It sticks to the precepts of mainstream economics but introduces elements of *fiqh*, or jurisprudence. Above all, however, Siddiqi is responsible for the popularity of profit-and-loss sharing contracts (e.g., *mudarabah*) over other contractual forms involving deferred payment or mark ups (e.g., *murabaha*).

The enduring legacy of Siddiqi, to my mind, is that many new books on Islamic banking and countless stories from newspapers or other media begin by mentioning the prohibition of *riba* and then immediately jump to a description of such contractual forms, without lingering over the finer points of Qur'an, *hadith* or *fiqh*. Indeed, the bulk of such books, whether written by and intended for "insiders" or "outsiders," is given over to a discussion of the contractual forms that Siddiqi legitimated and popularized. For example, Muhammad Taqi Usmani is a Pakistani who formerly served on the Shari'a Appellate Branch of the Supreme Court of Pakistan, and is a permanent member of the International Islamic Fiqh Academy in Jeddah (which operates under the Organization of the Islamic Conference). He currently sits on the *shari'a* supervisory board of the Accounting and Auditing Organization for Islamic Financial Institutions in Bahrain. His book, *An Introduction to Islamic Finance* (2002), contains only two prefatory pages on "an Islamic way of life" (pp. xiii–xiv); the rest of the book is devoted to the ins and outs of contractual forms like *musharaka*, *murabaha*, *ijarah*, *salam*, and *istina'*, as well as investment funds and limited liability, each of which occupies a chapter. Similarly, Paul Mills and John Presley's (1999) *Islamic Finance: Theory and Practice*, spends only fourteen pages on the religious and institutional background before going into the dynamics of profit-and-loss sharing.

International training and certification programs in Islamic banking and finance also stress the contractual forms above almost everything else. The student is to learn contracts and how to use them. Larger questions of Islamic ethics, behavioral norms, the role of the state in collecting *zakat* or the place of individual *sadaqah* (voluntary alms), or the relationship between Islamic economics and Marxism or Keynesianism may serve as interesting background information, but one is rarely, if ever, tested on it. The goal is to teach a tool kit. When I began this research in 1998, there were two international Islamic banking certification programs, both using a distance-learning model over the Internet.[6] I enrolled in one of them, and spent several hours a week from June 1998 to September 1999, studying lessons e-mailed to me and seventy-five other students, asking and answering questions, Socratic-style, using e-mail. My fellow students were from the United States, Canada, the United Kingdom, Australia, New Zealand, Indonesia, Malaysia, Hong Kong, Saudi Arabia, the United Arab Emirates, Bahrain, Lebanon, Kuwait, Morocco, Tunisia, Kenya, Tanzania, South Africa, Turkey, Spain, Bosnia, Russia, India, and Pakistan. Most were academics: postgraduate students, dissertation writers, and professors like myself. The rest were bankers and financial consultants.

The course consisted of three "modules." The first was on the "foundations of Islamic finance."[7] For one week, we focused on the sources of Islamic law, and the relationship between the Qur'an and *sunnah*, or the rules of law deduced from *hadith*, or stories from the life of the Prophet. We circled back to these initial lessons throughout the course. We also learned methods of interpretation: *ijma*, the consensus of the community of Muslims, and *ijtihad*, individual interpretation based on acceptable hermeneutic techniques. We were taught *qiyas*, reasoning by analogy, as the primary such technique. After that first week, Module 1 consisted of learning the various contractual forms developed in Islamic banking with reference to their status in *fiqh*, the Qur'an, and the *sunnah*. It was as if we were being empowered ourselves to engage in *ijtihad*, to think creatively, and analogically, about things like currency options with reference to various *hadith* or Qur'anic verse. There were very soft boundaries between what "we" were legitimately capable of producing, new knowledge that had the status simultaneously of "religious" law and "financial" practice, and what powers of interpretation were reserved to higher or more powerful others ("*fiqh* scholars," or "experts in *shari'a*" as they were often called). Sometimes they were too soft for the comfort of many participants: were we "learning," or were we "making"? This led to discussions about the limits of *ijma*—who could produce it, how many scholars it takes to make a consensus, and did we ourselves count as such scholars if we hit on a new financial innovation that seemed, to us, to have legitimate grounding in Islamic law? My question to one of my instructors: "In a modern world characterized by Durkheim's 'organic solidarity,' do specialists in particular areas get to form *ijma* for their own specific part of the social organism? E.g., do Islamic financial specialists get to find/declare *ijma* about certain aspects?" His response: "Islamic financial practices should not merely strive to remain in the 'permissible' domain, but explicitly seek to achieve higher and higher levels of Islamic values. Islamic law should not be used as a 'screening' device." The implication: interpret, and interpret some more, lest *shari'a* become a dead technique rather than a striving toward perfection.

The remaining two modules focused on "products, services, and markets," and "accounting and regulation." First, we took the tools we had learned in Module 1 and applied them to various banking models (commercial banking, development banking, consumer banking), insurance, project finance, money markets, and stock exchanges. Then, we studied accountancy procedures and talked a lot about capital adequacy norms. If an Islamic bank is structured using profit-and-loss sharing contracts rather than interest-bearing debt, it will have a liquidity problem if depositors/investors seek to withdraw their money in a hurry, much as George Bailey's Building and Loan faced a liquidity crisis the night Potter closed the local bank. But it was the lessons from Module 1 that stuck with us. Modules 2 and 3, furthermore, were made up primarily of scholarly and practitioner articles—already formed knowledge, as it were—while the material for Module 1 came from primary sources or descriptive, documentary texts about the Qur'an, *sunnah*, and *fiqh*. We were to read the reports in Modules 2 and 3 and assess them, using our knowledge of Islamic law. We could refine and critique, and perhaps suggest new avenues of research, using the tools from Module 1. The most important lessons were the bases for coming to judgments about the permissibility of various contracts, and the contractual forms themselves.

The coming together of new knowledge formations and a new community of interpreters through Islamic banking training programs became a cause for concern for many involved in the field during time of my research. Many decried "self-proclaimed *shari'a* scholars" and warned that people with "no real credentials" were selling themselves to financial institutions—Islamic or otherwise—as "experts." At the same time, people chafed against established voices of authority, and some vociferously defended the "right" of everyone to interpret as they saw fit. I discuss this conversation more fully in the next chapter.

One aspect of it that went completely undiscussed was the role of language. Debates were always conducted wholly in English, with a smattering of Arabic terms from *fiqh* and Islamic banking. Indeed, the specific status afforded English in Islamic banking, and the dissemination of ideas through the medium of English, has produced a distinct language ideology in Islamic banking and finance that resonates with debates over interpretation and the putative universality of neoclassical economics.[8] English is the presumed universal standard. It brings more people together in Islamic

banking than any other tongue, even (or especially) Arabic. It also provides
an important bridge between centers of intellectual production and implementation in the United States, the United Kingdom, and India and Pakistan, on the one hand, with those in Malaysia and Indonesia, on the other.
For many Malay/Indonesian speaking and reading publics, the dissemination of knowledge in English has been critical to the formation of Islamic
banking in the "Malay world." It was the English texts of Siddiqi, Mannan,
Afazlur Rahman, Anwar Iqbal Qureshi, and others that impacted the development of the field there to a far greater extent than the Arabic texts of al-
Najjar or Qutb.[9] Arabic terms thus function in Indonesian/Malay Islamic
banking as they do in English: as supplements to a universal standard. Several interlocutors in the United States made explicit to me the role of Arabic as a supplement to English on several occasions. They stressed that
English, or sometimes "America," like economics, was inherently perfect-
ible through the addition of Islamic or Arabic terms. "Just as America became a better place because of burritos and tacos, so America will become
a more perfect place because of Islamic banking," as one explained to me.
"Can you imagine the English language without all the French words in
it? This is how it will be when everyone knows the meaning of *riba*." Arabic
is not simply the language of revealed knowledge or the divine word, but
a crucial, necessary (and possibly sufficient) supplement to another (near-
perfect?) tongue. Arabic terms function similarly in the Indonesian/Malay
language texts—and, often, analogously to the way English terms do. Such
"foreign" terms become "Indonesian," replicating New Order ideologies
of encompassment (see Boellstorff 2003; Siegel 1997). The potential universal encompassment of English or Indonesian, depending on the context,
is further replicated in diagrammatical representations of Islam as a universal field of knowledge formation and human activity. The form of the flow
chart produces an aesthetic of infinitely extendable bureaucratic "neutral"
knowledge that, here, is simultaneously the infinite reach of God (compare
Riles 2000; see figures. 1.1 and 1.2). And God's reach is wide, indeed: I
have seen flow charts identical to figures 1.1 and 1.2 reproduced in other
Islamic banking presentations; a colleague sent me another version of figure 1.1 after attending an Islamic banking conference in Sri Lanka. The
reach of these images seems to transform the question of whether there is
an "original" into a theological problem about the definition of the ineffa-
ble and the status of that which emanates from it.[10]

I have lingered over dissemination, field formation, and language to mirror the form of Islamic banking and finance as I came to know it during
my own education, as well as during archival research, fieldwork in Indonesia, and conversations in London, the United States, Indonesia, and online.
I continually found myself wanting, or being explicitly called on, to adjudi-
cate disputes over interpretation, historical analysis, or economic or legal

Skema Bangunan Islam

Figure 1.1 A "Diagram of Islam's Structure." (From Muamalat Institute 1997:3, an Indonesian-language text; note the use of Arabic and English words)

principles as a member of the field. Maintaining a "critical distance" became impossible but also improbable as a means of generating "new" knowledge that hadn't already been conjured, argued over, or dismissed by the field itself. At times, this was a little unsettling. I once found myself hopelessly out of date when I presented a paper at an Islamic banking conference comparing Christian and Muslim takes on the prohibition of interest, only to have my "findings" shot out of the water by the next speaker. He thanked me publicly for laying out all manner of misconceptions so clearly that he would not have to spend time discussing "wrong" interpretations; for an example of such wrong interpretations, listeners could simply hark back to Professor Maurer's talk. I was not being challenged as an outsider; I was being challenged as an insider with old theory. I took some comfort from the fact that my interlocutor was seen as a "radical" by others in attendance, who found comfort in my simpler frame. But I couldn't shake the feeling that I had missed the train to more lively and cutting-edge debates. I have the same worry here, too. In making the revelation that it is the impact of figures like Siddiqi and their emphasis on the trade

GAMBAR 1
ISLAM A COMPREHENSIVE WAY OF LIFE

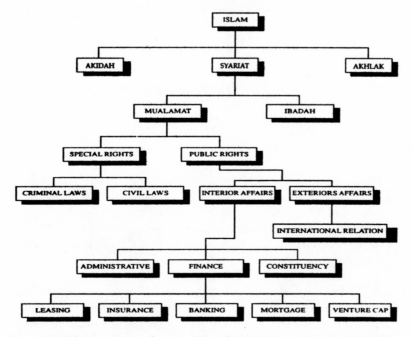

Figue 1.2 "Islam, a Comprehensive Way of Life." (From Antonio 1997:224, an Indonesian-language text; note the use of Arabic and English words)

and profit *ayah* that accounts for the focus on profit-and-loss sharing, I am echoing others in the field who have made much the same observation already (e.g., Haneef 1995). I fear that I will be taken by Islamic banking colleagues and their critics as laying out yet another (dated) grand theory about something, whether it be the "real" reasons for the prohibition of *riba*, or the finer points of *fiqh*, or a sociological-historical account of the origins of Islamic banking, or a critique. Timur Kuran, for example, a long-standing critic of Islamic banking, has taken me to task in print for my seemingly uncritical insider's perspective (see Maurer 2001a; Kuran 2001), while in Indonesia, I found myself explaining certain aspects of profit-and-loss sharing contracts, and even Qur'anic injunctions, to "experts" (including one imam) who sought my advice as an "impartial outsider."

I would like to claim the mantle neither of an insider nor an outsider, but of a fellow traveler who has been trundling alongside the knowledge formations of others as I try to formulate the lineaments of our own divisions as we do the work that we do in eliciting each other's regard, whether with approbrium, acceptance, or indifference.[11] Thus, I do not see the present work as adjudicating the relationship between "theory" and "practice": fieldwork in Indonesia and explorations of Islamic finance in the United States were not attempts to "test" the presuppositions of Islamic economics against "reality"; nor were they attempts to see if, "in practice," Islamic banking strays from its "official" line, or if practices "on the ground" work to revise or supplement "theory." Those kinds of approaches would depend on the stabilization of theory and practice, or idea and reality, as separate and discernable rather than continually intertwining. They would aim for a critical metalanguage, above and distinct from the phenomena they observe. The effort in this book is to speak in a paralanguage, a language alongside those of the people with whom I have spoken and lived over the course of the research, and with whom I continue to question our mutual entanglements.

With that said, I will outline the two kinds of origin stories about Islamic banking and finance that have been circulating in IBF worlds as part of people's efforts to specify "what it is" (myself included). The first centers on the meaning of the Qur'anic verses, and is a scriptural origin story. One variant of this kind of origin story proposes that the Muhammad, a merchant by trade, incorporated fair and just economic principles into his teachings and in his daily life.[12] These principles have been passed down through the *hadith* to the present day, a font of economic wisdom waiting to be tapped once Muslims worldwide could look beyond the economic precepts of maximizing, calculating *homo economicus* in order to foster a revived *homo islamicus*. Another variant is that the revealed word of God in the Qur'an itself embodies rational economic principles that are quite in line with the modern assumptions of neoclassical economic theory. As a form of universally applicable theory about human beings' economic behavior, economic theory necessarily is in accord with and confirms the source of universal knowledge, the Qur'an: *homo islamicus* and *homo economicus* are one and the same. These two variants circulate in IBF worlds today. Sometimes they vie with one another; more often, they exist awkwardly side by side. The first takes is cue from interpretations of Islamic law that emphasize social justice and redistribution (e.g., Chapra 1992). Its focus is on understanding the Qur'anic prohibition against *riba* (glossed here as interest, but also as indicating the time-value of money) as a means to mitigate inequality between lenders and borrowers. *Riba*, this logic goes, allows the lender to insulate himself from the risks involved in a business venture, while exposing the borrower to the risks of both business failure and default. Eliminating *riba* eliminates the risk-free accumulation of the lender and throws him, with everyone else, into the world of uncertainty into which God has placed human beings (see Vogel and Hayes 1998; Gambling and Karim 1991; Mills and Presley 1999). The second takes its cue from interpretations of Islamic law that emphasize rationality and formal equality. Its emphasis is on understanding the Qur'anic prohibition against *riba* as a means to ensure that decisions are economically rational by compelling parties to a transaction to mark their activity to market, that is, to ensure the optimality of the market mechanism (El-Gamal 1999, 2000a). I discuss this in greater detail in chapter 3.

The other kind of origin story is sociopolitical. It essentially brackets the question of the original meaning of the Qur'anic scripture, and seeks instead the beginnings of IBF in twentieth-century Muslim politics in the Middle East and Indian subcontinent. In one variant, classical Islamic contractual forms animated by the Qur'anic injunctions were "eclipsed" by European colonialism and the rise in the West of the methods and institutions of the modern financial system, which were exported to and instituted in the colonial world (Vogel and Hayes 1998:4). Decolonization and independence movements, coupled with Islamic revivalism, fostered the rediscovery or reinvention of classical contractual forms and doctrines (Saeed 1999). The oil boom provided the wealth necessary for an alternative system of finance to grow and mature. Another variant of this origin story does not challenge these understandings of the beginnings and causes of Islamic banking and finance so much as it queries their underlying ideological agenda. In this variant, IBF is less concerned with economic assertion and creating a true alternative to Western institutions as it is to foster a sense of collective identity and, especially, bolster the position of national elites in the face of assertions of resurgent "Islamic" identities that might supersede them (Kuran 1997). In both variants, the history proposed for Islamic finance is the same, but one variant views IBF emerging to serve an economic need, while the other views it emerging to serve a political need. The former locates it within a broad tradition of Islamic revivalism, including Islamic socialism and modernism (often at odds); the latter locates it squarely within "fundamentalism." Both stress the importance of key texts, written in the first third of the twentieth century, that married Islamic assertion with Keynesian and/or socialist economic theories (e.g., Maududi 1975; Qureshi 1946). Both also credit the Muslim Brotherhood in Egypt and the Jama'at-i-Islami in the Indian subcontinent with fomenting reflection on Islamic economic alternatives (e.g., Saeed 1999:9), and the tension between modernist and neorevivalist interpretations of scripture (the modernists emphasizing social justice, and neorevivalists emphasizing the legal form of the prohibition of *riba*; Saeed 1999:41ff). One variant of the sociopolitical origin story tends to see IBF as potentially viable and practical alternatives to "conventional" finance; the other tends to see it as impractical, as rarely living up to its promises, and as sidestepping the prohibition of *riba* through simple accounting tricks or linguistic sleights of hand.

This may seem like a dumb question to many on this board, but I have recently heard that Sharia is final and all Ijtehad has been banned since the age of the Caliphs. If so, then how come we are arguing about Riba? Has the ban on Ijtehad been lifted or is the person dead wrong? If he is, I would like to know why and I would like some references on the nonfinality of Sharia.[13]

It is tempting to attempt to locate the first kind of origin story, the scriptural story, solely within IBF worlds, and the second, the sociopolitical, wholly outside such worlds, looking in. The first kind clearly comes from the position of a believer reading the sacred texts and engaging in the interpretative work, *ijtihad*, that many believers hold to be incumbent on the faithful. The believer doing the work of *ijtihad* is specifically situated, in an Islam that considers the "gate of interpretation" to be "open," that is, an Islam that does not consider all questions of ethical practice to have been settled in the first centuries after Muhammad's revelation. Questioning whether the gate is indeed open renders the entire enterprise of Islamic banking and finance suspect.

The second kind of origin story clearly comes from social-scientific modes of inquiry into social, historical, and political origins, the causes and consequences of human activity, and whether or not those humans ascribe their actions to divine guidance or divine plan. This story also depends on *its* believers, who are specifically situated in an inquiring practice that takes the human as its object and that predicts observable regularities in human activity. In discussion and debate with others interested in Islamic banking and finance but not "of" it, I have often felt that we talk past each other, not least because the words we use to talk about it create the illusion that we are speaking of the same thing. On more than one occasion such conversations have included almost ritualistic invocation of Max Weber and Benjamin Nelson, the sociologist whose *Idea of Usury: From Tribal Brotherhood to Universal Otherhood* (1969) explores the changing exegeses of Deuteronomy.[14] Scholarly communication itself is an illusion in these instances—when, often, very little is actually communicated! The problem has been particularly acute for me in cross-disciplinary discussions, when words stabilize referents the very status or existence of which I am often unsure, or when I am trying to convey the slippage between the ontological and the moral, often within the terms of Islamic banking itself, and only the ontologies get through.[15] Nelson and Weber are invoked "inside" Islamic banking, of course, and so the distinction between analytical level and the apparatus being analyzed once again becomes almost illegible. Furthermore, these origin stories, their variants, and their analyses intertwine with one another, sometimes in apparently contradictory ways, sometimes not, and get voiced in all manner of forums and settings, both "inside" and "outside" IBF worlds. Indeed, their circulation calls into question the very notion of an inside and an outside to and an ontology of "Islamic banking and finance."

The distinction between Islamic and conventional finance—the term most often used by people involved in IBF for financial activities that involve or touch on *riba*—could be said to hinge on religion or faith. Yet questions of faith or belief usually take a backseat to questions of technique or instrumentality in contemporary IBF forums. In a sense, "Islamic banking and finance" *is* the debate over its own origins and the debate over *riba*: how it is defined, how it is avoided, and how it has become the absent center of IBF practice today. As an ongoing debate among an enormous number of participants, not a thing or clear-cut set of practices, it cannot be said to have an inside or an outside. As an ongoing debate often grounded in specific techniques or contractual forms, whose formal properties more than their transcendental status ground the debate, IBF also cannot be said to be strictly speaking a "religious" phenomenon, unless any and all debates over putatively economic activities and practices are simultaneously over putatively religious or transcendent concerns. (This is a proposition this book does not challenge, and ultimately supports.) IBF practice holds a mirror to conventional practice and reveals its nonmodern character, a character where the work of purification and stabilization of "religion" and "economy" is revealed as continuous, not settled in the Renaissance, or with Weber, for that matter (Latour 1992; Asad 1993).

Within the logic of the exemplary that warrants social-scientific ontologies, Islamic banking and finance provides a perfect case of what economic sociologist Michel Callon describes as the "performation" of the economy, the processes through which explicitly articulated economic theories serve "as a frame of reference to institute each element of the market" (Callon 1998:22). Islamic economics configures and formats the new object called "the Islamic economy" or "the Islamic financial system." Just as Callon delineates "the essential contribution of economics in the performing of the economy" (p. 23), I would like to draw attention to the essential contribution of Islamic economics in the performing of the Islamic economy represented by IBF, and also of "the economy" itself, Islamic or otherwise. For the mutual imbrication of IBF and conventional finance—understood as ongoing debates that call forth, purify, and stabilize the objects they name even as those ongoing debates represent intensively proliferating hybridizations between "Islamic" and "conventional" finance—reveals that the performation of the Islamic economy is simultaneously the performation of "the" economy, particularly its supposedly rational and secular character. Thus, the Saudi prince can write things like: "Basically, the Islamic system of economics has very little variation between it and the economic system in the West. The difference is in the basic philosophy, not in the implementation and the instrumentalities" (Al-Saud 2000:3). The role of

Islamic economic theory in performing the Islamic economy is nowhere more evident than in the linguistic slippage in commonly heard (or read) phrases like "Islamic finance faces many challenges today" (Obaidullah 2000:131), where the phrase "Islamic finance" indexes both a scholarly or disciplinary activity and an on-the-ground reality. This kind of absent distance between the research and the reality it represents points up a dense network of connections that ultimately obviates any neat compartmentalization of Islam, Islamic finance, conventional finance, and the secular. It also accounts for the way almost every Islamic banking speech act or text includes a reflexive definition of what it is, or how it does or does not differ from conventional banking.

This also, I believe, is why IBF is frequently, if not almost exclusively, always so preoccupied with discussions of technique, apparatus, engineering, instrument, and rationality. The instruments of Islamic finance—contractual forms like *murabaha*, *musharaka*, *ijara*, and *mudarabah*—occupy center stage in nearly all accounts of IBF. (Even this book, an attempt to cut through the debate in a different fashion, must eventually come down to them lest it be read as not sufficiently descriptive or detailed on what Islamic finance "really is" or how Islamic finance "really works.") Still, as Islamic economist Mahmoud El-Gamal remarks, while "Arabic terms . . . [such as these] are very common in Islamic banking . . . good translations of those terms are readily available" (El-Gamal 2000a:146). "In contrast," he continues, "the use of the English terms 'interest' or 'usury' . . . has all but replaced the use of the term *riba*, for which no English translation is available" (pp. 146–47). The notable exception is the occasional use of the expression *lariba* to refer to Islamic banking, as in the name of the American Finance House–Lariba. In this case, however, "Lariba" signifies doubly, as *lariba* and as the acronym for Los Angeles Reliable Investment and Banking Associates.

In claiming that IBF and "conventional" finance are part of one field, not two, and are densely interconnected, indeed, constituted as separate objects by their very interconnection and their attempt to purify their constant hybridization, I am writing against the discourses of difference and deviance that sometimes characterize discussions of IBF.[16] Charges of difference and deviance go both ways, of course. Regulatory agencies might castigate Islamic banking as shady or disreputable just as IBF practitioners deride the lack of transparency and "fictitousness" of debt-based financing, as opposed to the clarity and groundedness in "reality" of asset-based financing organized through profit-and-loss sharing contracts like *mudarabah* or leasing contracts like *ijara*. Still, the growth of conventional finance cannot be understood to be separate from the development of Islamic finance, and vice versa. The political economy of decolonization, the the oil price rise of 1973, and the creation of new kinds of objects of property like

TABLE 1.1
A Sampling of Common Islamic Finance Contractual Forms

Name of Contract	Approximate Equivalent	Technique
Ijara wa iqtina	Lease-to-purchase	Borrower pays rent based on equity share (initially determined by down payment) plus predetermined and unchanging portion of the principal. With each payment to the principal, borrower's equity share increases, and so rent decreases. Rent determined by marking to market.
Istisna'a	Manufacturing partnership	Finance company funds construction of a house, factory, or business, or the purchase of a piece of equipment for the borrower on the finance company's property; borrower then purchases through ijara or other process.
Mudarabah	Limited partnership	Borrower and finance company enter into limited partnership and form a corporate entity; borrower rents from the corporate entity, increasing borrower's share in entity over time until it is completely owned by the borrower. The object of the contract is the corporate partnership itself, which over time is bought out by the borrower.
Murabaha (bai bi thamin al ajil)	Deferred payment sale	Borrower pays finance company, which holds title until complete payoff of principal plus administration costs.
Musharaka	Joint venture	Similar to mudarabah, but finance company and borrower share title as "co-owners" of the property rather than as partners in a separate corporate entity. The object of the contract is the property, not the corporate partnership.

petrodollars, together with their associated forms of knowledge—"economics" and "Islamic economics," "finance" and "Islamic finance"—signal the mutual frames of reference that performed and formatted each. What is necessary to understand IBF and conventional finance, then, is an "anthropology of entanglement" (Callon 1998:40). This would close off such questions as "What is the place of Islamic banking in the world?" which imagine a place for a specific entity within a larger, more encompassing entity, or "What is the distinctiveness of Islamic banking?" which imagines distinction on the model of difference or on the model of the theory/practice divide. An anthropology of entanglement would simply hold that the logic of encompassment as deployed in such questions misapprehends entanglement as embeddedness (cf. Granovetter 1985), or takes recombinations for relationality. It necessarily queries other modes of analysis that would unproblematically accept the slippage between finance as an activity in the world and finance as an intellectual project.

COMPLEMENTARY CURRENCIES, SHORT CIRCUITS

> *Are HOURS legal?* The IRS, Federal Reserve, Treasury Department, Secret Service and FBI have repeatedly told the media that there is no law against HOURS, as long as HOURS have a dollar equivalent (for paying taxes), as long as they do not look like Federal Reserve Notes, as long as each note has at least $1.00 value. Each participant must report taxable HOUR income, at $10.00 per HOUR.[17]

Quantitative descriptive modality of social scientific inquiry: Ithaca is a small hamlet with a population of around thirty thousand, located in upstate New York at the southern tip of Cayuga Lake. Cornell University occupies a hill overlooking the town, and accounts for the town's disproportionate population of twenty-to-twenty-four year olds. It is also the town's largest employer, providing jobs to about nine thousand people, while the next largest employer, Borg Warner, an auto-parts manufacturer, provides work and wages to around eighteen hundred. Ithaca College is the next largest employer. Seventy-four percent of the residents checked the "white" box on the 2000 U.S. Census form; 6.7 percent checked "black or African-American," 13.7 percent "Asian," 0.4 percent "American Indian and Alaska Native," and 0.1 percent "Native Hawaiian or Other Pacific Islander." In addition, 3.4 percent checked "two or more races," and 5.3 percent indicated "Hispanic or Latino (of any race)." The median income is $21,441 per "household," and $42,304 per "family."[18]

Qualitative descriptive modality of social-scientific inquiry: Ithaca is ten square miles surrounded by reality. The town/gown divide is strong, despite the incredibly heavy reliance of the local economy on Cornell. Still, in this predominantly progressive and environmentally aware town, one resident told me, Cornell is "the place where corporate America and the government come together," a part-public, part-private institution funded in part by large federal research grants. Or, as others sang, "High above Cayuga's waters, there's an awful smell. Some say it's Cayuga's waters; we know it's Cornell."[19]

Since 1991, a local alternative currency, the Ithaca HOUR, has been circulating in this town. HOURS are notes printed on natural fiber paper (originally made from cat-tail pulp) and come in six denominations (2 HOURS, 1 HOUR, 1/2 HOUR, 1/4 HOUR, 1/8 HOUR and, since 2003, 1/10 HOUR). Each HOUR is equivalent to ten U.S. dollars, or, alternately, depending on whom you ask, one hour of labor-time. Since 1991 over ten thousand HOURS have been issued, and the total value of all transactions conducted in HOURS since that time is estimated to be around $2 million. Nearly five hundred businesses accept HOURS in partial payment for goods and services, and over one thousand individuals currently list themselves as offering goods or services in exchange for HOURS in the "HOUR Town" Annual Directory, which, since 2002, has served as a sort of telephone book for people seeking to make transactions in HOURS. The Alternatives Federal Credit Union accepts deposits in HOURS, and will accept HOURS for membership, loan, check bounce, and automatic transfer fees, as well as in exchange for a "Socially Responsible Investing" packet. Several grocery co-ops will accept them, as well, and several establishments offer employees the option of receiving part of their wages in the form of HOURS. More than sixty vendors at the weekend Farmer's Market will also accept HOURS, generally for full payment. All businesses and other vendors that accept them do so at the $10.00/HOUR exchange rate.

Almost more impressive than the circulation of HOURS has been the global circulation of media stories about them. HOURS have been featured in over 100 news stories in Ithaca-area newspapers. Over 450 stories have appeared in media outlets globally, from CNN and the *New York Times* to *Family Circle* and US Airways' *Attaché* in-flight magazine. Newspapers around the world, from Sweden to Thailand, Argentina to Bangor, Maine, have also carried stories about the currency since its inception, the rate peaking in 1998–99 at about 50 and slowing to about 10 a year since then. Interest in HOURS displaced earlier media attention to other alternative currency experiments in western Massachusetts: Great Barrington's "Deli Dollars," and the "Berkshire Farm Preserve Notes," the former issued by the owner of a deli who was unable to secure a bank loan when faced with the possible closure of his establishment, and the latter issued in conjunction with SHARE, the Self Help Association for a Regional Economy, to support local farms. Today, it is Ithaca HOURS that clearly garner the most interest. Stories about other local currency experiments invariably make mention of HOURS, and often report interviews with one of the founders of the Ithaca money, Paul Glover.

The currency itself, however, has been emplotted in narratives of the history of barter, money, and local sustainability that make it rather difficult to specify. People familiar enough with HOURS to know something about their origins write them into histories of barter, agriculture, small businesses, and environmental awareness. "There's a tradition of exchange," I was told. "There's a history and tradition of cooperative societies," too. I was directed to Janet Fitchen's (1991) ethnographic study of the transformation in dairy farming in upstate New York, *Endangered Spaces, Enduring Places*, which chronicles the decimation of small-scale dairy farms by the mechanization and economic restructuring of the industry. The book also pays careful attention to the transformations in the meanings and identities bound up with notions of the "rural" in the region. People in Ithaca emphasize its history as a market town, with "a lot of spokes coming into this central area," bringing together farmers and others from the surrounding countryside. In these narratives, features of the landscape—the hilly, rocky terrain, the gorges—prevented the mechanization of dairy farming in Tompkins County and contributed to the failure of the industry. Ironically, those same geological features are also proudly hailed as integral to local identity: "Ithaca is Gorges" is the tourism slogan, and an engraved image of Ithaca Falls adorns the local currency.

The failure of the farms heralded their renaissance, and breathed new life into Ithaca's unique social formation. Already a center for artists, intellectuals, and environmentalists, Ithaca benefited from a new migration to the bankrupt farms:

> When the Farmer's Market started up again in '73, it was all the hippie friends of mine who had bought farms and had a kitchen garden and a few goats and a few chickens, and they were just selling their surplus in a parking lot from their pickup trucks. And they discovered, hey, you fools, you'll pay me lots of money for what I have extra, so they started putting in bigger kitchen gardens and on purpose raising things for this market. Then local restaurants started saying, hey, people around here pay more for fresh local products, blah blah blah. . . . So, the farmer's market gave a market for the farmers, it was a self-fulfilling prophecy.

In such narratives, today's "hippie" farmers are seen as an outgrowth of yesterday's dairy farmers. And today's barter among them is seen as a simple extension of the barter networks and cooperative societies that structured farming in an earlier era. Contemporary farmers with some familial connection to that past are virtually erased from present recollections. One resident had to correct herself in midsentence: "A lot of the agricultural component [of the local economy] started at the Farmer's Market—well, not completely, a lot of them are people that have been farming for a long time in the area." That "them," while often elided into the community of new, postbankruptcy farmers, is nonetheless central to narratives of continuity that link past barter activity with present alternative currencies.

Barter networks, especially among farmers, long predate the Ithaca HOUR and are interwoven in some people's lives and memories with their more recent bartering activity. Such activity seems to have taken place on a limited scale since the Depression, and continues into the time of this writing (2004). Hence, people will relate histories of "continuous bartering" in Ithaca since time immemorial. Most of the barter took place "directly": one person with a good or service would swap with another, making a trade without reference to any currency whatsoever. And most of it was relatively dyadic. As one person who barters regularly and has done so since the 1980s put it, "Usually, it's not a circle. Usually, it's a lot of straight lines between two individuals." Such direct barter is often the barter of a service, and rarely of a good. People explained to me that direct barter generally involves "people who have a production skill," skills that ranged from balancing checkbooks and computer repair to landscaping and babysitting.

The origins of the Ithaca HOUR rest in efforts to expand barter dyads by means of a currency that people could exchange with strangers for goods and services. One person called it "go-between barter" in contrast to "direct" barter. It is unclear, of course, why it should be considered "barter" at all, if the currency is used as a means of exchange and a universal equivalent. "Barter" as a term to describe what Ithaca HOURS facilitate seems to have its origins in the imagined histories of barter in Tompkins County, making HOURS part of an unbroken line of local economic practices with great historical and presumably cultural depth ("there's a tradition of exchange"). The term probably also has its origins in Internal Revenue Service regulations that demand all income earned by "barter" be recorded on people's income tax returns. Since there is no other way to record HOUR income, it has to be recorded in the "barter" category. The tax code, and efforts to resist it, occupies an important place in people's consciousness of HOURS, and will be discussed in greater detail below and in subsequent chapters.

According to the received history of Ithaca HOURS, the first attempt to expand barter dyads was a short-lived "Local Exchange Trading System" or LETSystem instigated by a visit to town from Michael Linton.[20] Linton established the first LETS on Vancouver Island, Canada, in 1983, in a context of severe unemployment. He designed a computer program that kept track of exchanges, denominated in terms of a notional currency unit, within a membership-based organization. People's accounts began at zero, and were credited or debited when they sold or bought something. Barterers negotiated prices in the notional currency. They then reported their exchanges to a central accounts manager, who would enter the credits and debits (see Solomon 1996:37–38). LETS took off in the early 1990s, especially in the Anglophone Commonwealth. By 1994, for example, there were three hundred LETS in the United Kingdom representing about fifteen thousand people (Thorne 1996). The notional currency and central account permit exchange relationships broader than simple barter dyads.

The acronym is remarkably polysemic. LETS stands for anything from Local Exchange Trading System to Local Energy Transfer Scheme to Local Employment and Trading System. One person I interviewed and at least one Web site (that of the Australian National University's QBC LETS) put it more directly: "What does the E stand for anyway?" There is considerable debate over the political and moral valence, not to mention intellectual property ownership, of "system" versus "scheme," the former denoting something more total than the latter, and the latter understood to be supplementary to the broader economy. Linton himself claims ownership over "system" and stresses the "self regulating" nature of "system" as opposed to the planlike nature of "scheme."

> A scheme is basically a plan, or a procedure for doing something. A plan tries to draw up every part, or show every step, in advance. A system, on the other hand, can respond to changes in its environment. Once established, it can be naturally self-regulating throughout its life. This is why we use the word "system"—"a complex whole, a set of connected parts." . . . The Pocket Oxford Dictionary also defines "scheme" as "an artful or underhand design." (This is not something we wish to be associated with.)[21]

Scholars of LETS also seem to come down on either side of the system/scheme divide. On the "system" side, they ask questions about whether LETS represent a form of "reembedding" of the economy in social relations (Thorne 1996) or a kind of "moral money" (Lee 1996), stressing reintegration of "complex wholes" of the anthropological kind. On the "scheme" side, they ask questions about whether LETS could become a "useful strand of community economic development policy" (O'Doherty, Dürrschmidt, Jowers, and Purdue 1999:1639), or "a new source of work and credit for the poor and unemployed" (Williams 1996:1395). It is noteworthy that the questions and answers are determined in advance by the people involved in any given LETS and take the same form as those of the scholars. One of Roger Lee's informants in a study of LETS in the United Kingdom said that the people in the network constituted a "community of philosophy"—the informant's phrase—or a culture, a complex whole or "a set of shared beliefs and prior commitments," Lee's phrase (Lee 1996:1387). Another of Lee's informants noted that LETS are made up of "people who think about the environment, vegetarianism, people who think about the humanities" (quoted in Lee, 1996: 1387). It also comprises people who want "to stand to one side" of the rest of the world economy (quoted on p.1386). Indeed, one of Lee's informants described LETS as a "new moral economy" (quoted on p.1392).

Michael Linton came to Ithaca in 1986 to meet Paul Glover, an Ithacan whose writings on sustainable urban ecologies had attracted Linton's attention. Linton and Glover began a conversation about creating a LETS in town, and linked up with the Community Self-Reliance Center (CSRC), a loosely organized entity that facilitated community events, political action activities, and skills-building workshops (from seminars on herbs to antinuclear political organizing). CSRC also produced a newsletter, *SPROUTS!* which, among other things, listed items people were willing to swap with others (Jennings 1992:31). CRSC was willing to sponsor a series of LETS workshops and raised funds to bring Linton back to Ithaca for a second visit, during which he established the first LETS in Ithaca in October 1986. The membership began at around thirty, almost without exception people already involved with the CSRC. The most important piece of technology for the system was a telephone answering machine. People would call and leave messages about their trades, and the system administrator would later listen to the messages and record the transactions in a computer database (p. 31). The administrator sent out monthly balance statements so that people could see whether they had run up large credits or debits and act accordingly. The unit of account was called the "green dollar," as in other LETS organized by environmentally conscious people. In a little over a year, membership had grown to seventy-five. In March 1988, however, the CSRC closed due to financial difficulties, and publication of *SPROUTS!* ceased. When the venue for listing possible trades vanished, trading itself slowly sputtered out (pp. 35–36).

Those involved with the LETS attributed its failure in part to its inability to reach beyond the small network represented by the CSRC membership (Jennings 1992:41). LETS members also cooled to their system when it became apparent that the Internal Revenue Service would want an accounting of all the "barter income" it generated. Having a computerized database facilitated such an accounting, but also raised concerns about government intrusion into the system, especially for tax resisters who may have joined the system to avoid the IRS in the first place. Another reason for the LETS's failure is proposed by Patrice Jennings, who has conducted an extensive historical study of the rise and fall of the LETS and the emergence of HOURS. She argues that since Ithaca's "economy" was relatively stable in the late 1980s, the LETS did not serve any real financial need for its members (p. 44).[22]

Jennings's research on LETS cannot be meaningfully separated from the development of HOURS. In the course of her research on the LETS, she came to interview Paul Glover, and before her research was completed, she became involved in an effort to create an alternative scrip currency— "coupons," at first—that would obviate some of the problems the LETS experienced that her research was documenting. Coupons had the advantage that they could be used beyond a small network of friends, and that they would not require a membership structure in order to function. Transactions would be easier and membership automatic, in a sense—anyone who has a coupon can use it with anyone who will accept it. Both Glover and Jennings had read about the Berkshire currency experiments, and, within a month of their first meeting, began to plan a similar scrip currency for Ithaca, which Glover named the "Ithaca Hour." To exploit the homonymic potential of the name of the currency, its founders began spelling it "HOURS" and renamed the *Ithaca Money* newspaper *HOUR Town*. HOURS would be printed up and distributed to Ithaca's "alternative organizations," especially those that had faced budget cuts. The early 1990s recession was beginning to hit town, and these "alternative" organizations were among the first to suffer. The plan was to encourage people to accept HOURS from these organizations in place of dollars. HOURS would also be distributed in the form of grants to community organizations, to fund projects now in jeopardy due to budget constraints. Finally, HOURS would be distributed to people who agreed to list their names and their products or services in an "Ithaca Barter Network" (Jennings 1992:48–49).

The design of the HOUR preceded the actual formation of the network or distribution of the currency. Glover set up a bulletin board at the Farmer's Market to pitch the idea and discuss it with others. Glover and Jennings established an "Ithaca Barter Board" (IBB) that would be responsible for printing and managing the currency. The first run of 1,500 HOUR notes and 1,500 half-HOUR notes was printed up, complete with serial numbers and signatures of the "Treasurer" and "Secretary" of the IBB, and the bills were deposited for safe-keeping at the Alternatives Federal Credit Union (which took some convincing as to their legality and assurances that their distribution would be accompanied with full disclosure of IRS guidelines on reporting "barter" income). Meanwhile, Glover began compiling a list of people who said they would be willing to accept HOURS, and eventually published five thousand copies of the first issue of the newspaper, *Ithaca Money: Ithaca's Largest List of Goods and Services to Trade*, on October 22, 1991. The newspaper specified an exchange rate of ten dollars per HOUR, based on Glover's assumption that ten dollars represented the average hourly wage in Ithaca. It was distributed to "alternative businesses," cooperatives, the Credit Union, and other places around town. The first issue contained the names and phone numbers of 80 individuals and businesses listing 273 offerings of, and requests for, goods and services. The newspaper also contained a coupon so that others could join the system: potential members were asked to attend a biweekly "barter potluck" where they would receive four free HOURS (later reduced to two). The first barter potluck was held on November 12, and by that time there were 500 HOURS in circulation and 120 individuals and businesses that had agreed to accept them (Jennings 1992:54–56).

As early as 1992, however, Jennings expressed some reservations about the new currency. Her fear was that it would be taken as "a new economic institution," or a "new financial regime," rather than as a "tool." She concluded her study:

> I do not believe that any of these tools should exist any longer than is required for them to perform their function. When we allow them to remain unchanged and no longer useful, wearing out their welcome, we numb ourselves to other possibilities in the world. We learn to live with systems that almost, or partially fit. When a reporter asked me to estimate how long the Ithaca Hours list would be around . . . I found that the only answer I could honestly give was "hopefully as long as it needs to be and no longer." (Jennings 1992:68)

In interviews, many expressed the sentiment that this particular tool had been around for too long. People were especially critical of the "hypocrisy" of the currency. Founded by the "alternative" community and as a means of economic empowerment, it had become a "hobby" of the "white, middle class." "Because we set it up to be self-perpetuating," one former IBB member related, "you would almost need to reform, revitalize the barter border, and bring in specific people . . . sort of a diversity approach." Indeed, for many, the "success" of Ithaca HOURS—the media attention, the appearance of the currency in tourist brochures, the institutional support of the Alternatives Federal Credit Union—represents profound failure. An employee of a local grocery store who agreed to accept HOURS as part of her wages brought home for me the paradox, indeed, the intertwining of success and failure. She receives HOURS in partial payment of her wages, but at the ten-dollar-to-one HOUR exchange rate rather than at one HOUR per hour of labor. Her hourly wage is $8.50. Similarly, a manager reported to me, in an utterance in which HOUR's homonymy nearly confounds as much as it clarifies: "I had a new employee actually ask me if they . . . chose to be paid in HOURS would they get an HOUR for an hour, as opposed to their hourly wage for an hour, which was a very interesting question, but not how the [store] pays." HOURS may be backed by "our skills, our time, our tools, forests, fields, and rivers," as the inscription on the bills states (see also fig. 1.3), but, on payday, are underwritten by the U.S. dollar.

There is also skepticism of the motivations of those who accept HOURS as payment, such as landlords, who may use them to hide their true natures: "You know, they *look* benevolent by taking their rent in Ithaca HOURS." There was also a sense that Ithaca HOURS were "contributing to Paul Glover's personal glory," as one person put it, and this sentiment is perhaps responsible for changes in the HOURS governing structure that took place in 1998–99. In October 1998 "Ithaca Hours" incorporated as a New York State not-for-profit corporation and elected a board of directors who began serving two- and one-year terms in 1999. Not-for-profit standing required the solidification of the exchange rate at $10/HOUR. It also enabled closer

Why do many businesses take HOURS for part
of the price instead of full price?

Figure 1.3 What's Behind the HOUR?

ties with the Tompkins County Chamber of Commerce. To those outside the board, the most visible change it brought about was the creation of the Annual Directory to supplant the *HOUR Town* newspaper listings. Rather than listing goods and services desired as well as for trade, the directory only lists those for trade. Here, "barter" looks more like "sale" and the "network of traders" takes the form of a business telephone book, a list of entrepreneurs.

The other major change in the HOUR system has been the extension of interest-free loans and outright grants to businesses and community organizations as a means of injecting more HOURS into the money supply. One of the first charges of the newly formed board was to determine how many HOURS actually were in circulation and to address the perception that the number of HOURS was shrinking, mainly, many surmised, because of the large number taken out of the county as souvenirs. Another concern was that the success of HOURS—especially the increasing numbers of businesses that accepted them—would dilute their efficacy "as an actual monetary system" and make them "almost interchangeable with dollars" (*Ithaca Journal* July 22, 1999, 2A). One member of the board remarked that "There are so many places that accept Ithaca Hours now that it could get to the point where it had no effect on spending patterns," thus canceling out any gains the local currency might make toward the goal of keeping money in the community (p. 2A). Loans and grants were seen as a means of getting more HOURS into circulation and of gaining more publicity for the currency. Grant recipients have included Big Brothers/Big Sisters of Tompkins County, the GreenStar Cooperative Market, and even a $25,000 (2,500 HOUR) loan for a private house renovation. The largest loan to date has been to Alternatives Federal Credit Union, the banking institution that helped launch the currency by providing depositor and security services. Ithaca Hours, Inc. lent the AFCU 3,000 HOURS ($30,000) in the form of an interest-free construction loan to build a new branch headquarters—a story first reported in a news feature written by Paul Glover himself, in the spring 2000 issue of *Ithaca Today*.

ALTERNATIVE ECONOMICS?

The next chapter takes up the question of the falsity or counterfeit nature of Islamic banking and local currencies, a question leveled at them because of their entanglements with that which they supposedly reject or seek to stand apart from. Here, however, I am concerned with their materiality, and in what sense that materiality presses against their self-reflexive congealing as "alternatives" and, at the same time, as "economies," understood to be made up of tangible, real material—whether those materials are pieces of paper (contractual forms or scrip), goods traded, or services rendered.

What would it mean for there to be an "alternative economy?" Timothy Mitchell (2002) and Mary Poovey (1998), among others, have traced the concatenation of the idea of "the economy" in post-Enlightenment Euro-American organizations of experience in terms of the apparent sundering of representation from reality. Understanding the world as capable of being represented creates the effect of a real, of facts or of data, preexisting the representational moment and standing apart from it, to be enlisted later in productive or scientific planning and enterprise. There is a temporal incongruity between their respective arguments, however. Poovey locates this separation of value from fact, and the concomitant congealing of "economy," in the long period following the invention of double-entry bookkeeping in Europe, stretching from the sixteenth to the early-nineteenth centuries. Mitchell locates it more firmly in the nineteenth and early-twentieth centuries, and sees it as part and parcel of colonial forms of knowledge that rendered the colonial subject open to technical reorganization. Both look to the history of certain procedures of calculability and mathematical precision as signal features of the history of abstraction making possible "economies" as separable and manipulable domains. Mitchell is the more direct in this regard. "There was no economy before the twentieth century because the economy belonged to a world that was being reorganized around a new axis," he writes, "the axis that appears to divide the world into image and object, representation and reality. This could not be a transformation only at the level of representations, for the modern belief in a disembodied yet secular realm of representation was one of the outcomes of this kind of transformation. Many quite real things had to be reorganized to make the world appear to separate cleanly along its new divide" (Mitchell 2002:93). The goal of their projects is to obviate the logical coherence of "the economy" and instead inquire into its constitution and performance, and at the same time to give weight to the materialities pressing back on their enlistment and reconstitution for diverse human projects. It also brings to the surface the noncapitalist formations operating "within" capitalism in the creation of new markets and calculabilities, "not," Mitchell writes in another context, "for making any general points about the impact of market reforms [on such noncapitalist relations] but to argue against general points" (p. 261).

I defer the problem of historical location until later, as the next chapter, in considering the truth or falsity of alternative currency, invokes "past" alternatives, and more directly engages the temporalities of the financial and monetary forms with which this book is concerned. If "economy" emerges as the reality-effect of a regime of representation, however, where are contemporary "alternatives" to be situated? Mitchell's attention to noncapitalist relations "inside" capitalism serves to unseat the latter's solidity and uniformity, complexly involuting its forms and boundaries, and ultimately questioning whether capitalism has "some universal social form" at all (Mitchell 2002: 269). James Ferguson, too, in his examination of twentieth-century development discourse, seeks to capture a sense of the "messy spreads . . . [and] dense 'bushes' of multitudinous and coexisting variations, continually modified in complex and nonlinear ways" (Ferguson 1999:42). This is offered as a means of capturing "changing realities" (p. 42) and complexities without falling into teleological histories, neat narratives of progress, foreordained outcomes, and predictable futures. The "alternative" in both accounts seems to reside in the coexistence of forms presumed by capitalist historiography to have been superseded or left behind.

Both Mitchell and Ferguson echo the work of Julie Graham and Katherine Gibson (Gibson-Graham 1996), which seeks another set of representational practices to query capitalism's supposed dominance, both in the world and in theory. Gibson and Graham want to uncover noncapitalist relations within capitalism and lying alongside or cooccurring with what has generally been understood as "the economy," in order to generate a theory of "economic difference" and to "liberate a heterospace of both capitalist and noncapitalist economic existence" (Gibson-Graham 1996:5).[23] They thus question the teleological ladder of economic development that sees capitalism as a stage of a history understood as a sequential ordering of human existence, and replace it with Stephen J. Gould's vision of the other "branches and pathways" captured better by the image of a multiply branching bush than a straight or linear tree (p. 115). The bush of economic variation ultimately casts doubt on whether it makes sense to call the economy "capitalist" at all (p. 262).

Interestingly, however, this line of analysis tends to leave untroubled the category of the economic that Mitchell would have us rethink, and to leave intact the practice of representation itself in the guise of analysis. Mitchell dislodges this practice (and thus undercuts his own use of it). By pointing to the interlinked representational and reality effects that call forth the economy as a separate domain, Mitchell unseats the quest for new representational strategies that he sets out for himself, as well as those indicated by Ferguson and Gibson and Graham. The problem is representation, and the presumed adequation of a representation to its realities. I am not taking issue with the dilation of discursive possibilities each author, and especially Gibson and Graham, affords. Without such an opening, a lot of the language of contemporary critical examinations of capitalism and the economy would be unutterable. Yet each author's project sits within a critique of *representation* and as such leaves closed the black box of *adequatio intellectus et res* as the access to truth, not to mention the notion of truth itself as an outcome or desire of a social inquiry turned toward a social reality.

Ferguson has a telling footnote. In it, he clarifies that his own use of Gould's bush metaphor is not meant to imply any identity or similarity between the change over time of "human societies" and "biological species." "It is not the actual processes of biological and social change that I am claiming to be analogous," he writes, "but the linear, typological sequences through which both are so often misrepresented and misunderstood" (1999:274 n. 3). This very move, however, depends on the separation of representation from reality, a separation that institutes those "actual process" as actual, and as able to be brought under the scope of human inquiry in its most Cartesian form, privileging knower over known but grounding the knowing in a preexistent reality that exceeds its representation. Ferguson effects a sharp division between epistemological forms (the linear, typological sequences humans use to understand or misunderstand) and ontological ones (the actual process of change over time). It is also telling that those actual processes stand in the text, as coexisting variations, through the material metaphor of the bush. It is a double-entry analytic: it leaves unanswered the question of how the ostensibly real (or counterfeit) relation between "fact" and "argument" is itself conjured up and subsequently canceled out, reconciled, to produce a profitable account that generates intellectual interest.[24]

The analytical work of specifying alternatives very quickly leads to a descriptive enterprise that does little to reshape the work of inquiry, even as the categories of inquiry are themselves complexly intertwined with the realities being described. The emphasis is on existence, being, ontologies in the world whose complexity has not heretofore been captured by an adequate representation, and on "bad" representations, deceptive, indeed counterfeit, which blind observers to other worlds and close off conversation. Improper representations, however, are often bound rather tightly to certain objects, which move in the world just as much because of those improper representations as they do because of their representations' adequacy or their own ontological veracity. Money, whether genuine or counterfeit, has efficacy as representation and reality in the same instance; its status as genuine or counterfeit only comes into being when its circulation is halted and its veracity, not exchangeability, is brought into question.

Deleuze has said of Michel Foucault that he "should not be seen as a historian," making new representations of an archive or seeking truths through descriptive adequacy. Rather, Foucault is "a new kind of map-maker—maps made for use not to mirror the terrain" (Dreyfus and Rabinow 1982:128). Dreyfus and Rabinow introduce Deleuze's comment after a discussion of the methodological failure of Foucault's archaeology of knowledge, a failure on the order of the one I am sketching here. Foucault's archaeology seemed to reinstitute description as the primary modality of inquiry, placing the archaeologist as a "split spectator, both sharing and denying the serious meaning that motivates the production of the plethora of discourse he studies" (pp. 90–91). As Dreyfus and Rabinow summarize, "Any enterprise which hopes to explain modern thought will itself have to avoid introducing yet another discourse that posits the world as picture and itself as not involved in what it posits" (p. 99). Hence, Foucault's shift from archaeology to genealogy, a method that seeks to diagnose phenomena from within (p. 103).

I would simply supplement Deleuze's comment on Foucault by emphasizing that the map provided here, from within and inseparable from the intermeshed time-space of description and object, explanation and explanadum, is not necessarily "for use" in any direct sense. It is more on the order of what the Situationists called a *dérive* (Debord 1958), a noninstrumental wandering, a becoming, carried along by the alternative currents of Islamic banking and local moneys. The goal of descriptive adequacy is unattainable but continually haunts the endeavor, lying alongside, but in another time, and speaking back, like the immaterial ghosts of prophecy, or the value of a currency.

CHAPTER 2

Of Law and Belief

well I'll take it I'll fake it for real.
—paulmac[1]

PEOPLE IN ITHACA generally speak of HOURS with approval. "I am definitely pro-HOURS," one woman told me. And yet, in searching for a
definition of what it meant to be pro-HOURS, I almost always received
responses in the negative: "It means to be anti-government," or "it means
you're against the IRS [Internal Revenue Service]." Rarely did people invoke discourses of community or locality in discussing their faith in
HOURS, except indirectly, in statements like "It keeps the money from
going to Syracuse," the nearest urban center. And being pro-HOURS
sometimes went along with a deep skepticism of the money. "They are not
valued for their equivalent," one woman complained. But equivalent to
what? Sometimes, the equivalence sought was to the hours of labor supposedly backing the currency. Other times, it was to U.S. dollars. There was
a slipperiness here, as people's conceptions of equivalence tacked back and
forth between labor and dollars, putting into play the labor theory of value
and the logic of the wage relation from which HOURS derive their currency. I heard countless stories of laborers who would agree to accept
HOURS in return for their services but then "back-calculate" a figure in
HOURS based on their hourly wage in dollars, and refuse to complete a
job unless that dollar equivalent was paid. I also heard stories from well-
intentioned people who agreed to accept HOURS for rent on storage space
(an important commodity in a college town) but who felt that the "rent"
they received was essentially worthless. A lot of people had never even seen
an HOUR bill, and few could list establishments that would accept them,
outside of one local bookstore and stands at the Farmers' Market. Even at
the Farmers' Market, HOURS sometimes caused confusion. "How do
these work?" one vendor asked me as I tried to purchase some pie. "It's
ten dollars to the HOUR, one HOUR is worth ten dollars," I explained,
making tight the relation between the HOUR and its dollar equivalent.

   The issue of whether or not HOURS are a "gimmick" or even a "sham"
repeatedly came up. This was the case especially in discussions over
whether people had anything to trade. Trade was a sort of gold standard
for HOURS. People who did not use HOURS, but thought they were a

good idea, bemoaned the fact that they themselves had nothing to trade, especially no tradable skills. (It was college students who most often claimed this.) Lacking something to trade, a skill or service for which one would accept HOURS as payment, meant one would use HOURS only occasionally and almost always in payment for a good, not a service. HOURS worked like coupons in these instances, or, even, like dollars, as a currency and not as an index of "barter" or any other kind of relationality. "The meaning of HOURS gets diluted," someone told me, when they operate like dollar bills. But this, of course, was the innovation of HOURS in contrast to the earlier LETS system: they permitted the same anonymity, the same Simmelian freedom of exchange, as standardized state-based currencies like the dollar. So, their gimmicky quality is at the same time the secret to their long-standingness, if not their success. Rendered into dollars, they cease to have "real" meaning. And this is what makes them work so well.

Discussions in the worlds of Islamic banking and finance also often come back to questions of the veracity of the endeavor as "Islamic" or as anything other than an ideological smokescreen for something else. Published texts almost always question the difference between Islamic and conventional finance, and propose answers like the following:

> Islamic economics differs from that of the West rather in its philosophy than in its implementation or instruments. (Buckmaster 2000:38; compare the quotation from al-Saud in chapter 1)

> This concept that the removal of the element [of] *riba* would convert secular banking into Islamic banking is a fallacy. The two are different because they are products of two distinct philosophies. One is based on the law of the jungle, where you either eat or you are eaten. The other is based on the timeless and divine principles that are universally applicable. (Qayum 2000:79)

Defining the "philosophical" basis for the difference between Islamic and conventional banking becomes complicated when the notion that Islam is not a "religion," strictly speaking, gets put into the mix: "Islam is not a religion in the western sense of the word," Qayum writes, it is a "code of life" (2000:77). Assessing the difference between Islamic and conventional banking is even more complicated set against excited statements of approval like, "Islamic banking overlaps with standard banking one-hundred percent!" or concerns that "What we are doing is just like conventional finance," or even, "Is this only about marketing?"[2] Furthermore, the idea that Islam presents universal principles can also lead to convergence with other supposed universals, reflected in statements in print or in conversation such as:

An Islamic economic system operates on the fundamental principle that the forces of supply and demand should work freely in the determination of prices in all markets. (Presley and Sessions 2000:131)

[In Islamic banking] all the things we hold dear—transparency and accountability—come to the fore.

These convergences are cause for revelation about deep unities between neoclassical economics and Islam, as well as cause for alarm or skepticism. As with Ithaca HOURS, I found a degree of cynicism about Islamic banking, even among its most vocal proponents, as well as a sense that Islamic banking was mainly "about conferences and meeting people" and not (just) about devising a new economic system or an alternative to conventional financial products.[3]

This chapter takes the skepticism about HOURS and Islamic banking as the starting point, and asks how the series of questions participants and outsiders level toward these "alternatives" are obviated in practice by their continual transactional veracity, the manner in which they "work" for particular practices and in particular times. In the remainder of this section of the chapter, I sketch out the forms and forces of such skepticism. Then, I turn to the legal warrants subtending Ithaca HOURS. In particular, I rehearse the American case law that circumscribes any effort to create a currency alternative to the U.S. dollar. Next, I examine the traditions of legal reasoning that flow into contemporary debates over Islamic banking. Along the way, I criticize utilitarian approaches to meaning and method that try to fix these alternatives in terms of their otherness or difference, rather than allowing them to oscillate between the various worlds they inhabit and construct. I also suggest that several critical conceits about exchange and about ideology capture the imagination and redirect people's critical engagement with Ithaca HOURS and Islamic banking, even as people's practical activity with HOURS and Islamic banking continues to trundle along.

Part of the reason for the skepticism has been the divergence between "Islamic economics" and "Islamic finance." The former indicates an endeavor seeking to remake "the economy" in toto, and to remake it along with the revisioning of all of human life in accordance with "Islam." The latter indicates an endeavor seeking to create "replacement products," as one man put it, for an emerging global market niche. Islamic economist Mahmoud El-Gamal has even modeled the paradox between the two using the tools of neoclassical economics. He formalizes it as a conflict of interests between jurists and bankers. Jurists' preferences give "higher weight to considerations of equity (*al-'adl*) relative to the weight given to considerations of economic efficiency (*al-kafā'a al-iqtisādiyya*)" (El-Gamal 2000b:7).

Bankers give higher weight to efficiency. Available financial technology "allows for linear trade-offs between efficiency and equity" (p. 7). Some fall within the boundaries of what is permissible according to *shari'a*, and some do not. Those more concerned with juristic principles tend to favor technologies closer to the equity end of the curve; those more concerned with efficiency tend to favor technologies that approach the edges of the *shari'a* boundary toward the efficiency end of the curve. El-Gamal argues that this mapping of preferences, which he demonstrates graphically, explains the different positions currently held by Islamic economics and Islamic finance proponents, respectively. Islamic economics tends to seek an ideal point on the equity side, which may fall beyond the technologically feasible. Islamic finance tends to seek an ideal point on the efficiency side, which may be very close to the boundary of the permissible or even fall— or seem to fall—beyond it. Those who want the best of both worlds, and to operationalize the principles of the Islamic economists, that is, to "maximize" "jurist preferences . . . subject to the current financial technological constraints," often end up with technologies that are highly inefficient. These people, "who attempt to use interest-free loans and other Islamically permissible contracts for poverty alleviation," for example, "play a qualitatively important role," but "their approach cannot possibly be successful in developing an Islamic finance industry" because it is so inefficient (El Gamal 2000b:8). El-Gamal later refers to these people as playing more of a "public relations role [that] adds credibility to the 'Islamic' label" than anything else (p. 9).

The next paradox that arises, however, is that scholars who put forward technologies closer to the efficiency side often bemoan those very technologies' success. They do so because of those technologies' distance from equity and thus, in this framework, "Islam" itself in its purest form. El-Gamal calls this "the paradox of criticizing one's own work" (2000b:9). One example is the success of *murabaha*, or cost-plus contracts, relative to *mudarabah*, or profit-and-loss sharing contracts. To many, cost-plus looks just like interest, especially if the markup is defined in relation to a benchmark interest rate, like the London InterBank Offered Rate (LIBOR). El-Gamal provides a more complicated example. In order to initiate *murabaha*, a bank first purchases the item to be financed before selling it to a client on a cost-plus basis. There are thus two contracts involved: the initial purchase by the bank (a simple sales contract) and the subsequent *murabaha* cost-plus contract. Jurists differ on whether the two contracts can be collapsed into one, based on the client's guarantee that he/she will in fact purchase the item from the bank once the bank has bought it. If they can, then *murabaha* begins to look very much like conventional finance—indeed, to be "virtually indistinguishable in the eyes of some observers" (El-Gamal 2000b:9). For El-Gamal such paradoxes point up the main question,

"[W]hich Islamic finance should we strive to develop?" (p. 12). And it is these very paradoxes that lead to skepticism and sometimes outright puzzlement over whether there is "really" any difference between Islamic banking and conventional banking.

For both Ithaca HOURS and Islamic economics/Islamic banking, there is a continual movement back and forth between an "is" and an "as if." When participants attempt reflexively to specify what these alternatives *are*, they also in the same instant configure a durative hypothetical, in an imaginary time-space parallel to the now, or else in a past contingent or future conditional (what it would have been or what it might become, if only . . .). At issue is whether these alternatives can be seen as true and genuine, or whether they are false and, in a sense, counterfeit. Even if false, however, the alternatives continue to circulate. What interests me in this chapter is that continuing circulation, and the obviation of possible falsity that permits it, is made effective through and also, at times, against law.

The Ithaca HOUR's veracity hinges on its position as a real alternative to the U.S. dollar, as well as its status as true currency and not counterfeit currency. People have repeatedly asked the question of whether printing HOURS constitutes counterfeiting, and also what a local currency system can do to prevent counterfeiting of the local currency itself. These questions of counterfeiting have to do with the exchange function of HOURS. This is because a counterfeit is only known when its circulation, its flow, is halted. If it circulates, even if it is "false," it is nonetheless "true" in the now of the transaction: it is efficacious. Islamic banking's veracity hinges on the place of "religion" or "faith." People worry whether it reflects "real" Islamic values or "real" Islam, and whether those involved in it are truly committed to a whole "Islamic system" for life or are merely "on the bandwagon" out of strictly "economic" interest.[4] Yet in the now of its transactions, it works, and it makes other things happen despite the lingering doubts about its purity or its being-in-the-(divine)-true. It, too, has efficacy.

Essentially, people ask of HOURS and Islamic banking: Are they really something, or are they nothing, or nothing different from the conventions they supposedly replace or supplement? I do not wish to overdraw the symmetries between the two, but, again, the method is not strictly speaking comparative because the cases are intertwined with each other and with the conventions of anthropological scholarship underwriting the book before you. In addition, the charges against Ithaca HOURS and Islamic banking are homologous, despite the former's "small scale" and the latter's "large scale," obviating, in effect, the scalar logics that attempt to define each (as discussed in chapter 1).

The concerns over veracity are concerns over whether or not these alternative currencies have any true meaning. How one assesses meaning, as a theoretical and practical project, determines in large measure how one assesses these alternatives. This chapter moves between two related criticisms of functionalist accounts of meaning: that advanced by the philosopher Hilary Putnam against the cognitivism of the philosophy of mind, and that advanced by the anthropologist Roy Wagner against the utilitarianism of the anthropology of myth and symbol. Hilary Putnam (1996) presented a thought experiment. Imagine that there is a twin Earth, identical to our own in every respect except that water on that twin Earth has the chemical structure XYZ, rather than H_2O. Yet all the properties of water on the twin Earth are identical to those on our Earth; it fulfills all the same functions and is understood in all the same ways. When a twin Earthling thinks about water, s/he is thinking about twin water (*twater*); and when an Earthling thinks about water, s/he is thinking about non-twin water (*water*). The only way to discover the content of the thoughts is with reference to their external worlds. Meaning, thus, "just ain't in the head" (Putnam 1996:13). It is external, not internal, to thought, and indeed demonstrates thought's own externality and extensivity. Even further, as Donald Davidson summarizes, "two people might be in physically identical states, and yet mean different things by the same words. The consequences are far-reaching. . . . If meanings ain't in the head, then neither, it would seem, are beliefs and desires and the rest" (Davidson 1987:18).

For anthropology, asserting the publicity and context-dependence of meaning is not particularly newsworthy. It was Geertz, after all, who reintroduced similar philosophical strands to the discipline. Yet I find it useful to return to Putnam's Twin Earth story in the context of the kinds of contexts anthropologists increasingly contend with. Anthropologists encounter peoples whose encounters with Western knowledge formations precede the anthropologist's encounter with them. This makes the use and, significantly, the critique of positivist social scientific metalanguages problematic. Simply asserting that we attend to "their" metalanguages rather than imposing the metalanguages of social science (e.g., Taylor 1987) will not create new knowledge, if the people anthropologists study speak those metalanguages and their critique right back, making for anthropology a new kind of "data" that looks surprisingly like and does the same work as their "theory" (see Riles 2000). Initiating an important dialogue on late-twentieth-century reflections on the nature of anthropological knowledge, Webb Keane argues that anthropology should recognize the "ground of the ethnographic particular" as characterizing a "space of encounter in which people seek or deny one another's recognition" (2003b:242–43) These encounters are shaped by a "dialectic between estrangement and intimacy": we objectify and move away, yet our engagements "return us to them" (Keane 2003b:243). While sympathetic to Keane's vision, I worry that intimacy and estrangement may not capture social fields in which people may "know that they share" (p. 231) but the metalanguage providing their actions with a description of what they are doing may not jibe at all with that of the people with whom they share (see Boellstorff 2003). Or, alternately, as with *water* and *twater*, the metalanguage guiding action may be identical to that of those with whom they share but have neither the same sense nor the same referential warrants (cf. Frege 1966).

I have been using the term *obviation* rather indiscriminately up to now. As Roy Wagner introduces it, the English word *obviate* can mean, "to anticipate and dispose of," and, via the Latin root *obviam*, "in the way," it is etymologically related to "obvious," "apparent, easily perceived" (Wagner 1978:31), since something obvious is in our way, before us, *sous les yeux*, as Leenhardt had it (see the introduction). Wagner uses this paradoxical bundle of associations to discuss metaphor and myth. Metaphor, he writes, inserts "an unconventional element 'in the way of' conventional reference, so that the new relation comes to supplant, to 'anticipate and dispose of' conventional effect" (p. 31). In the workings of metaphor, then, "to anticipate and dispose of," and "to render apparent" can "become a single operation, that of circumventing the arbitrariness of some expression or situation by discovering and making 'obvious' an analogy that motivates it" (p. 32). By making obvious motivating analogies, obviation "doubles back" even as it blocks or lies in the way of other meanings by overlaying them with new semantic or pragmatic relationships (p. 257). It is a process of innovation that is simultaneously analysis and reanalysis; in making new relationships through its overlaying or eclipsing of others, it continually "mines" new meanings, analyses, and realizations out of its initial configurations (p. 257). Thus, "a myth does not *say* things but *makes* them, and then disappears into its result" (p. 252).

And it makes *us* at the same time. In our desire—not internal, and much more than context dependent—to interpret and understand (and thereby remake and represent) myth's meanings, those meanings " . . . grasp *us*. Myths in this respect are like metaphors, using shared associations in such as a way as to elicit novel or comparatively unshared ones" (p. 252, ellipsis and emphasis in original). Later, I will compare obviation to Alfred Hitchcock's "McGuffin" device—the object that is seemingly of no consequence and is often forgotten, and yet drives the plot forward by compelling novel associations while we are in its grip.

That both Islamic banking and Ithaca HOURS can continue, despite what would appear to be grave concerns, even among adherents, as to their truth, suggests that something else is going on in their operation. For Ithaca HOURS, the exchange function lies in the way of the store of value function of the currency, where store of value refers not to wealth but to moral precepts and commitments, as well as "memories" of an imaginary time before. For Islamic banking, the discussion of religion or philosophy lies in the way of the techniques of finance and the tools of jurisprudence, as well as "memories" of the Arabia of Muhammad and the true or pure markets the Prophet helped institute. These moral precepts and techniques, as well as these memories, if followed along their narrative trajectories, lead participants, and analysts, right back to the starting point of the question of truth or falsity, genuine or counterfeit. But in the process of that movement they lie to one side of the definition of truth as adequation of representation to reality, and "grasp us" as analysts and context for novel and unshared associations. This, to me, is their import. Ithaca HOURS and Islamic banking set in motion another kind of truth, one not bound to the logic of reference or *adequatio*. The remainder of this chapter attempts to track this movement, and to unpack the assertions I have just made, via Ithaca HOURS's and Islamic banking's legal warrants. The next chapter explores the work of memory and history, and the possibility of translating among pasts, futures, and memories in the now of alternative moneys.

Detox and the Dollar: Counterfeit Currents

A 2001 essay in the magazine *Harper's* caused a stir among Ithaca HOURS proponents. The author, Mark Wallace, derided HOURS because of their attachment to the U.S. dollar. Despite the rhetoric of being "alternative," Wallace claimed, HOURS betray all the trappings of authoritative currencies—"signatures, serial numbers, and watermarks" (Wallace 2001:54)—and are themselves merely a rhetorical flourish to what he saw as a socialist-style, protectionist scheme to keep money in the community. It is also a scheme founded on an illusion. Wallace made fun of the "anti-corporate views" of Paul Glover, HOURS's founder, as well as of the "economic puritanism" that, he wrote, is a luxury that only communities like Ithaca—"afloat [on] a sea of affluence fed by Ithaca's universities"—can afford (p. 54). If the goal of HOURS is to end Ithaca's dependence on U.S. dollars, in spite of their being backed by U.S. dollars, then "Ithaca may be faced with a difficult detox" (p. 54).

Wallace's article did capture some of the unease of those Ithacans who view HOURS skeptically, and who question whether they merely function as a "general equivalent based on dollars," as one put it. This is one kind of counterfeit: Ithaca HOURS as "fake" because not truly "alternative" to the U.S. dollar—a counterfeit alternative.

But might HOURS themselves be considered counterfeit money by the U.S. government? This is another oft-expressed concern. The U.S. Constitution has reserved for Congress the right to mint coin,[5] but a series of appellate and state supreme court cases have left open the capacity of citizens to print paper and circulate it in return for goods and services—in short, whether citizens can make paper "current." Lewis Solomon, of the

Is It Legal?

Surprising as it seems, Ithaca Hours and other local currencies are completely legal. Neither the U.S. Constitution nor federal statutes generally prohibit private groups from issuing paper currency. In fact, current federal law permits the issuance of paper money as long as the notes are valued at $1 or more.

Federal law *does* prohibit private coinage, however. From 1830 to 1860—and especially during the Gold Rush days of 1849—private coins were manufactured in several parts of the country. Congress responded by banning private coinage in 1864.

It is important to note that all income derived through Ithaca Hours or other local currencies must be declared for the purpose of federal income tax.[6]

George Washington University Law School, has written a book considered by many to be the bible of local currency experiments, *Rethinking Our Centralized Monetary System* (1996). Its chief contribution is to assess the legal aspects of local currencies, and it provides a compendium of U.S. case law and jurisprudence on currency, bills of credit, minting, taxation, securities, and so forth. It also makes policy recommendations, most significantly, the repeal of the 1864 act prohibiting the issuance of private coinage,[7] and the repeal of laws making illegal "fractional paper currency with a value of less than one U.S. dollar" (Solomon 1996:127).[8] The 1864 act has remained essentially unchanged since its creation:

> Whoever, except as authorized by law, makes or utters or passes, or attempts to utter or pass, any coins of gold or silver or other metal, or alloys of metals, intended for use as current money, whether in the resemblance of coins of the United States or of foreign countries, or of original design, shall be fined for more than $3,000 or imprisoned not more than five years, or both.[9]

Ithaca HOURS proceed from the legal universe Solomon outlines, in that they are paper, not coin, and they do not appear in denominations less than one dollar. They also proceed from the legal definitions of current money and the distinction between current money and tokens in the cases he cites. Legally, then, they are not counterfeits.

The cases defining "current money" in the United States each rest on two principles that distract their reader, and alternative currencies, from another notion. The first is that money itself entails a relation of similitude, an adequation between representation (a paper bill) and value (its worth). The second is that money, like language, achieves its definition through human exchange and mediation. These principles function very like Alfred Hitchcock's "McGuffin" device: a thing that drives the plot, and that captures the attention of the characters in the film as well as the audience, but that ultimately is merely a prod to other kinds of motion. The stolen $40,000 in *Psycho* is all but forgotten once we enter Bates' Motel, yet without it, the story would never have moved forward. The McGuffins in these court cases, and in discussions of alternative currencies—similitude, and exchange—lead us into realms of memory and temporality, the store of value(s) function of moneys that are implicit in their durative becomings and efficacies. Money is a "memory bank" that makes other things, including itself, work; it not simply a medium of exchange or a metamedium of mediation (see Hart 2000; Rutherford 2001). A detour through the case law Solomon musters makes apparent the efficacies of alternative currencies that are already evident in their practice, and also demonstrates the work of obviation in their formation.

One such case concerned a business's private issuance of metal tokens as promotional gimmicks, and it set into play a definition of "current money" picked up by subsequent courts. The Clark and Boice Lumber Company had produced tokens inscribed with the name of the company on one side and the words, "Good for 50c in Merchandise" on the other. The Minnesota District Court held, in *U.S. v. Roussopulous* (1899), that as the token "differs in its devices and inscriptions plainly from all coins of the United States, and is not liable to be mistaken for any of them, even by careless or illiterate persons," it therefore "cannot have been intended to circulate as money."[10] Here current money was defined in terms of similitude and human interpreters: a thing is not money if people cannot mistake it for money, based on the money's and the thing's appearance.

In another Minnesota case important to the defining of current money, *State v. Livingston Quackenbush* (1906), the court had to rule on a different matter altogether: whether a banker who knew his bank was insolvent could legally accept a deposit from an unsuspecting client.[11] Quackenbush, the banker, lost the case. He admitted his bank had been in difficult straits, but he argued that the indictment against him did not specify clearly enough the money in question and so should be ruled invalid. His former client, Philip Edelkam, had deposited one hundred dollars with him and was now seeking the return of that money. The indictment against Quackenbush read that the money was "the sum of $100 . . . good and lawful money and current as such under the laws of the . . . state of Minnesota, and of the value of $100, a better description of which said money is to the grand jury unknown." Quackenbush essentially demanded, Show me the bills or coins that make up these one hundred dollars supposedly in my possession, exploiting the absence of indexicality in the demand, the lack of any spatio-temporal framing of definable objects in the world ("that" money, not just any money). To Quackenbush, designating "a sum" and "a value" was insufficiently specific, and further the reference to "the laws of the state of Minnesota" left open whether the money was "lawful money of the United States" at all.

The court, in rejecting Quackenbush's arguments, asserted that it is in the nature of "current money" to be a bulk commodity. Money *is* its designated value, not individual coins or notes—a principle, incidentally, established by an 1851 *British* statute cited by the court here. The Minnesota court cited a number of precedents in U.S. courts where describing money as a "sum" was deemed sufficiently specific. Even where "the kind of money was unknown," "money, currency, a circulating medium of some kind" is what money *is*; it is *not* its "kind" that matters but rather its "value."[12] To Quackenbush's argument that the indictment "describes something that is nonexistent," namely, money current under the laws of Minnesota—presumably, for Quackenbush, referring to a territorial currency no longer considered legal tender (see Helleiner 2003)—the court replied that the reference to Minnesota laws was merely "surplusage," words without meaning. Money is currency, and currency is:

> whatever is lawfully and actually current in buying and selling, of the value and as the equivalent of coin. "Current money" means money which passes from hand to hand and from person to person and circulates through the community. It is synonymous with "lawful money." [It is] [w]hatever is intended to, and does actually, circulate as money. "Current money" [is] that which is generally used as a medium of exchange.[13]

In *Quackenbush*, then, money was the sum of value, not kind, plus human mediation and circulation—"hand to hand."

A third case from Minnesota married *Roussopulous* with *Quackenbush* and similitude with human circulation, and has become the benchmark precedent for cases involving definitions of currency. In *United States v. Gellman et al.* (1942) the issue was whether the manufacturer of metal slugs of the shape and size of U.S. five-cent, ten-cent and twenty-five-cent coins was guilty of counterfeiting.[14] The slugs bore various inscriptions, such as "No Cash Value" or "Good for Amusement Only." But they just happened to be the correct size, shape and weight to make mechanical vending machines work, including "music boxes, cigarette machines, telephone pay-station boxes, parking meters, and other types of machines which are adapted for use or service by the insertion of certain genuine United States coins." The court found Gellman not guilty. Despite "this modern mechanical vending age," the court saw no reason to substitute a "'mechanical test' for the discrimination in accepting proffered coins commonly and usually employed by average, prudent persons." "Obviously," the court wrote, "these tokens or slugs were never intended for circulation as money. The very inscriptions . . . dispel any doubt in that regard," citing *Roussopulous* on the issue of tokens. "Money is a medium of exchange," the court wrote. "It is something which has general exchangeability as such." The tokens in question do not. That some machines accepted them does not change the fact that no person would.

The (possibly very naïve) court found that the producers of such slugs were not guilty of counterfeiting. "While historically speaking, and in a comprehensive sense, many commodities have been used as a medium of exchange, one cannot reconcile the adaptability of certain metal devices in operating mechanical machines in place of money as fulfilling the requirements of a medium of exchange," because no person would accept them in the hand-to-hand circulation that is the defining feature of current money. Therefore, anyone who might use such slugs in vending machines would not be guilty of passing counterfeit coin. They would be guilty of fraud, but the court judged that relief from such fraud did not come into their purview in this particular case, as it was a legislative not judicial matter.

These cases frame currency in terms of an exchangeability among persons that is made possible because of the similitude of objects to an agreed-upon standard object that gives value its form. A counterfeit is only a counterfeit if the average person would be fooled. If you fool a machine, you're committing fraud, but not passing a counterfeit. The implication is that inanimate objects cannot read meaning, and that meaning inheres in the relationship of the adequation of a representation to reality. If you can fool other people with a clever representation that seems to effect that adequation, then you are counterfeiting.

These cases themselves, however, replicate the operation of deception that they outline. In stressing similitude, exchange, and human agents, they fool their inheritors with the logics of representation and adequation, and the centrality of human exchange. They leave to one side the efficacy of the objects in themselves, and the efficacy of any number of current moneys. For, despite the case law, but implied within it, is the proposition that *anything* can become current. One rationale for outlawing private coinage mentioned by the court in *Gellman* was to prevent other currencies from "competing" with the U.S. dollar. Here, "resemblance and similitude is not necessarily an element," the court wrote. Yet the argument for letting Gellman and company off the counterfeiting hook hinged on resemblance. Competition with the U.S. currency poses another problem of efficacy, and the cases could not address the aporia staring them in the face: that other moneys will "work," even when their humans can see plainly that they do not resemble the real thing, *if they work*. If people and machines started accepting something that was not the "real" thing, it would become current money. Meaning, similitude, and exchange are McGuffins, moving the plot but inconsequential, in the end, to objects'—*any* objects'—own efficacy. With mechanical machines, the human agent is superfluous. One could very well imagine a slug-bearing person claim before a post-*Gellman* court, "I didn't do it; the machine did! If it wasn't good coin, why did the machine accept it?" It is a small step from "the machine-subject did it!" to "the human-object who accepted it did it!" Hence the focus of counterfeiting interdiction is on those who produce, not those who pass, counterfeit money. But this is disingenuous at law, since counterfeit money becomes "money" in its circulation and use, not in its production—thus Gellman, at least, walked away a free man. It bears noting that mechanical tests, not human ones, in fact determine the veracity of true and current money. Cashiers are trained to look for special devices on bills, but more recently have been encouraged to mark a bill with special ink that will reveal money's truth. If the ink makes a mark of the right color, the money is true— a logic directly contrary to that part of *Gellman* that stressed human exchangers, yet completely consistent with that part of *Gellman* that warranted, even as it obviated, efficacy over similitude and meaning.

Indeed, cases subsequent to *Gellman* brush aside resemblance and move more quickly to use, tightening the relation between "current money" and "exchange."[15] Conflating use with exchange creates another McGuffin, however, for it obviates use as value storage. Thus, the First Circuit Court of Appeals found that the making of fake Krugerrands (gold South African coins) did not constitute counterfeiting, since the coins "were never intended for use as current money."[16] They were rather "collectibles," stores of value, whether monetary or memorial. "Collectibles," the court reasoned, are nonfungible, while "current money" following *Quackenbush* must be fungible. For current money, it is not the object that matters, but its use. Nonfungible items, by definition, will not be used as a medium of exchange, for to do so would be to make them fungible. If collectibles are held because they contain memorial value, the implication is that memories can't be traded.

People purchased (fake) Krugerrands to store value and presumably to "protect" it from the vagaries of currency markets, the market in gold taken to be more "stable" over time, as well as outside the control or purview of sovereign states. Yet here is an inkling of a memory, a memory of a sovereign freedom reserved to individuals and communities against the centralized state. It is a memory imbued with notions of efficacy and efficiency. Setting in motion numerous, competing private currencies would allow an efficient market in currencies to develop. "The market," in effect, would decide which currencies have more value relative to others. The market would thereby be empowered as an agentive, emergent entity, separate from its humans. This is the vision of the "free market" economist and Nobel laureate Friedrich A. Hayek, who is cited by Lewis Solomon (1996) as well as right- and left-libertarians. His *Denationalisation of Money* (1976) has become a core text of the alternative currency movement. And the hypostatization of the market is on the lips of Ithacans involved in HOURS, sometimes almost in spite of themselves: "The market is an essential interaction for strengthening communities," I was told. And HOURS "obey the laws of supply and demand." Indeed, the HOURS currency board continually worries about the possibilities of deflation, since the supply of HOURS cannot keep up with the demand for them. That demand comes not only from people wanting to trade, but also in good measure from people who remove them from circulation. Why? As "collectibles."

I am suggesting that the McGuffins of human exchange and the similitude of a currency to a state-based current money lie in the way of considerations of efficacy and use. I am further suggesting that efficacy and use, when conflated with exchange, produce another McGuffin that lies in the way of value storage. That value storage is not just about monetary value, or the abstract value that money supposedly materializes. It is about memorialization, an invocation of a conception of freedom and the market at the core of alternative currencies. Memory evades the logic of adequation. I return to this point in the next chapter. For now, suffice to say that bound up in alternative currencies are temporalities that do not simply reflect the logic of adequation or the abstraction of value in a means of exchange, but what Keith Hart calls a "memory bank," like one of those mechanical machines of the *Gellman* case, which trundles along despite the intentions of its humans.

What is the difference between HOURS and dollars? Are HOURS fake, indexing the difficulty of a real detox? I would simply call to mind that U.S. dollars and coins are collectibles, too, efficacious more than as means of exchange or stores of monetary value. Do HOURS intend to compete with U.S. dollars, despite their formal equivalence to dollars? If they do so intend, then of what moment is their formal equivalence but a McGuffin leading people down narrative and historical tracks only to return to where they started?

REAL RELIGION, CRITICAL CASUISTRY

Many commentators on Islamic banking locate it within the new fundamentalisms and revivalisms of the twentieth century. As part of such movements, Islamic banking comes to be seen as deriving from an "ideology," where ideology is understood to mean a set of representations, often considered "false," that hide or mask other interests besides those explicitly articulated. Fazlur Rahman (1919–88), for example, the renowned professor of Islamic thought at the University of Chicago, viewed efforts to eliminate *riba* as part of the "anti-Western," "postmodernist fundamentalism" that sought to elaborate upon those characteristics that most distinguished Muslims from the West (Rahman 1982:136). Among the "pet issues" of such fundamentalisms were "the ban on bank interest, the ban on family planning, the status of women . . . [and] the collection of *zakat*" (p. 136). Timur Kuran, an economist and contemporary critic of Islamic banking, similarly views the attempt to eliminate *riba* as filling ideological functions, and as "an instrument of identity creation and protection" (Kuran 1997:301). The "main purpose . . . is not to improve economic performance." Rather, Islamic banking is a method of "fighting assimilation" for "[g]uilt-ridden Muslims" who "contribute to religious causes, support religious movements, and undertake acts of religious piety," thereby "inflat[ing] the observed religiousity of the Muslim world" (Kuran 1996:438). He claims Islamic banking specialists share Samuel Huntington's (1996) diagnosis of there being a "clash of civilizations" between the West and Islam (Kuran 1996:439).[17] Islamic banking is a "symbol" of "defiance and separatism" (p. 442; see also Kuran 1995, 1996). As Islamic banking is not economically efficient, according to Kuran, it unwittingly leads to a clash of "selves" within Muslims, which "pits . . . *Homo Economicus* against *Homo Islamicus*" (p. 442). Abdullah Saeed, of the University of Melbourne, similarly places Islamic banking within the Islamic neorevival and offers important critiques of contemporary practice. Islamic banks "have been unable to eradicate interest from their transactions," he writes, interest "which is practiced under various guises and names" (1999:146). As he concludes, "it is not enough to have the label 'Islamic,' to be an Islamic bank" (p. 146). Finally, like Rahman, Kuran, and Saeed, Frank Vogel and Samuel Hayes, of Harvard University, whose *Islamic Law and Finance: Religion, Risk and Return* (1998) has become a standard text for insiders and outsiders alike, also situate the movement within the "recent surge of Islamic self-identity" (p. 4). Vogel and Hayes's, however, is a much more sympathetic account. Rather than being duped by false prophets peddling Islamist ideologies, Muslims interested in Islamic banking are "inspired by religious piety . . . seeking greater conformity between their lives in the modern world and the precepts of their faith" (p. 5). "Islamic banking," they write, "makes that conformity possible in the realm of commerce" (p. 5).

That Vogel and Hayes differ from the other authors here only on the valence of piety is significant for assessing statements about the truth or falsity of Islamic banking. Is piety "real," or it is hiding guilt or self-interest, or is it causing an internal, psychic conflict of values? For Rahman, Saeed, and especially Kuran, piety is an analyst's misrecognition of something else: political reassertion, and especially the politics of cultural identity. For Vogel and Hayes, piety is not misrecognition, but the truth of the matter. Whether real or ideological, however, "religion" operates similarly in each text. It consists of beliefs and meanings, as well as intentions, motivations, and interests. The difference between Vogel and Hayes and the other authors lies in their assessment of those intentions, motivations, and interests. The former see no reason to doubt the explicit representation, or to view it as "ideology" in the negative sense. So, the question becomes, does Islamic banking represent religion in the service of ideology, or religion as true piety?

I want to suggest that this question, like the issue of whether HOURS are truly alternative, is another McGuffin, an obviating feature of the discourse around Islamic banking and finance that does certain work while allowing other, quite different work, to muddle along. (In a moment, I will analogize this other work to casuistry, but of a specific sort.) There are various permutations of this McGuffin, each overlaying the others and producing new associations, relationships, and analytical possibilities, all of which seem to have been exploited at one time or another. It is not only the question of whether "religion" is put in the service of less noble ends, but also whether "Islam" *as* a religion is a true or false one, for presumably a true religion would not truck in profane, self-interested political ideologies. This question is itself a permutation of the Orientalist conceit that Islam is not a religion in the Western sense of the term, but a total way of life, a position, as already noted, adopted by many Islamic economics scholars. If Islam does not participate in the partitioning of the world into separate domains, then Islamic economics is not a curious hybrid but a just-so term capturing an essential unity. As one Islamic economist writes, "Islam does not accept the Western concept that economics is divorced from morality" (Ali 2000:63). It rather participates in the fullness and plenitude of divine unity, or *tawhid* (Choudhury 1997). Islamic economists get themselves into interesting contortions on this point, however, for their criticism of conventional economics is that it, too, encodes a whole worldview. Ahmed writes that "Islamic economics is not value neutral," yet also notes that neither is conventional economics. The difference, then, is that conventional economics masks its values through an ideological smokescreen of efficient markets theory and the like, while "we" Islamic economists "do not hide our values" (Ahmed 2000:33).

The issue of the "Islamicity" of Islamic banking turns on the equity/ efficiency opposition discussed in the introduction to this chapter and modeled by Mahmoud El-Gamal. It also depends on a sense of Islam as a quantifiable metric: things can be more or less "Islamic." The assessment of the Islamicity of different financial practices according this metric hinges on instrumentality and, crucially "workability." It does no good to maintain a more pure Islamicity if the results are unworkable. Generally speaking, the argument on this point within the field has to do with the status of contracts like *murabaha* (cost-plus sale) and *ijara* (leasing). Because both guarantee a fixed rate of return, some have condemned them as less Islamic than *mudarabah* (profit-and-loss) and *musharaka* (joint partnership), which do not (El-Gamal 1998:5). El-Gamal argues that "in order to compete with fixed-return financial instruments, the use of the less preferred Islamic financial instruments is necessary and sufficient for long-term survival" (p.

5). While most Islamic banking and finance specialists still have a soft spot for *mudarabah* and *ijara*, however, some even criticize the more preferred contracts, arguing that, in practice, they are insufficiently consultative or participatory. Masul Alam Choudhury (1997), chief proponent of the "*tawhidi* approach" that sees divine unity and totality in the workings of the world, makes just such an argument. Muhammad Nejatullah Siddiqi, the intellectual grandfather of many contemporary Islamic economics and finance specialists, criticizes Choudhury on the grounds that "participatory finance and consultative decision-making in production, distribution, and exchange, to the exclusion of all other forms of financial management" are not "workable." He further argues that while it "always uplifts the spirit to have a grand vision in which everything hangs on everything else, and all are firmly rooted through a single stem," still "one should never confuse one's favorite path through the vast expanses of terrain with the terrain itself. The latter is wider than the former and leaves people the right to choose between alternative paths" (Siddiqi 1999:3).

One analytical move for an anthropology trying to make sense of this field might be simply to affirm the collectivist selves and participatory, communal nature of Islam and Islamic banking, and thereby to specify and define its difference from the West and conventional banking. Another analytical move might be to demonstrate that such claims to communalism and participation mask other interests, and to affirm that therefore Islamic banking is a ruse, an ideological formation built up from a specific conjuncture of political economy and culture. Anonymous comments on some of my earlier attempts to write about my research invariably pushed me toward one or the other of these two options.[18] In print, others commented in similar fashion, generating debates that I take to be special ethnographic moments in themselves, as they pushed my thinking in new directions and led me to further question the separations among the subjects, objects, and methods of my research.[19] Timur Kuran, for instance, responded to my article on Islamic options contracts (Maurer 2001a) that no matter any potential or actual prohibition against certain financial practices, "clever operatives will find ways around" them, and that Islamic banking is simply a self-serving tool of "regimes in desperate need of political legitimacy" (Kuran 2001:29).[20] That Islamic economics and Islamic finance themselves have already made both of these analytical moves, however, in internal debates as well as academic ones, complicates whatever analytical force one might claim for them. To put it another way, the metalevel debate between Kuran and Maurer has already been anticipated (and exhausted) in metalevel debates between, for example, Siddiqi and Choudhury.

To a certain critical anthropology, of course, the terms of such metadebates are already set in within a legibly modern grammar that makes them appear rather flat. They resonate with European Enlightenment humanism and its Romantic rebellions, which pitted individual against collective, reason against religion, profane against sacred, and so forth, and which then could only imagine alternatives as consisting in the neglected or subordinate term of the dichotomies. Thus, it really should not be surprising to anthropologists that sometimes Islamic economists and their critics alike argue that "Muslims" have "collectivist selves" rather than the "individualist selves" of "Westerners," or that "Islam" is a unified whole while "Western culture" is a set of separate domains.

Other times, when presenting earlier versions of this work, I received another kind of criticism. This criticism accepted the inherent interestingness of the material at hand (which was a relief, since so many have found the technical details tedious), as well as my caution against the sameness/difference reductionisms often proposed for its analysis. Rather than proffering the explanations of ideology, self-interest, or cultural difference, however, these critics recommended an analogy to Christian casuistry. Jonathan Benthall, for example, in a response to the Islamic options article (Maurer 2001a; see Maurer 2001b), urged me to consider the family resemblance between Islamic injunctions against usury and the similar ancient Egyptian, ancient Roman, and Abrahamic prohibitions. To Benthall, "the transnational financial community studied by Maurer has more in common with Christian casuists" than anyone else (Benthall 2001:29).

Now, Benthall probably had in mind the perjorative sense of the term "casuistry," as mere quibbling, evasion, or sophistry, as well as the historical sense of "applying the general rules of religion and morality to particular instances in which 'circumstances alter cases' " (*OED*). I would like to linger awhile in both senses, and chart the movement between them that occurs in contemporary Islamic banking, for I believe the work of casuistry wheels along next to and despite the discussion of "real religion" or "mere political interests." Writing of that dispute within Islamic economics, El-Gamal writes, "As the field of 'Islamic economics' tries to find its place (within economics, social science, Islamic studies, or any other field) not only must we continue to differ in our opinion about the nature of the field, but we must also continue to misunderstand each other" (1998:5). Hilary Putnum (1983) would have put it in a related manner: we muddle through together. I attempt to convey a sense of that muddle and misunderstanding next.

Nabil A. Saleh (1986) concludes his definitive study of the prohibition of *riba* and *gharar* (uncertainty, risk and speculation) in Islamic law with the following concern: there are two means of developing Islamic banking instruments. One devises operational techniques that seem to "overturn the prohibitions of *riba* and *gharar*" through the niceties of legal reasoning and strategy. The other stresses adherence to the letter of the prohibitions in the name of ensuring the "legitimacy of its means and objectives" lest "the whole system . . . be perverted" (pp. 117–18). Saleh worried that the growing rift between these two approaches, which map onto El-Gamal's efficiency/equity dichotomy, endanger the future of Islamic banking. He also worried that the resort to legalistic stratagems, *hiyal*, allowed Islamic banks adopting the former approach to "achieve objectives which are not necessarily lawful" for the sake of "flexibility" (p. 117).

The invocation of *hiyal* raises an important consideration. At what point do legal stratagems become illegitimate? When does splitting legal hairs render an entire activity suspect? In my training course, the question of *hiyal* was left open. While the Maliki and Hanbali schools of *fiqh* rejected *hiyal*, the Hanafi and Shafi tended to accept it. If the gate of interpretation is closed, then *ijtihad* cannot proceed. Rather, *taqlid*, imitation, must be the chief means of attempting the creation of entities adequate to changing historical conditions. Yet *taqlid* for Islamic banking would mean imitating conventional economics, which contains forbidden elements like interest. Therefore, one could either achieve Islamic banking through *taqlid* with the imagined past of Islamic market relationships characterizing Muhammad's Mecca, or, one could make a case for opening the gate of *ijtihad* and using its methods of reasoning by analogy (*qiyas*), comparing benefits and harms (*istislah*), and even, possibly, devising *hiyal*.

Yet in the ongoing discussions of Islamic banking, *hiyal* and *qiyas* take center stage in the working out of practical problems and in speculative ruminations.[21] For example, many Islamic finance institutions offer the gamut of Islamic contracts, like *ijara* and *murabaha*. Offering both under one roof mixes contracts considered to be "more" Islamic with ones considered to be "less" Islamic. If conventional banks have Islamic "windows" (like HSBC or Citibank), they mix Islamic and conventional products and procedures. Is either case of mixing acceptable in the name of efficiency and practicality? Would one eat food marked as *halal* at a non-Muslim restaurant? "Don't you ever wonder what goes on [there]?" Some compared these questions to the Austrian Glycole scandal, in which wine bottlers mixed industrial alcohol with cheap wine and were able thereby to spark a price war with their competitors. It was only after several hapless wine drinkers went blind that the crime emerged. Alcohol, in fact, comes up a lot in discussions like this. (So does pork.) Are derivatives, for example, like alcohol taken for medicinal purposes, because they can mitigate risk? Or, since they can also lead to frenzied speculation, are they more like alcohol drunk for the sake of getting drunk? If the former, they may be permissible. If the latter, they are not. Are derivates like cooking with alcohol? Alcohol denatures at most temperatures used in cooking, but, as there is no tradition of cooking with alcohol in Islam, is it permissible even after it has been turned into water and sugar (as someone noted, "I don't assume that many Muslims are eager to pour Bourbon in their lentils or drown

BELIEF: Like knowledge, belief is not an obvious category referring to a psychological state. It is an artifact of the distinction between construction and reality. It is thus tied to the notion of fetishism and is always an accusation leveled at others.[22]

their kabobs in Grand Marnier")? Perhaps cooking with alcohol, and therefore using derivatives to hedge risk, is neither *halal* nor *haram* but *makruh*, not recommended.

Similar issues of *hiyal* or *qiyas* arise in conversations over "branding." Is "Islam" merely a sort of brand name attached to products for marketing to a Muslim niche? For example, there may be conventional financial products that are perfectly acceptable in Islam and about which there is no controversy. Should such products be labeled "Islamic" for the sake of attracting clients? Analogize this to oranges. Oranges are always *halal*. So, is there any good to be obtained in labeling them as such in order to sell them to Muslims? Or does such labeling actually do a harm, by "confusing the masses" by playing around with "names"? What if the orange is genetically modified? If it remains an orange, then perhaps there is no problem. But if a financial product is slightly modified, it might suddenly become *haram*. Alternately, should Islamic products be developed and marketed *without* the "Islamic" label, in order to reach a wider audience and in order to avoid the negative repercussions that might follow from naming something "Islamic," especially post–September 11 in the West? Thus, should Islamic investment funds be renamed "ethical," or perhaps "faith-based?"

Occasionally, these kinds of questions lead some to throw up their hands in frustration and demand a return to strict *taqlid* to classical Islamic practices. It also leads to charges that only qualified *shari'a* scholars should issue *fatwas* on such matters, or, alternately, that everyone should be skeptical of "so-called" *shari'a* scholars who may be in the pay of one or another agency. In the meantime, however, when the sources of authority are not being called into question, work is getting done. Contracts are being drawn up. Innovations are being made. And Islamic banking and finance trundles along.

I want to suggest that such debates are casuistic in the classical sense of the term. They are forms of moral practical reason that take place "whenever extraordinary new issues arise," (Keenan 1996:123), and, like casuistry, they take the form of analogies to actual cases rather than the use of rules as algorithms fitting all cases. They involve working, practical knowledge and a "thick" understanding of particular problems and situations (see Jonsen and Toulmin 1988). They depend on a conception of *shari'a* as dynamic, not static, and *fiqh* as "not a compendium of religious duties but a system of subjective rights" (Asad 2003:242; see Hallaq 1997). Furthermore, the deployment of terms like *halal*, *haram*, *makruh*, and so forth and the performative force of the sorts of debates and questionings discussed above operate not simply as the products of ethical judgment or deontics. They themselves are a form of practical activity that work to "cultivate virtuous thought and behavior" (Asad 2003:246). The McGuffin of whether or not Islamic banking is mere ideology or true belief lies in the way of the practical unfolding of this kind of virtue in the world.

If what distinguishes Islamic banking is its Islamicity, it will no longer do for analysis simply to assert that religious meanings are "outside" rather than "inside" the person, that religion is entangled in "public" symbols (Geertz 2000). It will also no longer do to assert that it is the meanings that are the important things in a religion. For, "what . . . if they gave a meaning and nobody came" (Wagner 2001:20)? What if "belief" as such is moot, as people carry out the practical activities that cultivate virtuous thought and action?[23]

HEADS OR TAILS? FALSE OR TRUE COUNTERFEIT ECONOMIES

In the cases at hand, it is as if proponents of alternative currencies and Islamic banking are continually oscillating between two worlds. Sometimes, the externalities creating meaning are *water*, sometimes, *twater*— dollars, or HOURS; forbidden *riba*, or something else arrived at through *ijtihad*. Meaning, sense and reference are less significant than that work of oscillation. The images, representations, meanings, debates and dichotomies overlay one another and supplement each other, but also lie in the way of each other, eclipsing or obviating one another in the motion between the two worlds. This motion is obviated by the charges of fakeness, counterfeiting, pie-in-the-sky idealism, ideological smokescreening, and so forth leveled by participants and critics (and hybrid participant-critics and critic-participants) of these financial practices. Yet, and because of this obviation, the motion continues.

My method has attempted to capture that motion and its obviation. Rather than an exegesis of the debates and discussions about truth and falsity in the land of alternative currencies, I have tried to "extend the symbol[s]" of that land (Sperber 1975:34, quoted in Strathern 1988:17). The extension of the symbols here is an effort to create a parallel knowledge to that of the people whose words and texts impinge upon the setting down of my own. The form of the analysis is recursive and processual, and, like the indigenous conversations it "reports," it returns back to its beginning point after detours through that which it has blocked from view. Like a myth, the analysis is "an expansion of a trope," constituted by "a series of substitutive metaphors" (Wagner 1986:xi). In the aphoristic "glossary" to his book, *An Anthropology of the Subject* (2001), Wagner "defines" obviation as "the art or technique of using pragmatic error to isolate and define itself as efficient causality" (p. 254). Error becomes cause, the spark that sets other things in motion. Pragmatic error itself is the product of "mistakes," Wagner writes, the mistakes internal to incorporating "objects . . . into one's world" (p. 254). Such "mistakes" are at issue both in the attempt at analysis and the attempt at setting alternatives in motion.

Speaking of counterfeits, Heidegger wrote that:

> False coin is not really what it seems. It is only a "seeming" and therefore unreal. The unreal stands for the opposite of the real. But counterfeit coin too is something real. Hence we say more precisely: "Real coin is genuine coin." Yet both are "real," the counterfeit coin in circulation no less than the genuine. Therefore the truth of the genuine coin can not be verified by its reality. (Heidegger 1949:294)

In countering the notion that adequation of representation to reality was the sole access to truth, Heidegger further noted, "Intellectus and res are thought of differently each time" (p. 296). Ithaca HOURS and Islamic banking, similarly, are thought of differently each time. A post-reflexive anthropology sets aside belief and truth while carrying itself along in these alternative currents.

CHAPTER 3

Of Monetary Alternatives and
the Limits of Values Past

> It is not a question of "returning" to the presignifying and
> presubjective semiotics of primitive peoples. . . . We will never
> succeed in making ourselves a new primitive head and body,
> human, spiritual, and faceless. . . . We will always find ourselves
> reterritorialized again. . . . We can't turn back. Only neurotics,
> or . . . deceivers, attempt a retrogression.
> —Gilles Deleuze and Felix Guattari[1]

WHAT DO YOU DO when your natives have not only read Richard Posner's
(1977) book, *The Economic Analysis of Law*, but believe to have discovered
heretofore hidden passages in their most sacred texts that seem to anticipate it?[2] Up to this point, this book has been preoccupied with the flows
of knowledge between its objects and its analytical tools, flows that precede
the writing. This chapter sidesteps the obvious questions these flows suggest: questions of redefinition, recombination, or appropriation. Instead,
it turns back to the problem of the alternative discussed in the introduction
and chapter 1. Islamic banking and Ithaca HOURS are self-conscious ret-
rogressions that place the "alternative" behind in time rather than ahead
in the future, thereby confounding the temporal anteriority assumed in
such concepts as redefinition. When taken to mean defining again after the
initial definition is set, a redefinition places the initial, nonalternative or
foundational definition behind it in time, and may point toward a future
alternative. Retrogression, in contrast, moves backward, and places the past
ahead of the now. That past precedes and anticipates the supposedly foundational definition, and so the alternative becomes not a variation on a
pregiven theme, but the pregiven background itself. Unseating the claims
of reference embedded in conventional temporality, further, brings back
into focus the problematic relation between the status of the science and
the status of its objects, especially for a science that claims to describe
things "from the native's point of view." This chapter looks at memories
without any referents in the past. It is not that these are on the order of
the imagination (cf. Appadurai 1996). Rather, these memories confidently
proclaim their own foundational status, and, as it were, quizzically confront
those who cannot see that they have been there all along.

This is a chapter about time, specifically the temporalities imagined to set alternatives in motion and to "back" them—to warrant them, and to have preceded them. Like the previous two chapters, it is concerned with the very possibility of "alternatives" to the encompassment of capitalist modes of production and modes of analysis. It begins with the collapsing temporalities involved in the discovery of market efficiency in sacred texts. It then turns to the way Islamic banking and Ithaca HOURS both seemingly reinvent justifications for class society, and thus turn out over time not to be "alternatives" after all. The analytical concern that this failure generates—linked to the problem of the truth or falsity of these alternatives, their being "mere ideology" or "just a game"—is itself ethnographic data for the argument that follows. Indeed, I argue that that analytical concern can serve as a model or replica of Islamic banking and Ithaca HOURS themselves.

The apparent temporal confusion of Islamic banking and Ithaca HOURS is found in attempts to postulate analytical or political alternatives to capitalism, and so I spend a good deal of time in this chapter on texts that exemplify this kind of confusion. I do not do so to criticize them so much as to hold them up as exemplars—again, "data"—of the kinds of lateral movements and becomings I track for Islamic banking and alternative currencies. Thus, I discuss some debates in Marxism over intellectual abstraction via the work of Alfred Sohn-Rethel. I turn to Mary Poovey's attempt to find non-market-based "values" for the humanities. I am not interested in treating the historical muddles these authors get themselves into as problems in their analyses or logic (as other critics have suggested, e.g., Jacob 2001) that need to be sorted out, but as homologous to the mutual muddling along of this book, its objects, and my position as "ethnographer" here.[3] The chapter continues with a reflection on other narratives of the refusal or repudiation of market values—Melville's short story, "Bartleby, the Scrivener," Mauss's *The Gift*—and places them alongside some Indonesian texts that effortlessly truck in impossible temporalities: past contingencies, memories not backed by anything and that may precede the events they reconstruct, potentialities and possibilities that alternate, transact, oscillate, and move alongside the "dominant" forms that supposedly encompasses them.

FIRST, HOWEVER, a word on maximization and market efficiency.

Richard Posner's text begins from the premise that maximization is a norm. The norm of maximization may have nothing to do with material goods, but instead refers to maximization in terms of other normative principles.[4] Posner is a federal judge and one of the founding fathers of the "law and economics" movement, an assortment of legal scholars and jurists committed to the marriage of neoclassical economics and the law. Critics of Posner generally start by attacking the premise that people do maximize. To assume that people maximize also assumes that their identities are consistent over time, that they make choices they do not later come to regret, that they are rarely ambivalent about the choices they make, and that they know what they want in the first place and set about trying to get it. People making these sorts of criticisms sometimes trot out the anthropologists or critical theorists to make their case, but more often cite social psychologists who demonstrate that people are "dynamically inconsistent" in their decision making.

Responses to these critics generally argue that maximization is a strategy for analysis. It does not matter whether people actually maximize. Using maximization as a research strategy within one's own theoretical apparatus can still provide generalizable results and have predictive value. Maximization in theory building, beyond mere analytical strategy, is another kettle of fish. The social-psychological data, in fact, encouraged some economists to do something they were itching to do anyway, at the level of theory: abandon realism. Our models still work given the conditions with which we set them out. Besides, physics abandoned realism, so we can, too.[5]

Economists, in short, maintained a strict commitment to what Dierdre McCloskey (1998) calls economic modernism, by which she means, broadly speaking, that economics is in the business of model building. Economists sought to operate as if the realist principles on which their theories rested were true.

The social-psychological data help economists get around the nonpredictive nature of their models. Take a model of efficient markets. When, in reality, markets are inefficient, it may be because of people's dynamic inconsistency. If the essence of the market is to be efficient, then when it is demonstrably not efficient, we need something to make it so, in order to make the implications of our assumptions—our models—consistent with reality. Precommitment mechanisms come to the rescue. For Richard Posner, the law needs to embody precommitment mechanisms consistent with the model of the market as efficient in order to produce efficient markets and the social benefits that supposedly spring from them.

Whence the precommitment to efficient markets in the first place, however? For anthropology, this has always been the central question. As Frank Cancian wrote, in an essay that sought to surmount the formalism/substantivism impasse in economic anthropology, "Economic man always operates within a cultural framework that is logically prior to his existence as economic man, and the cultural framework defines the values in terms of which he economizes" (Cancian 1974:145; see Cancian 1966). Cancian sought to demonstrate that "comparisons of economic and noneconomic influences on economic behavior pose a bogus question" (1974:142): "our customs do not hinder our efficiency. This is not because we have peculiarly distinct customs, but because we define efficiency in the context of our customs" (p. 147). It is not, as Posner would have it, that we need precommitment mechanisms to help us get to efficiency, but rather efficiency is already a normative precommitment. Dierdre McCloskey remarks, "Intoned so often in harmony with others, such phrases have become incantations. Economic modernism is a revealed religion" (1998:146).

The problem, however, is that the response to economic maximization depends on several tricks of scale. Finding efficiency, the analyst simply changes the focal point of the lens and discovers that it is backgrounded by other precommitments (pre-precommitments, as it were). The scale trick can proceed endlessly, as in a hall of mirrors, and knowledge production turns into replications of those reflections at infinite levels of scale. Such moves in anthropology led to the crisis in representation that demanded alternative perspectives be brought to bear on any phenomenon, and, later, the crisis in perspectivalism that pointed up the limits of perspective as an analytical tool (Strathern 1991).

Qur'an as Precommitment Mechanism

Does the anthropological answer satisfy when it comes face-to-face with practices that trouble the scale-making inherent to it? Mahmoud El-Gamal, one of the central contemporary theorists of Islamic economics, has written a series of essays that were widely presented at conferences, posted on Web sites, and disseminated in print during the time of my "fieldwork" (1998–2003). These essays attempt to demonstrate that the Qur'anic prohibition against *riba* is not a prohibition against interest per se, nor an Aristotelian objection to the fecundity of nonliving objects. Rather, he argues, it is a statement on human failings and the efficiency of markets that redress them. El-Gamal also explicitly rejects the claims of the earlier generation of Muslim thinkers who argued that interest constitutes injustice because it insulates the lender from the risk inherent in the universe in which God has thrown Man. In these important, indeed, epistemic papers, El-Gamal argues that God revealed to Muhammad a fundamental insight about the nature of humanity: that we are impatient, that we treat gains and losses asymmetrically, that we do not fulfill our plans, and that we seek to hasten evil. El-Gamal finds that God was talking about "discounting anomalies" that prevent people from truly maximizing. He then demonstrates that the equity-based contracts that Islamic finance has developed as alternatives to debt-based financing function to mitigate those anomalies. In short, Islamic equity contracts like *mudarabah* work to guide the believer away from his or her own inconsistencies and toward efficiency.

El-Gamal begins with a classic *hadith*:

Bilal visited the Messenger of God (peace be upon him) with some high quality dates, and the Prophet (peace be upon him) inquired about their source. Bilal explained that he had traded two volumes of lower quality dates for one volume of higher quality. The Messenger of God (peace be upon him) said: "This is precisely the forbidden *riba*! Do not do this. Instead, sell the first type of dates, and use the proceeds to buy the other." (quoted in El-Gamal 1999:30)

He then cites the authority of Ibn Rushd, or Averroes, the twelfth-century Andalusian Muslim philosopher, who argued that the prohibition against riba was intended by God to prevent excessive injustice, and that "justice" meant approaching equality in transactions. Barter and trade, of course, make equal transactions difficult. Money facilitates assessments of value that permit equal trades. In his commentary on the Bilal *hadith*, Ibn Rushd stated that justice is achieved by marking goods to market before exchanging them. He also stated that justice requires that the ratio of barter trade equal the ratio of prices, which in turn equal the ratio of "benefits," or utilities. El-Gamal writes (in an earlier version of El-Gamal 1999 posted on his Web site) that he "cannot resist the temptation" of placing the word *marginal* before the word *utilities*, since doing so gives him the conditions for Pareto efficiency in the market (see El-Gamal 1999:31). Had Bilal marked his poor-quality dates to the market by selling them for the highest price he could get, and then purchased high-quality dates with the money thus obtained at the lowest price he could find, he would have achieved an equality of the ratio of marginal utilities of the traders to the ratio of market prices. This is what the Prophet demanded of him. This is what Ibn Rushd six centuries later noticed. And this, in part, is how El-Gamal today finds Posner in Islam.

Posner is not enough, however, for efficient markets. People are dynamically inconsistent, and often do not act in their own self-interest. El-Gamal examines the experimental evidence for dynamic inconsistency, and finds a Qur'anic verse to illustrate each discounting anomaly discussed in the literature.[6] For Posner, efficiency is attained by making sure the law functions as a precommitment mechanism for achieving the justice of the market. For El-Gamal, efficiency is attained by making sure that humans follow the law of God. Posner's formulation is a tautology: you get efficiency through justice and justice through efficiency. For El-Gamal, there is no tautology, because efficiency is a value that comes from God. Islam itself becomes a precommitment mechanism. God gave humanity the Qur'an to enhance economic efficiency, and economic efficiency is the sign and seal of divine justice.

For things which are not measured by weight and volume, justice can be determined by means of proportionality. I mean, the ratio between the value of one item to its kind should be equal to the ratio of the value of the other item to its kind. For example, if a person sells a horse in exchange for clothes, justice is attained by making the ratio of the price of the horse to other horses the same as the ratio of the price of the clothes to other clothes. . . . As for fungible goods measured by volume or weight, they are relatively homogenous, and thus have similar benefits. Since it is not necessary for a person owning one type of those goods to exchange it for the exact same type, justice in this case is achieved by equating volume or weight since the benefits are very similar. (Ibn Rushd, quoted in El-Gamal 1999:31, some punctuation omitted)

Intertwined Knowledges and Social-Scientific Anxieties

One lesson here is that Western formalisms, our customs, the economic anthropologist might say, often have the power to shape others. Western forms are powerfully hegemonic world-organizing frameworks, and Islamic economics must engage with them in order to be heard. After all, Islamic economics today, finding Posner in the Qur'an, makes the same moves that Islamic economics seventy years ago did, when the author of one of the first widely disseminated texts in the field, not surprisingly for the time, found John Maynard Keynes in the Qur'an.[7]

I think this is too easy a lesson, however. One might look back to Keynes, and note that his early writings on money, debt, and probability theory derive from his conversations with members of the Bloomsbury group, architects of a different kind of aesthetic modernism than that which became dominant in art, architecture, and economics after World War II. In particular, Keynes was captivated by the artist Duncan Grant's Turkish studies, and, like any good Oxbridge boy, read the Qur'an and *Lawrence of Arabia*, the influence of which has been noted by Keynes scholars.[8]

Posner, too, is not immune from the intertwined histories of Islam and the West. It is not surprising that Mahmoud el-Gamal looks back to Ibn Rushd, who, as Averroes, is credited with refining theories of causal efficacy[9] that got taken up, after the Reconquest of Spain, in the Christian West. One could craft an intellectual genealogy for Posner that would include Ibn Rushd, either from the starting point of economics, or of natural law and legal reasoning.

Posner commits the error of believing his culture is the culture of no culture. Efficiency simply *is*, and there is no need to justify or explain it further. El-Gamal resolves the blind spot in Posner by finding precommitment mechanisms in God's word. In other words, for El-Gamal, efficiency simply is, as well, but its being is divine and transcendent, indeed, untranslatable because it has directly emanated from the mouth of God, and can only be approximated as we approach an eternity where truths are once again revealed. To McCloskey's tongue-and-cheek comment about the religion of the economists, then, El-Gamal might say, "Well yes, absolutely!" El-Gamal simply reveals a truth of economics, Islamic or otherwise. He is clear about the metaphysical origins of his (economic) faith in a manner that conventional economists, at least for now, can afford not to be.

The revelation is anxiety producing, however. Not only does it suggest that the fact making of social-scientific inquiry is an activity of practical ethics—casuistic, even—it also means criticism might want to assume the very techniques or apparatuses it seeks to criticize. Whither criticism as an operation of unseating or dislodging if it must take on formal elements of its objects and thereby obviate those operations?

This is precisely the conundrum posed at times by alternative currencies. If El-Gamal finds Posner in the Qur'an, Ithaca HOURS proponents find "perfect markets" in their local currency experiment, or, at least, strive to create them. Alternative currency and Islamic finance "puritans" (I found the term in both contexts) see themselves as subject to the same "natural" economic laws as the rest of us. Their alternative system is of the same genera as the dominant capitalist system, for it is subject to the same laws of supply and demand, inflation and deflation, and so forth. Thus, in Ithaca:

> There's an extent of hoarding as people trust the money more, [HOURS] are regarded more as a store of value. A lot leaves town as souvenirs and as gifts to family and friends. This is deflationary. . . . Initially, my obsession was to prevent inflation by talking to as many prominent participants as I could and helping them to spend what they earned. And now it's swung in the other direction so we're paying attention to deflation.

The "economic forces" here "swing" this way and that, as if with a power all their own; and money here takes on some of its "traditional" functions, as a "store of value," as if these things are natural and given.

A very specific sort of nature enters into Islamic finance as well. Speaking of Islamic mortgages, one Islamic financier notes that they will

> satisf[y] the natural instinct of ownership in the citizen. Knowing that he or she owns a house—"a piece of the rock"—makes the individual proud of his or her citizenship, deepens the feeling of engagement in civil society, and enhances the real estate in general as owners strive to beautify their owned properties through continual maintenance and improvement. Finally, owning a home strengthens the feeling of responsibility towards the citizens' own families and the community at large.

Further, on the abstraction of labor in capitalism,

> *Me*: Is it correct to say that riba always has to do with paying money for time— that is, paying money for the period of repayment of a loan, paying extra for a commodity because of a deferment of a contract, etc.?

Instructor: Yes, in the context of a loan contract.

Me: Since a "period [of time] is not a valuable property" [and here I am referencing course material which explained that one cannot buy time since time is not inherently valuable and since buying time is a means of hedging against risk, which is immoral] . . . does this mean that time cannot be valued in terms of money [ever], and, if so, what of wage labor, where a worker works for a period of time and is paid after the completion of the labor? Would wage labor be a form of riba . . . ?

Instructor: As we will discuss later, a wage contract is a form of Ijara [or leasing]. You only substitute the benefit expected from a productive asset [as you do in a lease, where you predict ahead of time the expected benefit and charge rent accordingly], with [the benefit] expected from labor. The expected benefit is exchanged for a predetermined rent.

Islamic finance, it seems, is a system that, while remaking money, also remakes justifications for class society. As do Ithaca HOURS. I mentioned earlier the issue of defining the value of HOURS in terms of labor value, at a set rate of $10 to the HOUR. However, as more and more professionals began to use and accept HOURS—dentists, doctors, and lawyers—more and more people started questioning the equation of one hour of labor for one Ithaca HOUR. Several professionals justify charging as many as ten HOURS for as little as fifteen minutes of their own labor by reimagining their overhead costs in terms of the labor contributed by their receptionists, janitors, hygienists, gardeners, and so forth. And, interestingly, to most people I talked to, this seemed like a fair and equitable valuation of professional labor.

I put the question of exclusion and class to two of the founders of Ithaca HOURS. One responded by explaining her growing disenchantment with the system and her renewal of direct barter ties with some of her old friends. To her, HOURS are coming more and more to resemble "real money"; that is, they are coming to take on the classic functions as a measure of value, a store of wealth, a method of payment, and a means of exchange, instead of being used exclusively for the last two functions. At the same time, to many business people I interviewed, who take in comparatively large quantities of HOURS, HOURS are also coming more and more to be a "waste of time" because, for them, it's difficult to "get rid of" all the HOURS they accumulate. One woman who estimates that she has 700 HOURS (the equivalent of $7,000) sitting around at home told me that she "blows them all" around Christmas time for gifts and luxury goods for herself—not, perhaps, a model of sustainable consumption intended by the system's promoters and expressed in its newsletter ideology.

The other founder of HOURS to whom I put the question of exclusion responded this way. First, he echoed Durkheim's social evolutionary narrative of the transition from mechanical to organic solidarity:

The foremost purpose of a market is to be an actual place, where neighbors learn about each other's resources and where they maximize their creative participation in the process not only of exchange but of ideas and affections. The market is traditionally an essential interaction for strengthening communities, which are the foundation of society. We basically have to decide whether we are humans or termites.

Or again:

We already have social limits and social boundaries by being constrained to compete for scarce dollars, so, in fact [HOURS] are helping to dissolve internal barriers. Likewise, were every community to have local currency, then each community and its residents would be more able to travel more often, to meet people from far away and to import and export from far away. If I don't have enough dollars, I'm not going to go to Europe. But if I can save dollars because I'm using a local currency [for daily needs] then I'm more likely to travel and then I'll be dissolving social barriers.

ALTERNATIVE VALUES

Rather than trying to overcome the anxieties such statements produce in those who would want a "true" alternative, I want to let them sit here for a while and ask whether they are not the symptom of a misrecognized trauma in the work of social analysis. One reading of the preceding "data" would argue that these contemporary alternatives are little more than ideological flourishes to dominant modes of capitalist production, circulation, and exchange. One could well argue that it is mere solipsism to belabor the confusing temporal referents they put forward for their practices and beliefs—Posner already anticipated in the Qur'an, natural barter society springing out of the waters of the Finger Lakes—since "everyone knows" these to be the products of sloppy, romantic, or unreflective thinking.

Yet, as suggested in the last chapter regarding casuistry, there may be marginal utilities, of a sort, to engaging analytically in such solipsism, or at least to trying to replicate its form in this analysis.[10] Indeed, I would suggest that when participants in Islamic banking or alternative currencies make statements that place their activities in another time from that of dominant forms of commodity exchange, they themselves are engaging in a form of practical solipsism that replicates commodity exchange itself. The Marxist theorist Alfred Sohn-Rethel imagined a situation of primitive commodity exchange in which nothing need be said in order for items to be traded, similar to the archetypal Ithaca HOURS conception of barter as the passing of goods from hand to hand. From the point of view of the parties involved, the exchange operates as having to do only with their own or others' needs. That point of view need not be self-interested; rather, the "exchange nexus" itself determines the form of the action such that, retrospectively, it could be identified as self-interested, but it need not. "Accordingly," he wrote, "commodity exchange does not depend on language, on *what* we communicate to each other. Nothing regarding the essence of things needs be communicated" (Sohn-Rethel 1978:41). Yet commodity exchange, he argued, "impels solipsism": "The doctrine that between all people, for every one of them, *solus ipse* (I alone) exist is only a philosophical formulation of the principles that in practice regulate exchange" (pp. 41–42). He thus analogizes commodity exchange to Bertrand Russell's "private language," the very conception of language criticized by Wittgenstein, Putnam, Davidson, and others.

The act of exchange, Sohn-Rethel maintained, is itself an abstraction, because it can proceed only from the "reciprocal exclusion of ownership" (p. 42), and, more importantly, because that which makes commodities exchangeable is their "existence as one," or "the singleness of their existence" (p. 43). The abstraction entailed in exchange is the making-one of the things of the world, indeed, the ontology that precedes their enlistment as empirical data for any situated human observer. It is that thingness that Sohn-Rethel wants to open up, the very "reality" of the real world made legible by the bourgeois sciences and philosophy. This is why Slavoj Žižek finds him so compelling, for it allows Žižek to develop the argument, discussed further in the next chapter, that "even if we do not take things seriously, even if we keep an ironical distance, *we are still doing them*" (1989:33).

Sohn-Rethel writes:

> Money . . . acts as the concrete, material bearer of the form of exchangeability of commodities. That this form can be expressed as the oneness of the commodities' existence explains why there attaches to money an essential, functional unity: there can, at bottom, be only one money in the world. There can, of course, be different currencies, but so long as these do effective monetary service within their own orbit, they must be interchangeable at definite rates and thus communicate to become one, and only one, universal money system. Thus all communicating societies of exchange effect a functional unity. (1978:44)

Once "trading in commodities has reached the stage where it constitutes the all-decisive *nexus rerum*," the social as a field of mediation comes into being, as well (p. 44). In other words, once abstraction is total, there is no alternative. Every alternative already communicates with the oneness of money, itself a replica of the oneness of the commodity at another level—the highest level—of scale. One *could* argue, then, following Sohn-Rethel, that Islamic banking and alternative currencies are activities only for dupes who do not care to see how their actions merely replicate the world of the commodity and money. For Sohn-Rethel, practical solipsism was an outcome of the "material necessity of the stage of development of [people's] productive forces—the umbilical cord that ties human to natural history" (p. 42). Indeed, the reference to natural history and certain difficulties of historiography (when did "natural history" cease?) destabilize his analytic and may place it on the order of a historical curiosity in itself.

But this is not what I shall argue. The dynamic of abstraction and exchange Sohn-Rethel formalized is interesting *not* as an analytical tool to figure out "what's really going on" in some causal sense, but as a model or replica of what people involved in Islamic banking and alternative currencies are doing; that is, it is useful for bringing into view the shape of *their* practical solipsism.

To take another example: Mary Poovey (2001) documents twentieth-century changes in the financing of American universities in order to make a case for challenging the corporatization of the university from a specific location in the humanities. "The function of the humanities," she writes, "is to preserve, nurture, analyze, interrogate, and interpret [the] living body of cultural materials. The function of the humanities, in other words, is to preserve, nurture, analyze, interrogate, and interpret the human" (p. 12). Temporality congeals this notion of the human: what humans possess that "animals and self-replicating robots" do not is "an imaginary relation to a past that can be remembered and a future that can be anticipated" (p. 12). Number erodes this notion of the human: quantification, Poovey claims, necessarily involves entry into the market equation because it entails the sort of abstraction Sohn-Rethel identified in commodity exchange. The human, for Poovey, falls into the category of "goods that are goods in themselves—that defy market evaluation because they are not quantifiable, thus not subject to commodification" (pp. 11–12). Poovey's primary moral claim is that value must become a function of something other than the market. "The only way we can evaluate the effects of market penetration into the university in terms other than the market's own," Poovey writes, "is to assert some basis for evaluation that repudiates market logic and refuses market language" (p. 11). And "[t]he only way we can inaugurate a discussion about alternative definitions of value," she concludes, "is to risk asserting that there are other goods that must exist if we are to remain human. Whatever being human turns out to mean" (p. 14).

It is not specifically the hypostatization of a particular category of the human that troubles me.[11] Rather, it is the manner by which Poovey arrives at the conception of value that is at stake in the essay and the world. Poovey concedes that her formulation of value is tautological. It must be, for only a circular notion of value can counter the equally circular notion of commodified value signaled through number and the market. Poovey seeks, as she puts it, to defy market evaluation, repudiate market logic, and refuse market language. A tautological formulation of value, alternative to dominant market evaluations, must not only stand outside but apart from that totality and be a totality, a closed circle, of its own. The risk of essentializing and totalizing, for Poovey, is worth it, has value in itself, is one of the goods that not only cannot enter into the mathematical commodity relation but by virtue of its value defies, repudiates, and refuses that relation.

What does it mean to defy, repudiate, and refuse the market? Participants in the networks of alternative currencies and Islamic banking often believe that, by transforming the money-form, they will arrive at a transformation of the economy. Within both networks, there are those who interpret their activities with alternative monetary forms as a refusal or repudiation of the market. Others see it as a modification. And still others view it as a return, a going back to an imagined past, a time before the money-form and the commodity-form were equated. For this latter group, the return often has a specific spatiotemporal referent: nineteenth-century America, before the establishment of the Federal Reserve system and the standardization of the U.S. dollar as the national currency. This return is also for them a giving back, returning to contemporary world society the lost alternatives to the market and money that they see represented in the system of territorial, noncommodity currencies they believe characterized nineteenth-century America.

In separating number from the human, Poovey allows number to maintain its animating mythology of anteriority. The myth of anteriority is that things precede numbers, that countable items in the world already exist before and independent of the act of counting. Numbers, in this logic, are not merely human abstractions but a language outside the human, a universal language of the universe itself. Witness the popular scientific and science fiction scenarios, from the Pioneer Plaques launched into space by NASA to Carl Sagan's *Contact*, wherein it is understood that the best means to communicate with extraterrestrial beings will be through number. As Brian Rotman (1987) and others have argued, anteriority is the presumed basis of both numerical and linguistic referentiality, the idea that things precede both numbers and words. Like language, however, number unsettles its own referentialist claims. Rotman begins with zero. Zero is a sign of "nothing." In that capacity, however, it is a sign about signs that indicates the absence of the other signs that belong to its sign system. Thus, zero is also a metasign that indexes the potentiality of enumeration, the whole sign-system of number, and the subject who counts. It is this metasign, Rotman argues, and not the presence of countable "things," that enables enumeration.

In separating number from the human and allowing number its animating anteriority, Poovey also grants ontological priority to a particular countable thing that undergirds her conception of the human and her conception of humane values: time. What makes humans human, she writes, is their capacity to remember the past and anticipate the future. Temporality here shares in the myth of anteriority behind number. In this mythology, time marches on. It can be counted independently of human beings. Humans remember times lost and think about times to come. Time precedes counting. And once humans start counting time, they create value. After all, the notion of time as a an a priori, countable thing permits the capitalist formations of value in the form of labor time and the time value of money that underpin finance, from futures contracts to interest payments to credit itself.

For Poovey, entry into the mathematical operation of quantification already locks into market valuation and commodity logic. I have been suggesting, in contrast, that the question of alternative values is askable only so long as we persist in treating value—not just the human—as conjured in relation to pasts remembered, futures anticipated, and time measured through quantifiable chronographies: the kind that make interest payments profitable, and true gifts impossible.

Bartleby and "Scrivening"

The temporalities of the people involved in Islamic banking and alternative currencies are not always so neatly linear as to enter into the logic of anteriority, however. The "lost" alternatives they imagine do not necessarily correspond to the alternatives that existed before the standardization of the national currency.[12] Like the American greenbackers in the nineteenth century, contemporary alternative currency proponents view poverty as caused by the "scarcity" of U.S. dollars. Creating scrip currencies by fiat increases the money supply and helps spread the local wealth. Contemporary efforts to make money "transparent" by making it merely a means of exchange and not a commodity derives from and encourages a species of realism without anterior referent, whereas proponents of fiat currencies in the nineteenth century were often cast as trucking in the imaginary, not the real, and troubling the connection between sign and substance.[13] In Ithaca, the HOUR is supposedly backed by worth, and evaluated in terms of one hour of labor time. This is the labor theory of value written right into the money form itself. At the same time, however, the commitment to realism also leads some alternative currency proponents to sound like nineteenth-century bullionists, since imagining a past time of barter and pure exchange wizards real, measurable, and unquestionable substances and energies as having value in themselves. Some even look back wistfully on the time when the U.S. dollar had its value fixed by the "reality" of gold and even before, in an imaginary primitive economic time when gold in itself supposedly functioned as a natural currency. In short, their positions, viewed from the point of view of "real" pasts, are a complex and contradictory muddle, a past not so neatly remembered.

Islamic bankers in the greater Los Angeles area, who have created interest-free alternatives to small loans and home mortgages, imagine a time when banks served community needs and a bank's capitalization was measured by the extent to which it was able to circulate wealth within a local community. Explicitly referencing the building and loan manager played by Jimmy Stewart in the film *It's a Wonderful Life*, and with images of old-time bankers serving local farmers and merchants, Islamic banking professionals nod toward the critique of banking in America's populist past. Like alternative currency proponents, some Islamic bankers take from their community-oriented vision a similar commitment to realism, to the solidity of what can (be imagined to) be seen: the social, marked by the term "community," imagined to be a visible and durable network of relations linking the inhabitants of a particular locale, or "the market," a continuously emergent phenomenon produced by the concatenation of human interests. As with alternative currency proponents, that realist commitment spills over into assessments of gold, historicized as the standard of currency before the commodification of money. If for some alternative currency proponents gold speaks to a set of coordinates outside the time-space of capitalism and within Mauss's primitive gift economy, for Islamic bankers it speaks to a set of coordinates outside the time-space of time-space compression, that is, outside the world economy before the end of the Bretton Woods agreement and the dollar's convertibility into gold.[14]

I linger over the quasi realism of groups seeking to create alternative values to point toward the complexity of that commitment as well as its contorted temporality. Herman Melville's short story "Bartleby, the Scrivener" also points toward another temporality different from that presupposed by Poovey. The story is not just about the capitalist contract, but capitalist time.

Bartleby, it should be noted, never actually refuses anything. Indeed, I am led to wonder whether the corpus of commentary on Bartleby's refusal is founded on a reading error (although the disciplinary conventions that divide up the universe into [written] texts and [social] contexts make me queasy even in writing this).[15] Bartleby "prefers not to"; he does not "refuse." It is the lawyer who employs him who consistently interprets Bartleby's formula as a refusal. The first interpretation of Bartleby's phrase as a refusal occurs during its third iteration, when his employer enjoins him to examine with him and his other two scriveners four copies of high court testimony:[16]

> "The copies, the copies," I said hurriedly. "We are going to examine them. There"—and I held towards him the fourth quadruplicate.

"I would prefer not to," he said, and gently disappeared behind the screen.

For a few moments I was turned into a pillar of salt, standing at the head of my seated column of clerks. Recovering myself, I advanced towards the screen, and demanded the reason for such extraordinary conduct.

"*Why* do you refuse?"

"I would prefer not to." (Bartleby, p. 13)

The lawyer, like the critics, persists in this reading error of mistaking *preferring not to* for *refusing*, as he resigns himself to Bartleby's apparent modus operandi:

Bartleby was never on any account to be dispatched on the most trivial errand of any sort; . . . even if entreated to take upon him such a matter, it was generally understood that he would prefer not to—in other words, that he would refuse point-blank. (Bartleby, p. 18)

To prefer not to is not the same as to refuse. To refuse is to disclaim, to disown, to reject, to abject.[17] Of course, preference is a key word of capitalism and the disciplines of economics and psychology that warrant it. But *to prefer not to* lingers at the threshold, as it were, neither disclaiming nor owning up to.

POTENTIALS AND GIFTS: IMPOSSIBLE TIMES

Bartleby's formula recasts both the notion of an outside space and an anterior real that motivate the separation of the human from number and the limited alternatives that that separation conjures. Giorgio Agamben notes that many European languages express the concept of the "outside" with words that mean "at the door" (1993:67). The outside is the threshold, a "passage," "the experience of the limit itself" (p. 67). For Agamben, Bartleby's formula is the pure potentiality of the threshold, the moment of the capacity for creation in the moment before creation (Agamben 1999).[18] This moment is irreducible to the realm of necessity or will from which refusal could emanate (p. 254). For Deleuze, the formula "send[s] language itself into flight," opening up "a zone of indetermination or indiscernability in which neither words nor characters can be distinguished" (1997:76). Bartleby forecloses particularity and reference (p. 71). His formula is not merely agrammatical, but anaphoric. The final word, *to*, "does not refer directly to a segment of reality but, rather, to a preceding term from which it draws its only meaning" (Agamben 1999:255).

This zone of indiscernability renders illegible a perpendicular set of distinctions, common to Western metaphysics and its modalities of evaluation, between language and economy on one axis, and gift and commodity on the other. Derrida reflects on the multiplicity of the term "gift" in Marcel Mauss's classic anthropological text and disclaims the possibility of a "general equivalent" that would unify that multiplicity within a single code (1992:51). That general equivalent would be the gold standard of semiotics, a "transcendental signified or signifier" occupying the place of a "transcendental given" (p. 52). It would be a true gift without obligation of return, a gift without a subsequent debt. Such a true gift would require both a forgetting of the gift and the forgetting of the forgetting (p. 17), a temporal logic without anticipatory futures (of the kind that make financial derivatives and interest payments possible). Mauss himself deconstructs the possibility of a transcendental given, putting a "hybrid"—his term—in its place. At the end of his essay on the gift, Mauss questions the transcendental unity of his object:

> We can dissolve, mix up, color, and redefine the principal notions that we have used. The terms that we have used—present, gift, *cadeau*—are not themselves entirely exact. These concepts of law and economics that we like to oppose: freedom and obligation, liberality, generosity, and luxury, as against savings, interest, and utility—it would be good to put them into the melting pot once more. (Mauss, quoted in Derrida 1992:55)[19]

Rather than attempt to sublimate the soup in the melting pot to arrive at clear categories or pure concepts, Mauss instead offers an "example," an ethnographic nugget from the Trobriand Islands that troubles the neat distinction between gift and commodity that seemingly animated Mauss's project at the beginning of his text. This, Derrida contends, is the "madness of this essay," and the madness of an economic reason that proceeds *as if* in the presence of transcendental commodity value and transcendental gift value despite the impossibility of either. Derrida's hope is that Mauss was like Baudelaire and other literary realists, who, Derrida claims, wrote with the knowledge that they themselves were "counterfeiters," self-consciously critical of their own fictions, the face values of which hid no deeper depths or hidden real whatsoever and so demonstrated the same for all language.[20] To write the real, for them, was always to counterfeit, to write on credit, on other fictions without originary foundation.

Bartleby, of course, goes one better: mistaken by the prison cook for a "gentleman forger" (Bartleby, p. 39), Bartleby is a counterfeit counterfeiter, a copyist who prefers not to copy. The ideal of a real counterfeiter still operates under the sign of an originary real. A counterfeit counterfeiter, however, introduces the possibility of a counterfeit counterfeit, unsettling the originary real of both author/copyist and original text and returning both to the moment when either both could and could not be. For Agamben, this means Bartleby opens up the "past contingent" that "retroactively acts on the past not to make it necessary but, rather, to return to it its

This root, ṢDQ, appears in the Qur'an in a number of forms. . . . [T]he basic
meaning of the root is "strength," or "hardness," whether of language or other
things. This original meaning . . . is still to be seen in the adjective sadq meaning
"hard, vigorous." Ṣidq is the "truth" of language, so named because of its
"strength" as opposed to the weakness of falsehood. In effect, the most usual
sense of ṣidq is to "speak truth," to give information which is true, i.e. which
conforms to the reality. This meaning of the word is seen in the most ordinary
sentences of the type: "They investigated the report closely and found that the
reporter had spoken the truth (sadaqa)." (Izutsu 2002:89)

potential not to be" (1999:267). The past contingent interrupts the originary real underpinning the remembered past. Memory, conventionally
understood, hinges on its relation to past reals, as it is always evaluated in
terms of its distortion or its accuracy. The past contingent recalls another
memory, rethought in terms other than those of that neat temporality (as
is the case, say, with trauma).[21]

In a footnote on his choice of the case of the Trobriand Islanders to
exemplify the composite assemblage that he calls "the gift," Mauss writes:
"We could just as well opt for the Arabic *sadaqa*: alms, price of the betrothed, justice, tax" (1990: 155 n. 24). *Sadaqa* is voluntary, not obligatory,
charity—it is not required of the believers, but recommended. And it becomes Mauss's example in the main text a few pages after the melting-pot
passage for a vision of a new economy he hopes is coming into being, one
rooted in mutual assistance and mutual cooperation. Mauss quotes from
the Qur'an, *surah* 64 on the Last Judgment, the end-times: "Fear God with
all your might; listen and obey, give alms (*sadaqa*) in your own interest. . . . If you make a generous loan to God, he will pay you back double"
(quoted in 1990: 77–78). Mauss continues, removing the *surah* from its
apocalyptic time, "Substitute for the name of Allah that of society and the
occupational grouping, or put together all three names, if you are religious.
Replace the concept of alms by that of co-operation, of a task done or a
service rendered for others. You will then have a fairly good idea of the
kind of economy that is at present laboriously in gestation" (p. 78).

Mauss in the early-twentieth century transcribed a passage from the
Qur'an from the late-seventh century referring to the End of Time, and
found in it a future time that is not at the apocalyptic end but rather in the
process of becoming, on the threshold of the present. This threshold, this
hybrid or melting-pot jumble, existed for Mauss also in the past of humanity and in the present of the so-called primitive societies like the Trobriand
Islands that occupied the ethnographic imagination. Like Islamic bankers
who remove the anterior subtending the American past and place interest-
free futures in the present, and like alternative currency proponents who
(a copy of *The Gift* in hand) herald a "return" to the barter economy,
Mauss's gift composes an alternative space-time on the threshold of the

market and the nonmarket, holding the potential for both while preferring not to cross into and thereby solidify or stabilize either.

Listen to Yahia Abdul-Rahman, a prominent figure in the field of American Islamic banking, speaking indirectly of the relation between Islam, a world religion founded in the seventh century, and the United States, a nation-state founded in the eighteenth:

> The globe belongs to God and it is wide open and full of resources and opportunities. Oppression in one location does not justify acceptance. It is the responsibility of everyone, in particular Muslims, to find another location where freedom and human dignity are prevalent. In doing so, a Muslim in his/her pursuit of business, carries with him/her the way of life of Islam. (Abdul-Rahman 1994: 8–9)

If it is the responsibility of all Muslims, indeed, all people, to find a location of freedom and dignity and thereby carry forward, realize the potential of, Islam itself, then the full flowering of Islam does not precede that place. For Abdul-Rahman, that place is America, imagined as the site of populist banking institutions serving local communities whose solidarity derives from the bonds of credit linking them to one another. As Jimmy Stewart says in *It's a Wonderful Life*, explaining to townspeople why their money is not literally in the bank: "The money's not here, why, your money's in Joe's house"—a line from a Christmas movie that served as an object lesson to instruct Los Angeles Muslims in the methods and morality of Islamic finance.

In this temporality of the threshold, Islamic banking *must* arise in America, as a historical inevitability. While other Islamic finance professionals cite the practical concerns of banking regulations and elite skepticism in Muslim-majority countries as the main reasons why Islamic banking emerged first on the Indian subcontinent and developed further in the West, Abdul-Rahman cites personal and national destines:

> Muslim . . . economists, social scientists and leaders living outside the Muslim countries in many of the developed countries of the world must carve a role for themselves to implement the theory of Islamic . . . financing in their communities . . . and try to branch out into the Muslim and developing countries worldwide in order to facilitate the bringing about of the dream of a world-wide community based [Islamic] financing system. (p. 33)

Abdul-Rahman writes in two times: the past contingent of what might have been (or ought to have been, or should have been if the future were to be as the present is now), and the future conditional of the logical process of abduction, in which an argument in the present is completed by a missing term that might come in the future (see Doyle 2003)—but that also must come; otherwise the present would not be as it is.

Derrida plays with the French figure of speech that the narrator of Baudelaire's "Counterfeit Money" uses to poke fun at his obsessive flights of fancy: "looking for noon at two o'clock." Derrida analogizes looking for noon at two o'clock to looking for the unitary meaning of the word *gift* in Mauss's essay. The impossibility of noon at two o'clock is akin to the madness of the gift and the madness of economic reason, the impossibility of finding the transcendental general equivalent backing money, gifting, evaluation, or signification. This does not necessarily imply, however, that looking for noon at two o'clock itself is an impossibility in the conventional sense. For what besides this are Mauss, Bartleby, and proponents of alternative monetary forms in fact doing in their conjuring of the alternative temporality of the past contingent, an anterior that is never always-already given?

THE LIMIT OF THE (CON)TEXT

As should be clear by now, I do not believe quantification, commodification, and capitalist modes of evaluation or abstraction are all they're cracked up to be. I also think that they often lead anthropologists and others down well-worn tracks to dead ends, toward answers we already know at the outset of our research, rendering the research activity itself the product of a foregone conclusion. The gift and the commodity, not to mention number and rhetoric, belong more properly to the melting pot into which Mauss ended up returning them. I do not think this means abandoning critique into some sort of desublimated slush, however. I do think it means we need to attend to number and quantification and their attendant temporalities more carefully.

Poovey's refusal of the market assumes an outside the market and ultimately locks in a temporal, numerical, and evaluative frame of reference where the only questions we can usefully ask have to do with insides, outsides, and the forms of efficacy that become legible within them. This, it seems to me, posits a necessary relation between present actions and future consequences and assumes a noncontingent outcome and definite trajectory to either invigorating the human or capitulating to quantification and commodification. It also inaugurates a new political and paradigmatic coherence for humanistic inquiry, lifting quantification, number, and time outside the scope of the human, returning to number its animating metaphysics of anteriority (that countable items precede numbers, that the past is knowable, and that the future predictable based on the present). Poovey unwittingly reveals the reification of the human and of number to be complementary, not opposed. What would it mean to abandon the reification of the human and number? What would it mean to come to grips with the radical openness of the future *and* the past,[22] the noon at two o'clock, and the impossibility of an anterior real?

The discipline inside of me wonders whether literary assessments of Bartleby's formula have suffered from a lack of familiarity with other traditions of "scrivening." To copy, in the tradition to which the lawyer's other two scribes, Nippers and Turkey, belong, is to stay inside the code of semantic regulation while disseminating a particular set of inscriptions. It depends upon a conception of language as natural or maternal, and textual form (the blank page, ruled lines on a piece of paper) as transparent.[23] But does copying always proceed from the given of the language? Take the language today called Indonesian or Melayu. A lingua franca, it was no one's mother tongue when its use was encouraged by the Dutch in their East Indian colonies. Its formation proceeded through a kind of inaccurate copying that lacked an original. The linguist H.M.J. Maier writes that Melayu "was the result of learning by reciprocal imitation."[24] Anthropologist James Siegel comments, "one learned the lingua franca by imitating what the other said while the other was doing the same" (1997:15). Emerging on the threshold of the colonial relation, Melayu was placeless, "a language without the built-in authority the taking on of which gives one not only a sense of mastery but, as a speaker, the reassurance of having a place in the world" (p. 16). Melayu was thought of, "even by many of those for whom it was a mother tongue, as a second language. Its function as a lingua franca continued and gave the impression that, after all, there was (another) first language to fall back on, even if one did not know it oneself" (p. 16). Interchanges between Dutch colonials and East Indians from different islands and linguistic communities were never quite translations, because translation implies moving between "code[s] already formed"; "in the case of Melayu," Siegel writes, "one is uncertain" (p. 19).

This linguistic flux disrupted the conventions of scrivening, or rather concocted other conventions that would have been unfamiliar to Bartleby's employer. Siegel describes the case of Muhammad Bakir, an early-twentieth-century resident of Batavia (now Jakarta) who owned a lending library and made copies of the texts in his possession. Unlike Nippers and Turkey, who copied what they saw and nothing else, Bakir inserted other words into the texts he was copying. There was nothing particularly unusual about this, for copyists, Siegel remarks, frequently made emendations in their copies. What was unusual here was the way Bakir introduced himself into the texts as a character, and composed a "Muhammad Bakir" who "oscillates between the text and the world" (p. 22). For example, in a story in which a princess relates to an audience that she is an orphan, and her listeners begin to sob, Bakir the Scrivener, who knew the pain of growing up without a parent, copies: "Many tears were shed, and the writer [i.e., Bakir, the scrivener] started crying as well, because his father died when he was still young and his mother did her best to comfort him." In other texts, Bakir copied dates that corresponded to his own time, not the mythological time of some of the stories he was copying. Through the medium of the new lingua franca, a nonmaternal language without spatiotemporal location or authority derived from any person's or group's mastery, Bakir the Scrivener created a world where "one finds oneself in the world and the text indistinguishably" (p. 21). The characters of the texts he was copying cried out to him; or, rather, to the writer of the "original" text. It is Bakir who hears them and who copies what they say—"O writer, enough, stop writing such things. I can't stand such pain. Change to another tale. Don't go on with this. O writer, who are you, and where do you stay, that you have the heart to make up such a story, so painful. You don't feel it, that's why you write whatever you like" (in Siegel, 1997:21)—leading Siegel to summarize, "The writer, who should exist before the character can speak, is spoken to by the character in a time that is paradoxically before the time the writer writes and yet, as evidenced by the existence of the text, after it as well" (p. 21).

In this historical moment of copying, the Indonesian word *pengarang* signified both character and narrator. Time and space accreted to each other in new arrangements in the copied texts, and there could be no question of pasts remembered or futures anticipated in this time-space, as copyists like Bakir composed stories from all over the world and of all kinds (from epics to gossip columns) for the newly constituting public that would become "Indonesians" (Siegel 1997:21). Bakir's copies thus reiterated the formation of the lingua franca itself. "He imitates the other who wrote the text before him and then, finding himself in the other's place, gives himself his own name in that place. He copies himself copying down the text, thereby introducing a series of duplicates of himself that began with making a copy of someone else's words" (pp. 23–24). Siegel does not mention this, but it is fitting that the root for *pengarang* (*karang*) refers to physical compositions and encrustations, and has the primary meaning of coral reef, that rhizomatic assemblage that provides chalk, a medium of inscription through dust, of impermanent and provisional tracing. The word also refers to things that are deeply rooted.[25]

LET ME ATTEMPT to distinguish what I might call the threshold of the past contingent from the analytic of insides and outsides, surfaces and depths. Marilyn Strathern uses the notion of merography (from *mero* = part and *graphy* = writing) to make explicit the modality of Euro-American common and critical sense that attempts to understand things by seeing them as parts of other things. We could call this contextualization, with the caveat that the merographic modality of knowledge is infinitely generative: contexts can be seen as parts of other contexts, and so on. The merographic effect is that of continually shifting perspective. Lots of perspectives, lots of contexts, create more knowledge. Schlecker and Hirsch summarize, "different aspects, brought into view through different relations (i.e., contexts), can add up to create an ever more appropriate representation of the object of study" (2000:71). Ethnographic practice, of course, has always been a merographic endeavor, with anthropologists situating one cultural element in any number of contexts in order to get different vantage points on it and ultimately arrive at a portrait of a "culture."

Strathern is concerned with the moment of merographic failure: what occurs to knowledge at the limit of contextualization? As Schlecker and Hirsch explain, "It became ever more apparent that any perspective was simply a perspective on another perspective or a relation to another relation. The debates effected a fundamental epistemological uncertainty about a given 'essence' of individuals and things before all perspectives or contexts: i.e., before all sense making" (2000:77). At the limit, no analytical purchase could ever be gained on the totality of contexts constituting a thing, person, or relation. Schlecker and Hirsch take this to be a problem with the extensivity of the ethnographic method that seeks to assemble as many contexts as possible in order to consider the nature of a thing. They call for an ethnography without "extensive ambitions," an "intensive" ethnography that would consider the description and its objects to be inseparable. It would be an analytic where "part and whole collapse into one" (p. 80), where contexts are revealed as confidence tricks—con-texts—not the purchase of new perspectives.

Reimagine, then, an exchanger of Ithaca HOURS who has a perspective on the national currency that reveals it to be constructed, not given. In place of the national currency, she constructs another currency. But the terms of those two constructions are self-identical—both are fiat currencies, created by acts of political will on different levels of scale. Seeing everything as constructed allows a proliferation of perspectives and constructions that returns us to the problems of will: you can't choose to exit your culture, for the very frame of reference by which you would do so is already inscribed within it (cf. Michaels 1987). At the same time, however, the Ithaca HOURS exchanger does not actually refuse the token currency of the national economy so much as return to it an imagined originary form. Before the standardization of the U.S. dollar, local currencies proliferated, images of the nation's founding linguistic and economic transactions between settler colonists and Native Americans copied into their designs, just as the founding transactions of the community currency are enshrined on the Ithaca HOUR paper note, which exploits the homonymic potential of "HOUR" and "our." They read: "ITHACA HOURS stimulate local business by recycling our wealth locally. . . . [they] are backed by our skills, our muscles, our tools, forests, fields, and rivers." Not "In God We Trust," but "In Ithaca We Trust."

Mauss might very well ask, what is the difference? The difference is that by giving "back" to the currency its "originary" local form, which is at the same time a counterfeit counterfeit form, Ithaca HOURS return to the U.S. dollar its potential not to become national but to be "merely" another local currency. I am reminded of the formation of a lingua franca in a place that became Indonesia. The exchanger of Ithaca HOURS, like Muhammad Bakir the scrivener, returns, gives back the moment of the past contingent, the threshold of potentiality where the money-form could become and could not become something else. The exchanger of Ithaca HOURS is in this sense a fake forger, a counterfeit counterfeiter. The difference between the constructedness of the givens of the national narrative and the (con)texts of past contingents is a problem of perspectives versus intensives. If we abandon perspectives, then memories can evade the logic of adequation. They might not be adequate to anything.

CHAPTER 4

Innumerate Equivalencies: Making Change with Alternative Currencies

> When all is said and done, the quality of uncanniness can only
> come from the fact of the "double" being a creation dating back
> to a very early mental stage, long since surmounted—a stage, inci-
> dentally, at which it wore a more friendly aspect. The "double"
> has become a thing of terror, just as, after the collapse of their
> religion, the gods turned into demons.
> —Sigmund Freud, 1919

EVERYWHERE THERE ARE indications that money, once supposedly welded
to its value as a natural characteristic of its very substance, is increasingly
abstract, detached from any grounding materiality, operating in the realm
of pure sign. From reflection on the democratic possibilities of the revelation that money is "only" information (Hart 2001) to appreciation of the
logics of circulation warranting the abstractions of contemporary finance
(Lee and LiPuma 2002), analysts of contemporary monetary formations
wonder what happens to the age old question of how a material object can
ever be adequate to abstract value when the object itself literally no longer
seems to matter. The story of money is repeatedly told in venues scholarly
and popular as an evolutionary tale of greater and greater distance from
actual things, of greater dematerialization, in a linear trajectory from barter
to metal coin, to paper backed by metal, to paper declared valuable by
fiat, and finally, perhaps, to complex financial entities like derivatives, with
future, not anterior, backing. The study of the social implications of these
monetary transitions has a long and esteemed lineage indeed, from Aristotle to Simmel and twentieth-century anthropology and sociology.

More broadly, however, because of its implication in the problem of
the relationship between a material reality and an abstract representation,
money in the Western philosophical tradition has often served as the sine
qua non of the problem of the possibility of truth itself. Barter, the story
goes, was direct, unmediated exchange of a quantity of one kind of thing
for quantities of another. People bartering did not have to reason any more
abstractly than the figuring of ratios (how many apples will get you a fish?).
Once money appeared, and mediation by a third term entered the exchange

operation, a new kind of abstraction had taken place. Traders (and analysts) got caught up in the curious dynamics of monetary equivalence, and the conundrum of money's very existence: how can everything be placed on one scale of value figured in terms of money, and how can this thing called money take on such mediating powers?

Anthropologists have long recognized that the "introduction" of money is never so simple an affair, of course. Paul Bohannan's (1959) classic studies showed that other schemes of reckoning abstract value existed in Tiv society before the impact of "general purpose" money came on the scene. More recent writers, like those in an exemplary collection (Akin and Robbins 1999), document the complexity of the interactions between general and special purpose moneys. Others, in sociology, demonstrate that general purpose money, deemed to dissolve all things into the flat wash of monetary value, has never been as straightforward as it has seemed, and that people rarely actually commensurate all things with money, or all moneys with things (Zelizer 1997).

Even though it is so trite and so old, the story of increasing abstraction always seems to cause flashes of revelation when new kinds of actual exchange make explicit the disconnection between money and whatever substance or power is deemed to underwrite it. The debate over the introduction of the greenback in the nineteenth-century United States resonates with contemporary conversations about derivatives, as it does with Melanesian discussions about Western-style moneys' interface with other items. We continually seem surprised by money's disconnect, or its failure "really" to capture worth. In his rich discussion of Melanesian currencies, Robert Foster concludes that Melanesians receive new national moneys in a manner that "exceeds the limits" of representation and abstraction, for "money can never represent or stand for anything else 'truly,' that is, fully and finally. . . . [T]he issue is no longer one of representation's arbitrariness, but rather its ultimate failure. In other words, money is always representationally flawed" (1999:230–31).

Attending to the representational failure of money occasions a reconsideration of the barter story, as well. Marilyn Strathern has argued that assessments of barter as relatively unmediated hinge on a misrecognition of the mathematics and pragmatics of such exchanges. She finds that value here hinges not on the commensuration of differences between things, but rather "a substitution of units" (1992b:185). These units are conceived "as body parts, from bodies (persons) which . . . must first be construed as partible" and also, therefore, as encompassing other things as well (p. 185). This process does not conjure objects separate from subjects, but partible persons/things and abstractable units that are substituted—not compared—with one another. This is not reification of the bourgeois kind. There, by contrast, comparison introduces numerical ratios between dif-

It doesn't build a bigger community, because it's just between the two of us. Now, maybe you say to a friend, hey, you can swap with her for this . . . but [then], if we have cliques swapping, and we have a dozen [people], then nothing happens. So, I guess I've broadened my concept of barter . . . to see how one could barter and trade with more than the person that you started with.

How would you compare [the] sort of barter relationships that you see now, that are direct, with something like the HOURS program?

They're nothing alike.

They're nothing alike? Tell me why.

Emmm . . . because one, one . . . Emmm . . . They're not alike, sort of, of, economically.[1]

---

ferent goods to commensurate value, and poses the problem of the adequacy of a representation (value) to its objects—the very problem that preoccupies the theory and practice of money. Substitution, by contrast, creates analogies, and equivalence in the exchange of gifts "will always (can only) appear as a matching of units" made to become analogues of one another (p. 171).

What if the abstraction of monetary mediation were really a form of substitution? What if the pragmatics of money—not what it does, but *how* it does—obviate that substitution because those pragmatics always seem to involve commensuration and calculation and, thus, comparison rather than substitution?[2] The adequation of substance to value might then be seen as an indigenous analytical procedure that takes the attention away from analogy and makes money appear to be a matter of abstraction and mediation instead, much in the manner that Sohn-Rethel thought it was, as discussed in the previous chapter. Loosening the grip of adequation may also help to turn around the implicit assessments of abstraction in many discussions of money. Is there a sense in which grain futures, for example, are irreducibly material, and grain highly abstract? Can we imagine a world where the problem of abstraction and adequation obviates the practical effectivity of money, despite, or because of, money's representational failures? Whither, then, social inquiry, a practice that defines itself in relation to the adequacy of its representations to a reality that supposedly precedes it? In other words, does acknowledging money's representional failure point up that of social inquiry, our intellectual currency, itself?

My central contention in this chapter is that accepting money to pose a problem of abstraction and adequation presumes a starting point from a state of fallen grace, a world where matter and spirit are sundered, and only the divine can make the Word flesh. And yet, it is unclear whether we have ever left that state of grace, or whether, instead, continuing in the now of the assumption that we have done so permits other work to take place.

Money's Equivalences

In most standard descriptions, modern money depends on its function as the general equivalent—the yardstick according to which all value can be measured, the solution into which all goods and services can be dissolved.[3] Scholars of money take various positions on the ramifications of that function. Does money's ability to render the qualitative into the quantitative flatten social relations, working like an "acid" on all humane values (Simmel [1907] 1990; see Bloch and Parry 1989:6)? Does money "homogenize" and produce a "featureless" world of "universal exchangeability" (Fine and Lapavitsas 2000:367)? Does it "disembed" social relations from their place and time, leading the advance toward modernity (Giddens 1990)? Does money's universal reach demand that there ought there to be limits to the placing of all goods and services on one scale of value (Radin 1993)? These questions assume that quantification necessarily involves standardization, homogenization, and universal commodification.

Those who are critical of the "money as acid" hypothesis draw attention to the myriad kinds and multiple effects of money. Money, they argue, does not simply or merely or universally flatten relations and meanings; it can enrich them, multiply them, complexify them (Akin and Robbins 1999; Bloch and Parry 1989; Carruthers and Espeland 1998; Zelizer 1997). Money may be earmarked for specific purposes; it may be separated out into distinct bundles between which convertibility becomes problematic if not impossible (Zelizer 1997). Nonetheless, these critics assume, monetization goes hand in hand with calculation (p. 12). Although money "commensurates incommensurabilities" (Carruthers and Espeland 1998:1400), the quantitative function of money "downplays, or even ignores those aspects of value that cannot be reduced to a single number" (p. 1401). In this line of inquiry, money's role in *commodification* comes under scrutiny. The distinction between the gift and the commodity is revealed to soften with use, and, more importantly, to be a distinction borne of the West's ideologies about itself (Bloch and Parry 1989). Arjun Appadurai has suggested, along these lines, that transcending the "us and them" oppositions implicit in arguments over money and commodification on the one hand and the gift on the other entails critical work to "restore the cultural dimension to societies that are too often represented simply as economies writ large, and to restore the calculative dimension to societies that are too often simply portrayed as solidarity writ small" (1986:12).

In these accounts, that "calculative dimension," equivalence as a mathematical operation, presents itself as common sense, much as it does in Mary Poovey's critique of market values, discussed in the previous chapter. The mathematical operation is accepted as doing what it claims for itself (as it were): that it calculates, equates, desacralizes, and rationalizes.[4] But is the conversion to number simply a reduction, a transformation to a lower-order level that permits a generalized abstraction of value across otherwise incommensurable domains? Highlighting the "social differentiation" (Zelizer 2000:385) of money sidesteps the problem: it does not address the question of whether the mathematical operation of equivalence actually rationalizes, but is an "additive" critique: money may rationalize and desacralize, but it also does different kinds of social and meaningful work. Since all analysts of money seem to agree that monetization goes hand in hand with calculation, we need to examine more than the "social networks" and "discursive regimes" in which money moves (Leyshon and Thrift 1997:38). We also need to attend to its mathematics: not whether and how the mathematics are used, not the meanings attached to it, not its metaphorical functions—but the mathematical form of the equivalence function itself. I will argue that this is a moral form.

Equivalence is not a straightforward or self-evident affair; it rotates around a specific numerological metaphysics that hinges on the figure zero and the algebraic function. Equivalence is also haunted by the possibility of its own failure, the lack of certainty at its core embodied by the figure zero in the algebraic equation necessary for any monetary conversion. Equivalence is haunted as well as by the uncanny doubling its potential failure facilitates, its rendering of difference into similitude, but not quite (Bhabha 1994; Schwartz 1996). It is this "not quite," this troubling remainder, that animated Renaissance European double-entry bookkeeping, and wizarded from accountants' books the mysteries of "income" and "profit," the sublime objects of capitalist ideology (Poovey 1998). To make this case, this chapter presents contemporary alternative numerologies of money and finance. I am interested in how, in their moments of apparent analytical, but not pragmatic, failure, these alternatives call into question the general equivalent and its attendant mathematics, and make explicit the messy but necessary remainders of those capital equations.

In the sections that follow, I explore specific mathematical practices among adherents to alternative monetary forms—the elimination of interest and interest-bearing debt in a mutual fund market framework and the making of change in a farmers' market transaction. The chapter considers whether and how these contemporary alternatives, in their moments of apparent breakdown, concoct new monetary, mathematical, and meaningful forms, and reveal something hidden in the old. I am interested in the morally fraught equivalencies that occur when Islamic conceptions of *riba* are translated into *zakat*, and when alternative currencies are translated into U.S. dollars. According to the explicit ideologies articulated around these monetary forms, such translations should not be possible. Yet, in fact, they continually recur. They also, I will suggest, work in concert with critical analyses of capitalism, in an ideological fantasy constituting possibilities of social change in frameworks of monetary transformation.

PURIFYING ISLAMIC MUTUAL FUNDS

In 1999, Dow Jones inaugurated the Dow Jones Islamic Market Index (DJIM). One of its family of stock market indices, the purpose of which is to aid investors and especially mutual fund portfolio managers in the selection of stocks, the Islamic Market Index was intended to provide "a definitive standard for measuring stock market performance for Islamic investors on a global basis" (Dow Jones 1999:3). Like other Dow Jones indices, it is updated and disseminated every fifteen seconds.

As is the case for most Islamic financial institutions, the DJIM submits to periodic review of a Shari'a Supervisory Board (SSB). Generally speaking, SSBs are made up of scholars, jurists, and clerics from a variety of countries representing the world community of Muslims. While members of SSBs adhere to one of the four main branches of Islamic jurisprudence, in practice they are bricoleurs, drawing from any jurisprudential source they deem appropriate for a particular problem. The several international clearinghouses for Islamic financial services information—from the Institute for Islamic Banking and Insurance in London, to the Harvard Islamic Finance Information Program, to the Islamic Finance Net Internet Listserv—routinely field questions from Islamic banking professionals seeking a particular legal school's opinion on a particular issue.[5]

The index proceeds from two assumptions about the relationship between Islam and the global market. The first is the assumption that something called a "global Islamic market" always-already exists. The index is simply a method of "measuring" it at any given moment. Measuring that market entails first determining which business activities make it up. To do so, Dow Jones devised "filters" or "screens" that would catch the elements of the already-existing global market that are "Islamic," and sift out those that are not. The second assumption follows closely on the first: any business activity *permissible* according to Islamic norms—themselves subject of considerable controversy—is itself *Islamic*. In other words, if I were to open up a widget company and sell shares of it on the stock market, my widget company would be deemed Islamic even if none of its activities had anything to do with any actually existing Muslims or any Islamic religious or financial principles. So long as I did not intentionally or unintentionally violate those principles, my company would be deemed to be (actively) following those principles.[6] The idea that the passive nonviolation of Islamic principles implies active acceptance of them is in line with the Islamic modernists who, at the beginning of the twentieth century, argued that any activity that proceeds according to "universal rules" (from the motions of the planets to the decisions of an entrepreneur) adheres, on the basis of that universailty, to the principles of the divinity. Such thinking allows contemporary modernists to claim that Islam permits the purest expression of the market form; and that, if Islam signifies justice, then the purest market signifies justice, as well (just as Posner thought it did).

At the same time, the operations of the Index proceed as if this global Islamic market is in a constant state of fraught conjurings. Dow guidelines provide two main screens to filter stocks deemed Islamically pure from the total universe of stocks. The first eliminates businesses whose activities violate Islamic law: those that deal with alcohol, tobacco, pork products, financial services, defense and weapons, and entertainment. The final element of this list is significant because it represents a path of least resistance: rather than assessing which hotels serve alcohol or pork, for example, or which motion picture production studios are involved in anything approaching the pornographic (which is considered prohibited in Islam), Dow Jones decided to eliminate all of them from the investable field. For the same reason, some Islamic mutual fund portfolio managers exclude all companies involved in any kind of meat production because, as one put it, "You never really know what goes on in those places." The global Islamic market, then, while assumed by the DJIM to be always-already there in the world, ready to be measured, is not quite as clearly bounded or absolute as it may appear. It is always at risk from unholy dangers, as well as mundane inaccuracies (for example, some meat or entertainment businesses may be operating in perfect accordance with Islamic norms but end up screened out of the global Islamic market by the operations of the DJIM).

The second screen deals not with what kind of business a company does, but the manner in which it operates. It consists of three separate "financial ratio filters" that sift out "companies with unacceptable levels of debts or impure interest income." The first excludes companies whose debt to assets ratio is greater than or equal to 33 percent. The second excludes companies whose accounts receivables to total assets ratio is greater than or equal to 45 percent. The third excludes companies whose interest income to revenue ratio is greater than or equal to 5 percent. In May 2001, the DJIM issued a revision of these financial ratio filters, such that corporate debt can constitute up to 33 percent of its market capitalization instead of 33 percent of assets, and interest is limited to less than one-third of market capitalization, instead of 5 percent of income. The revision has sparked discussion and controversy among members of several Islamic banking Internet discussion groups, who worry that the DJIM, in the interests of expanding the investable universe of stocks, has become more "liberal." The DJIM may re-

vise these filters further in light of these concerns, and many Islamic financial advisers currently, when in doubt, use the old guidelines.

These financial ratio filters seek to guard the Islamic market against *riba*,
often glossed as interest. As already discussed, the prohibition against *riba*
is hotly debated. Islamic economics, both as an academic discipline and a
field of professional expertise, hinges on the prohibition. In the calling
forth of a global Islamic market, however, the Dow Jones Islamic Market
Index—one of the movement's greatest and most visible successes—appears to turn that absolute into a calculus, a limiting function that does not
screen out *riba* entirely, but rather keeps it within specified parameters.

The transformation of *riba* into a limit function permits another. Although financial derivatives like futures and options are held by many in
Islamic finance to be a form of gambling, the technical and especially mathematical apparatus warranting them can become a tool for "purification."[7]
Islamic financial engineers can use derivative pricing procedures like the
Black-Scholes formula to "purify" a portfolio. An Islamic mutual fund
manager can use such a formula to estimate how much of a stock's return
derives from that fraction of a company's income that is derived from interest. The manager can then determine how much of the total portfolio's
return derives (theoretically, at least) from interest. That amount can be
"purified" by being given to charity. Now, the status of that charity is up
for debate. When I first heard presentations about the DJIM Index at conferences in the late 1990s, many equated that charity with *zakat*, obligatory
alms. By 2001, however, many were saying that it could not be *zakat* because the amount given in charity could never be predicted in advance and
meet the requirements of "true" *zakat* (generally defined as 2.5 percent of
one's income and assets per year).[8] At issue is the question of when charity
becomes *zakat* or when it is more properly *sadaqa*, the voluntary contributions discussed in the last chapter that have an etymological relation to
truth and to friendship. To some, however, these gifts to charity are not
properly speaking "voluntary," since not making them means withholding
forbidden *riba* or tainted income.

Alongside the debate over charity runs another. The use of mathematical
theory (e.g., Elgari 2000) points up Islamic financial engineers' understanding of mathematics in moral terms. The Black-Scholes formula, for example,
is a probability function designed to deal with a stochastic or random process. As such, it is a product of what economic historian Philip Mirowski
(1989) has termed the "probabilistic counter-revolution" in neoclassical economic theory. Mirowski has traced the rise of probability theory in economics to a repudiation of strictly determinist models and an elaboration of
statistical procedures designed to deal with real-world numbers and to
"eventually achieve numerical results." But, for the Islamic portfolio manag-

ers, those numerical results are moral results, even if—or because—the results are subject to "differences of opinion" (Elgari 2000:77).

Islamic financial engineers can also mathematically scale the *riba* calculus by attempting to approach the limit of the limit. In the words of one portfolio manager, "even though the Shari'a Board allows up to 33 percent debt and 5 percent interest, we try to keep it well below that, like, to 18 percent and 2 or 3 percent, because otherwise it's just wasted—we have to give it up in charity." In the "pure market" of the Islamic index, in other words, investors still demand returns and do not want to see their investments "wasted" on charity, regardless of any religious mandate. It is a mistake to view this as a contradiction between theory and practice. What is at stake is a matter of both a remaking of Islam through the bringing together of *riba* and charity, and the remaking of the market as moral even in the pursuit of individual profit without regard for others. For, in the Islamic banking formulation, Islam and the market are/ought to be "equivalent."

The mathematical operation of equivalence between *riba* and charity also reveals people's efforts to resist it in the name of economic profit ("we don't want to waste it in charity"). Even that resistance, however, by serving the laws of "the market," presumed to operate according to the dictates of individual profit-seeking, serves the modernist conception of Islam at the center of Islamic economics. The mathematics of Islamic financial engineering points toward the divine and the market, both of which are taken to index the greater good of social justice. Social justice is symbolized and made material, then, both in the giving of charity, whether as *zakat* or *sadaqa*, and in the effort to avoid doing so. The numbers that allow these moral mathematical calculations point toward "facts" that, far from being deracinated particulars, are always-already evidentiary. The equivalence function is never complete; there is always a moral remainder, as it were. That remainder is the uncanny presence of an abstraction of transcendental value—the value of God and the values of the market.

MAKING CHANGE IN LOCAL CURRENCIES

A young woman who had decided to leave the suburbs, college, and the predictable path of so many of her peers in exchange for the life of an organic cooperative farmer stood in the summer sun one Tuesday morning, explaining to me her use of a local, alternative scrip currency in lieu of the U.S. dollar. "A lot of people [here] don't support the government completely. . . . I definitely like to see the fact that we can keep a local currency, and I think it builds community more, and people get involved with the community as well."

At the same time, she articulated a particular anxiety that repeatedly surfaced in people's everyday use of the local currency. While speaking of the produce she sells in the farmers' market, she lingered over the very practical problem of "making change," both in the sense of returning to a customer the remainder of a market transaction, and in the sense of contributing to the building of a new society: After showing me that she sells bunches of carrots for a dollar each, she continued:

> most of our stuff is done in even prices, so, like an eighth of an HOUR is a dollar twenty-five, so, [if you purchase a bunch of carrots with a 1/8 HOUR note,] you get the twenty-five cents back. And that's one thing, that [is] kind of strange about it, . . . you know. . . . Um, just, because we're trying to avoid the currency as much as possible, and to exchange back and forth like that with it . . . kind of breaks the whole system in a way.

Her use of HOURs, she believed, was a small part of a shift away from American materialism and corporate domination and toward "community values" and "community solidarity." And yet, at the same time, she remarked, of American society more generally, "I really don't see it changing all that much."

Time and again I encountered people who, in the course of dealing in HOURs, had to make equivalence conversions that never seemed to sit well with them.[9] Some tried to settle their anxiety about making change in the farmers' market by simply trying to keep their dollars separate from their HOURs and maintaining this monetary boundary as strongly as possible. Sometimes, this could mean losing a sale. Mostly, however, this would mean simply turning down a customer's HOURs and accepting only dollars—even, and especially, when a market vendor is what people call a "diehard" HOURs supporter. The diehards' efforts to maintain a clear separation and to deny convertibility between HOURs and dollars more often than not results in their accepting more U.S. dollars than they would otherwise, if, for example, they would simply break change for an eighth-HOUR note and return to a customer the twenty-five cents owed on a purchase of a one-dollar bunch of carrots. People who made an effort to keep their HOURS and dollars separate often kept their U.S. currency in a lockbox, and their HOURS in an envelope. One diehard who used this method told me she started doing it because some customers would come to "buy the smallest thing they could and try to get cash back." This same farmer, the next day, was unable to break my quarter-HOUR note when I attempted to purchase some beans, and so insisted I pay in U.S. currency. "Wouldn't you know it. . . . I think the HOURS are in the other truck. Well," she joked, "there you have it. You try to use HOURs . . . " You try to use HOURs, and then you can't.

Fractional HOURS notes make the problem of the commensuration of HOURS with dollars more explicit, and more explicitly foreground the problem of the labor theory of value subtending the currency. Until 2003, the smallest HOURS note, the 1/8 HOUR, already pointed toward the pull of the dollar over that of labor time because while 1/4 HOUR can convert into a useful $2.50, an eighth of an hour of labor time is only 7.5 minutes—not a particularly "useful" amount of time within which to conduct a service. In 2003, the new board of directors began issuing 1/10 HOUR notes. Again, this is very convenient from the point of view of a dollar exchange—1/10 HOUR equals one dollar—but again makes explicit the HOUR's failure, after a fashion, as a currency tied to labor for its labor time equivalent is only 6 minutes.

At the same time, however, among vendors and farmers, HOURs seem usefully and tangibly to supplement U.S. dollars. HOURs and dollars mix freely in the repayment of debts and the settling of accounts between vendors and farmers, especially between farmers on the one hand and crafts vendors on the other. They are used together and interchangeably—often, as part of the same payment—for transactions that take place within the farmers' market on a regular basis. One pottery maker, having given a farmer a basket in which to display her produce two weeks before, received from her a mixture of dollars and HOURs. He then took the HOURs and went about purchasing vegetables for the week. People usually settle debts like this on a weekly or biweekly basis, and they are central to the continuing circulation of HOURs in this community.

Other important sites for the circulation of HOURs are the several large businesses that accept them and that offer to pay their employees partially in them. "For tax reasons," as one manager explained, HOURs and dollars at her establishment are not kept separate. "They're a lot like food stamps, the way we handle them," another manager explained. In people's everyday speech, HOURs' conversion into dollars is so complete that they are denominated almost automatically in dollar amounts. When I asked a store accountant "How many HOURs does each cashier keep in the drawer?" she responded instantly, "twenty-five." Twenty-five HOURs would be equivalent to $250, so, I asked for clarification. "Two hundred and fifty dollars, then?" She responded, "No, no. Twenty-five dollars," or, in other words, two and a half HOURs. Similarly, when I asked in another context how many HOURs a store took in during any given day, a clerk responded, "thirty-seven." Again, upon asking for clarification, I learned that this referred to $37, not $370.

But when people convert HOURs into dollars like this, what do they mean by "dollars"? The vault manager at one of the local credit unions that accepts HOURs showed me a page from her ledger book one afternoon. At the end of the working day, she records the *number* of pennies, nickles, dimes, quarters, one-dollar bills, five-dollar bills, ten-dollar bills, twenty-dollar bills, fifty-dollar bills, one-hundred-dollar bills, and HOURs that the credit union vault will hold that night. While there is a separate ledger column for each denomination of U.S. currency, there is only one for HOURs. In other words, there are not separate boxes in which to enter the number of eighth-HOUR notes, quarter-HOUR notes, half-HOUR notes, one-HOUR notes, and two-HOUR notes. I asked her to explain this, since, it seemed to me, the credit union would want an accurate tally of its holdings in HOURs each night. She told me that she is not required to enumerate HOUR notes in the same way she does dollars and cents. Instead, she converts HOURs into a dollar equivalent, using the ten-dollar-per-HOUR rate, and records their "value." As she explained this to me, her voice trailed off: "You know, it's so unreal. When you see all the money in there, and have to record it on a piece of paper like this, it's just so unreal."

Here is a clue, I believe, to the referent of "dollar" in people's near-automatic rendering of HOURs into dollars. It is not the dollar as a piece of paper, or the dollar signified by tally marks in a ledger book, or the enumerative presence of tangible objects held in a vault. Rather, the dollar indexed in statements like "We keep twenty-five HOURs in the drawer, I mean, twenty-five dollars of HOURs," is the dollar as abstract numeraire of value. In the ledger book, HOURs have presence as value, not as enumerated objects. That value is measured in terms of "abstract" dollars, not physical paper dollars. The disbelief of the vault manager—"it's just so unreal!"—is quite instructive: we know the dollars in the vault are just pieces of paper. Indeed, in the books, they signify *only* as pieces of paper, as objects in the world, one-nesses in the sense described by Sohn-Rethel and discussed in the previous chapter, pure things in themselves that are not beholden to any theory, person, or social relation for their presence but are just there. In contrast, HOURs are animated by the dollar as numeraire, as the abstraction of value.[10] Even in the paper dollar's negation as value in the ledger book of the bank accountant who is simply interested in counting objects qua objects, or in the cash boxes and envelopes of the diehard organic farmers seeking to stand outside of the dollar economy, the "abstract" dollar asserts itself, again and again. The remainder left over after the (attempted) transaction in HOURs, "making change" in both the monetary and social senses, is the uncanny presence of an abstraction of transcendental value—the value of the dollar and the values of the market.

EQUIVALENCE AND THE MOUSETRAP

What is at stake in the apparent revelation of transcendental value in these two monetary alternatives to contemporary financial globalization? In both instances, analysis reveals hidden terms, just beneath the surface. Diagnosis: fetishism! Actually, double fetishism. What analysis reveals is not the "real" truth of the matter, but another fetishistic spirit: Islamic banking and Ithaca HOURS are both haunted by transcendental value, which is simultaneously their greatest failing as true "alternatives" and their greatest mystery, the spirit that keeps them functioning. And what is this transcendental value but a fundamental misrecognition, a covering over of the really real relations of production that are structuring market transactions and, in the case of the local currency, literally "backing" value—labor power. This, however, is too simple an analysis. As James Ferguson cogently remarks, "The danger in thinking is not so much fetishism as it is the illusion that one has escaped it" (1988:490).

Equivalence, a reduction into sameness, is obviously part of the fantasy work of fetishism. For Marx and Freud, money, in rendering dissimilars into species of the same, participated in the uncanny. Marx referred back to Shakespeare:

> Shakespeare brings out two particular properties of money. 1. It is the visible god-head, the transformation of all human and natural qualities into their opposites , the general confusion and inversion of things; it makes impossibilities fraternize. 2. It is the universal whore, the universal pander between men and peoples. The inversion and confusion of all human and natural qualities, the fraternization of impossibilities, this divine power of money lies in its being the externalized and self-externalizing species-being of man. It is the externalized capacities of humanity. What I cannot do as a man, thus what my individual faculties cannot do, this I can do through money. Thus money turns each of these faculties into something that it is not, i.e., into its opposite. (Marx [1844] 1997:110)

For Marx, the transformation of things into their opposites spoke of the monstrous reduction of human relationships into relations among things, by way of the dismembering of the person into bourgeois self and alienated labor. "By turning his money into commodities that serve as the material elements of a new product, and as factors in the labour process, by incorporating living labour with their dead substance, the capitalist at the same time converts value, i.e., past, materialized, and dead labour, into capital, into value big with value, a live monster that is fruitful and multiplies" ([1865–66] 1997: 468).[11]

It seems we cannot escape monsters. At the same time, however, merely "revealing" what was previously hidden perpetrates three errors. First, it assumes that the hidden actually is or was obscured. In fact, in the Islamic banking and local currency examples, that which I could have identified as the latent content of the monetary equivalence, was, upon occasion at least, clearly articulated in the practices if not the consciousness of participants

themselves. I did not reveal a hidden term—God/dollars—so much as re-
fract it through their own discursive practices. Second, it assumes that the
analyst has some special access denied participants—a classic anthropological and critical hubris. Participants in these alternative monetary forms
know quite well that God and the dollar lurk just behind the surface, and
even, sometimes at least, know quite well that something else lies behind
even these terms—the social for Islamic banking, inflected through the
term *justice*, and labor power for the local currency, indexed most directly
in the very name of the money ("hours"). Third, and most important, it
does little to answer the question of why *equivalence-functions* and not some
other operation conjure the spirit of transcendental value in order to hide
the real spirit of value—labor—and replace it with the sublime. Why, as
Žižek puts it, should the content assume such a form (1995:300), the form
of the algebraic equation?

Diane Nelson provocatively indicates, "Playing detective and getting
down to how the fetish 'really' works completely misses the magic act"
(1999:77). The magic act here involves the three errors just articulated.
Attending to the magic act means breaking with the tradition of algebraic
reason—"solve for x"—that has characterized social analysis and that rests
on the stability of the distinction between fact and evidence (as well as
ontology and morality, profane and sacred, etc.). There is a "more" that
fascinates in revealing the secrets of the commodity-form and the equiva-
lence-function. This "more" drives the critical impulse, both my critical
impulse and that of the people whose monetary alternatives I have discussed. We are both, after all, members of "reflexive" communities that
"consciously pose [ourselves] the problem of [our] own creation" (O'Doherty et al. 1999:1646, quoting Lash 1994). This "more," I am suggesting,
following Žižek (1994), is the fantasy-work of the form itself. The question
better posed, then, is not what is at stake in revealing the latent content of
the fetish, but what is *on stage*, both when analysts, through critique, and
analysands, through monetary alternatives, attempt to do so?

Consider Islamic portfolio management and local currency transactions
as a drama within the drama of global capitalism, or a play-within-a-play.
In Alenka Zupančič's excursion into Hitchcock films, the play-within-a-
play represents a "moment where fiction is faced with its own exterior at
its own interior" (1992:82). In the play-within-a-play, that which is ex-
cluded from the fiction in order for it to function as narrative, all the background assumptions, technologies, and prediscursive elements that are the
conditions of possibility of narrativity, are condensed into the moment of
the fictionality *within* the fiction. For example, to stick with the filmic analogy, if the microphone boom or gaffer were visible to viewers of the film,
the magic of the movie would evaporate. However, the filmmaker *can* represent those technologies and background elements through a process of

doubling or duplication inside a fictional scene set within the film, in a drama that the filmic characters view, for example. In Hitchcock (e.g., *Murder*, or *The Thirty-Nine Steps*) this moment of fiction-within-fiction is right at the center of the larger narrative, and it constitutes the space of revelation toward which the narrative flows. The doubling effected by the play-within-the-film reveals the "sign of guilt" of the murderer, as well as the signs of guilt of the originary fictional act. The effect is that of a setup (for the murderer as well as the viewing audience), a "mousetrap."[12]

The mousetrap device stands in contrast to the "whodunit." In a whodunit, we "coldly and without emotion await the end to learn who committed the murder. The whole interest is concentrated in the ending" (Zupančič 1992:83). The detective in the whodunit plays the role of the scientist/analyst: he or she gathers clues and reconstructs the crime, and thereby deduces the identity of the murderer. But "if the climax of the whodunit is the moment when the murderer's identity is revealed," the mousetrap setup is quite different (p. 83). "The fascinating point is not the revelation of the murderer's identity, the reconstruction of the crime and the deduction of the truth, but *the manner in which the truth is displayed*—or is gazing at us, if we can put it that way, in the glint of the murderer's eye" (p. 84, my emphases).

Islamic banking and local currencies, as plays-within-a-play, are like Hitchcockian mousetraps. It is not the revelation of truth—"I have gathered all the clues and now can point the finger: the capitalist is the murderer! He has turned dead human labor into living nonhuman objects!" Rather, it is the particular staging of truth: in making change, or failing to do so, and in giving *zakat*, or seeking to avoid it, the actors in the play-within-the-play reveal the transcendental in the failures of equivalence, materialized in their social activity. That transcendental is uncanny precisely because it is so deeply familiar to social practice. As Žižek puts it, "the fundamental level of ideology . . . is not of an illusion masking the real state of things, but that of an (unconscious) fantasy structuring our social reality itself" (Žižek 1995:316). Or, in other words, the illusion "consists in overlooking the illusion which is structuring our real, effective [and affective][13] relationship to reality" (p. 316).[14]

The ideology-work, in short, is the act of critical analysis of the real, the attempt to be "nonduped" by ideology, whether in "my" social science fictions[15] or "their" alternative market forms. Because of our complicity in each other's critical projects, we perpetuate the illusion that we are beyond or above the illusion. Or, in other words, we perpetuate the facticity of the facts of both social science and monetary transactions: in a word, the enumerable, that which is capable of entering into the algebra of equivalence in the first place. This holds even for the human sciences, and not just the quantitative ones. In claiming social occurrence x as an instance of phenomenon *y*, I conjure a relation of equivalence through a function of enumeration; that which is enumerated as an "instance," before it becomes evidentiary as an "instance *of*," is an enumerable deracinated particular, a "fact." This is the kind of operation that allows us to ask about the effects of equivalence (does it provide instances of homogenization, or instances of social differentiation?) without querying the equivalence function itself. And it leaves us stuck in the same debates we have been having since Simmel.

MONSTERS, MARKETS, AND MODERN FACTS

As Brian Rotman (1987) has argued, Shakespeare's *King Lear*, written around 1606, is an allegory about new economic formations and new ways of perceiving the world. It is profoundly haunted by the figure zero, the possibility of absolute absence—the "nothing" around which new knowledge practices like double-entry bookkeeping found form. The tragedy begins with Cordelia's refusal to denominate her love for Lear in monetary terms, as her two sisters had already done in return for a third each of the kingdom:

Lear: . . . what can you say to draw
A third more opulent than your sisters? Speak.

Cordelia: Nothing, my lord.

Lear: Nothing?

Cordelia: Nothing.

Lear: Nothing will come of nothing.   (I.1)

The drama continues with Lear's ensuing madness and culminates in his death, his own rendering into nothing. Because of his infatuation with the numerologics of monetary equivalence, he forsakes his kingdom and eventually his life—his crown a great 'O' as well, as indicated by the Fool, who sees "nothing" in that symbol of Lear's royal station: "Now thou art an O without a figure. I am better than thou art now: I am a fool, thou art nothing" (I.4). The play is full of accounting metaphors, some not picked up by Rotman, beginning with the opening exchange in the play, between Kent and Gloucester ("equalities are so weighed that curiosity in neither can make choice of either's moiety").[16] I am particularly fond of the metaphorical reconciling of accounts that occurs in the resolution of the conflicts between the two evil sisters and the two Eds (Edmund and Edgar)—especially the latter, who are alike, but not quite.

Given the importance of the new knowledge practices of accounting in the play, we can also read *King Lear* as part of the history of academic disciplinarity. The literary historian Mary Poovey (1998) analyzes the separation of the sciences of fact from the force of rhetoric through the development of modern financial accounting. While others have taken Poovey to task for a certain laxity in the mustering of the facts of history (e.g., Jacob 2001), I am interested in how Poovey shows the manner in which Renaissance bookkeeping constituted a modality of argument that couldn't quite escape its status as rhetoric. In part this is because people could fudge the numbers and did so all the time for different rhetorical effects.

Poovey argues further that double-entry did not simply have rhetorical effects, but was itself a specific mode of argument. The balance book pivoted around zero, a number that troubled Renaissance accountants and their interlocutors (Rotman 1987). Double-entry was an algebraic operation, and algebra had entered into Europe via the deeply religious texts of Mohammed ben Musa (also known as al-Khwarizmi, from whom we derive the word algorithm), a figure overlooked by Poovey and Rotman. For al-Khwarizmi, algebra was a prayerful activity, something not lost on the Renaissance European importers of the technique. Enumeration was not a natural act but a metaphysical one. Solving for x did not mean finding the "real" value of a slave, cost of a bride, or exchange rate between wheat and barley (the examples that make up the bulk of al-Khwarizmi's text). It was, instead, partaking in, following along with, pointing toward the quintessence, the absolute.[17] "The balance," Poovey remarks, "conjured up both the scales of justice and the symmetry of God's world" (1998:54).

There were two sides to this divinity, however. Zero, like money, was possessed of unsettling, potentially demonic powers.[18] Indeed, this relationship between zero and money was made explicit in eighteenth-century ballads about the South Sea Company's rise to prominence and spectacular downfall, as in the following little ditty by Thomas D'Urfey titled "The Hubble Bubbles":

> A bubble is blown up with air,
> In which fine Prospects do Appear,
> The Bubble breaks the Prospects lost,
> Yet must some bubble pay the cost,
> > Hubble bubble bubble hubble all is smoke
> > Bubble bubble hubble bubble all is broke
> Farewell your Woods your Houses Lands your Pastures
> > And your Flocks.
> For now you have nought but your Selves in ye Stocks.
> > (in Dugaw 1998:52)

Like the hapless stock jobber in the song, the facts of double-entry depended on their being beholden to "nothing" but themselves, on their being deracinated particulars, stand-alone data that were not wedded to any theory. They could be enlisted as evidence, but supposedly were not, in themselves, evidentiary. At the same time, however, their pivot point, zero, could not escape its broader and more sinister metaphysical connotations. After all, "now you have nought but your Selves in ye Stocks" implied not just foolishness but heresy, heresy against the divinely ordained hierarchical social and legal order and the forms of property—woods, houses, lands, pastures and flocks—that mirrored and justified it. This heresy, as a religious modality of perceiving the world, belies the easy separation of ontological facts from deontological evidence.

Historians of mathematics trace the origins of the fact/evidence distinction not to algebra but to an apparent bifurcation in concepts of probability (Daston 1988, 1994; Hacking 1977). These scholars seek to historicize the separation between probability taken as a description of random processes in the world and probability taken as an assessment of the weight of arguments (e.g., "it is probable that . . . "). The former probability, based on recording and measurement, is central to the discursive fabrication of the kinds of facts we take for granted when we talk about empirical reality. The latter transmutes into rhetoric, discourse, language games, law. The bifurcation of probability into stochastic probability and argumentative probability lies at the root of the historical separation of scientific from humanistic inquiry. Take Blaise Pascal, a figure central to most historical accounts of probability. His correspondence with Fermat over games of chance is taken as the aleatory, descriptive side of probability theory, while his wager over the existence of God is generally taken as the rhetorical, weight-of-argument side of probability theory. The former relied on number, rendered a purely descriptive function of counting; the latter relied on words and arguments, the persuasive force of rhetoric. (Shades of the sciences/humanities division in the contemporary academy.)

What then are we to make of Pascal's experiments with magic squares, however (table 4.1; Darriulat 1994)? A magic square consists of rows and columns of numbers arranged so that carrying out the same arithmetic operation across the rows and down the columns results in the same number. Christian, Jewish, and Muslim mystics used magic squares to demonstrate miracles to the heathen in order to convert them, to deduce and manipulate the flows of divine knowledge in the world, and to marvel at the unity of creation (see Karpenko 1993). Number here did not describe countable objects or phenomena in the world; rather, number was a marvel, always-already evidentiary for God's design.[19]

In short, number did not become transparent, in the sense of merely reflective of countable, deracinated particulars in the world, in any simple or direct or complete sense. Indeed, turning to the number zero, the pivot of double-entry, we find that its rhetoricality and mystical properties were never really occluded, just refracted through new knowledge practices and

TABLE 4.1
A Magic Square

1	15	14	4
12	6	7	9
8	10	11	5
13	3	2	16

discursive struggles. The balance did signify the divine, but it was the particular divinity associated with miracles and portents, not the distant divinity who set the clockwork of the universe in motion and then receded from the world's view. Where Poovey sees the balance as sidestepping the association between number and necromancy (1998:54), then, I suggest that a different slice through the sort of divinity people had in mind during their calculations reveals these number games to be far from rationalizing or desacralizing.

Miracles and portents were not just figures of numerology. They were also found in monsters. With the consolidation of Baconian science, monsters became objects of the natural world. In Robert Boyle's formulation, monsters, as aberrations, give insight into the normal order of things, and thus confirm the natural world as one eminently explicable by the laws of science (Daston and Park 1998). While Enlightenment Europeans naturalized monsters, however, they invented at the same time new figures of fancy that had the potential to topple this natural order. Both popular class and elite Western Europeans wizarded up and then tried to cope with the new cultural domains of finance and of fiction, and became avid consumers of stocks and storybooks (see Hentzi 1993; Ingrassia 1995; Sherman 1996). Returning to the South Sea Company and the emergence of modern stock markets, then, there is more to the "nothing" of D'Urfey's "Hubble Bubble" than might at first glance be apparent: "now you have nought but your Selves in ye Stocks." Not only is the present rendered a nothing; not only is property dissipated into lack. The self is, as well. Having "nought but your Selves" is tantamount to Lear reducing his crown to an empty O. In a world where property and title had gone, apparently organically, hand in hand, the troubling lack conveyed in zero, paper stocks, and fictionality—the creation of nothing out of nothing for no (holy) purpose—called forth a new and terrible beast: the person as empty cipher, the subject as its own negation and absence. This was indeed a frightening monster. It recalls Shakespeare's depiction of Goneril and Regan, the evil sisters, as no mere humans but strange and vicious creatures—serpents, kites, and carrion fowl. Zero and algebra thus did not simply close off "the infinite proliferation of number signs" (or metaphysical signs) it seemed to bring into being (cf. Rotman 1987:32), but opened up the inhuman, the soulless, and the monstrous, through the interlinked practices of spinning fictional tales and making financial speculations.[20]

The fantastic creations of paper credit also redounded into natural science. As scientists brought monsters into the natural order, they did not always do so with a ready-made explanatory framework. What was important was not the existence of a rational explanation for a miracle or a monster, but, rather, the *possibility* of there being a rational explanation. Lorraine Daston terms this, appropriately, a "promissory naturalism": "It is the possibility in principle, not the actual availability of a natural explanation, that counted here. . . . This kind of promissory naturalism, based more on metaphysical faith than scientific competence, remained typical of attempts to naturalize marvels and miracles well into the eighteenth century" (1994:251). The promissory naturalism was akin to the promissory notes of the stock-jobbers—a species of faith and credibility in the possibility of realizing abstract truths or absolute value, and not the actualization of truth or value.

I wish to draw attention to this traffic among divine monsters, natural science, mathematics, and finance in the emergence of new forms of equivalence. Doing so does not reveal something previously hidden, some nugget of essential reality or truth. Instead, it simply fleshes out some of the ghosts in the machine of capitalist numerologies. The equivalence function was never a simple desacralizing operation; its mathematical form was never purely ontological. Instead it was always a moral form. This recognition permits me to describe some of the work involved in producing both commonsense and critical "truths" of money.[21]

Lorraine Daston and Katherine Park open their book about monsters with a story told by Robert Boyle that illustrates the promissory naturalization of the uncanny, and the tight relationship between wonder, marvels, and scientific investigation. In a scientific paper published in 1672 about "shining flesh," Boyle inserted a narrative about the "night before," and set up a mousetrap of his own, a fact-within-a-fact, so to speak:

> Yesterday, when I was about to go to bed, an amanuensis of mine, accustomed to make observations, informed me, that one of the servants of the house, going upon some occasion to the larder, was frightened by something luminous, that she saw . . . where the meat had been hung up before. Whereupon, suspending for a while my going to rest, I presently sent for the meat into my chamber, and caused it to be placed in a corner of a room capable of being made considerably dark, and then I plainly saw, both with wonder and delight, that the joint of meat did, in divers places, shine like rotten wood or stinking fish; which was so uncommon a sight, that I had presently thought of inviting you to be a sharer in the pleasure of it. (quoted in Daston and Park 1998:13)

The "pleasure" of the sight, Daston and Park write, kept Boyle going right through until the next morning; he even called for another shank of veal to be delivered to his room while he was undressing for bed (p. 13). I want to suggest, in the spirit of Daston and Park, that the pleasure here is not simply that of the scientist faced with a new challenge for his emerging explanatory framework. It is also the pleasure and terror of wonder itself—the excitement of an encounter with the uncanny, and the thrill that comes from the manner in which the "truth" is revealed in a mousetrap.

In a world dominated by strikingly uniform globalization slogans that proclaim there are no alternatives to neoliberalism, financial integration, or capital mobility, it is important to insist on the experiential metaphysics of this thrill of wonder, and to recuperate the uncanny within it. This seems especially pressing in light of the scholarship on money and commodification that readily accepts quantification's desacralizing and homogenizing claims and looks elsewhere, but never at the mathematics, to find hope in other meanings, other social practices, and other institutions in an additive and indirect critique. The veal shank's unearthly glow could, after sustained scientific investigation, be naturalized—the promissory note could be cashed in for gold. The fact that such promissory notes today cannot be cashed in for gold does not take away from their relationship to the sublime and the uncanny.[22] It is important, however, not to lose sight of the fact that the ghostly glow shimmers only on rotting meat, that the other side of the sublime is slime—the messiness of desublimation necessary to create the seemingly pure forms of monetary equivalence and the seemingly pure distinctions between gift and commodity, sacred and profane, that animate whole monetary, mathematical, and market worlds (Giblett 1996; Gibson-Graham 1996; Maurer 2000).

But which is the sublime, and which is the slime, in the alternative financial forms examined in this chapter? For Islamic portfolio managers, any income "tainted" by *riba* must be "purified." For local-currency diehards, government-issued currency is quite literally "dirty money." For both, however, their efforts to make change—literally and figuratively—hinge on a transmutation of filth into faith.[23] *Riba*, forbidden interest, becomes charity, a charity that speaks to truth, friendship, social justice, and the divine. U.S. dollars become the abstraction of transcendental value. As Freud remarked, gods and demons are doubles and duplicates of each other. The same could be said of the facts and fictions animating social analyses of social change. Revealing the hidden truths of the commodity fetishism, for example, in order to bring people to consciousness of their own "real" conditions of existence, would give us the answer only to "whodunit?" This kind of algebraic reason gives the illusion of standing above the fray and outside the time of the world rather than an essential part of its becomings. The alternative monetary forms here go one better. They do not reveal truths. They restage them. They give us the pleasure and terror of the truth "in the glint of the murderer's eye," a reflection of our selves—empty ciphers, like Lear's?—while lending new meanings to the ditty, "now we have nought but our Selves in our Stocks."

CHAPTER 5

Wiseman's and Fool's Gold

THE PRACTICE OF CHRYSOGRAPHY, writing with gold on paper, emerged among scribes of the Abrahamic faiths around the same time that metal coinage was invented, and ended in the twelfth or thirteenth centuries A.D. with the introduction of paper currencies that were exchangeable for gold (Shell 1982:186). Chrysography posed a particular theological problem, for it ran the risk of commensurating the "monetary value of the written letter" with the spiritual value of the Word of God. The "medium of linguistic exchange"—written words—were penned in the "substance of monetary exchange" (p. 192). Clerics feared that the golden representation of the word of God had the potential, for the foolish at any rate, to approach the aura of the Divine.

Chrysography presented a species of the problem of the limits of "likeness and adequation" (Shell 1982:194) a problem that preoccupied thinkers in the Western tradition from the Greeks to Enlightenment philosophers arguing over the tossing of coins and the figuring calculus, the mathematics of probability, asymptotic relations, and limits. These were problems posed by the attempt to separate the "moral arithmetic of belief" from the "econometrics of marginal evaluation," or epistemological probability from statistical probability (p. 194: see also Maurer 2002b). What happens to an imitation, an original, and the relation between the two when the imitation reaches the epistemological and mathematical limit of likeness; when, as a copy, it becomes both believable and empirically accurate? Gold letters suggested, to the point of possible confusion and equation, monetary value and spiritual value. The practice of writing in gold faded just when insubstantial paper gained value from an imagined relation to gold backing it. Here, the problem shifted onto the money-form itself. Was paper as signifier adequate to its signified referent, the sublime object of true value? Fiat currencies that emerged in the nineteenth century pushed the problem further, as they were backed by nothing but credit, faith, and the insubstantiality of state promises. And counterfeit money brings it to a head, for a really good counterfeit is efficacious only so far as its fakeness remains unknown and it circulates as "good and true money" (Derrida 1992:59).

This chapter considers a case where a possible counterfeit maintains its efficacy even after the revelation of its true nature, because its true nature cannot be captured within the logic of likeness or the problematic of the relation presupposed by adequation. It does so via an alternative currency that emerged in Indonesia around the time of the Asian financial crisis, and that demonstrated, or rather performed, the interzone between alternative currencies and Islamic banking. In the course of this research, I was continually surprised to find how remarkably self-referential alternative money and finance can be. This was another manner in which the encounter between Islamic banking and alternative currencies was staged in advance of my attempt at "comparison," and accounts, again, for my effort to replicate the form of that encounter instead of engaging in a comparative project in the strict sense.

In 1992 in Birmingham, England, Umar Ibrahim Vadillo organized the first of a series of barter markets for goods produced by Muslim immigrants. Seeking to stand outside of the national economy by creating self-sufficient networks of merchants and traders, Vadillo's Sufi-inspired (and, it is rumored, possibly fascist) "Murabitun Movement" became interested in the possibility of creating a global Islamic alternative currency. By 1995, Murabitun was minting gold (and later, silver) coins—"Islamic Dinar" (and, later, "Islamic Dirham")—and, paying visits to Ithaca to consult with the inventors of the HOURS system. Vadillo published a lengthy treatise titled "The Return of the Gold Dinar," in which he outlined the philosophical and economic principles behind the currency and its role in eventually reestablishing the caliphate. By 2001, Murabitun had established an on-line system for purchasing these coins as the basis of an alternative electronic currency. Account holders use a notional currency based on the coins to purchase goods and services on-line. The coins themselves are held in a central depository in Dubai, and the entire system runs through a registered corporation in Labuan, the Malaysian offshore financial services center.[1]

In 1998, Murabitun's activities attracted the attention of the World Gold Council (WGC), a transnational consortium of gold producers organized for the purposes of "inducing lasting-effect structural changes in gold markets" and promoting gold marketing and gold-positive attitudes in consumers (WGC, "Mission Statement"). Its monthly review of gold-related articles in the world press had picked up an item in *Final Call*, the magazine of the U.S.-based Nation of Islam, on the creation of a global Islamic gold standard (Muhammad 1998; WGC, "Notes and Quotes," March 1998). A few months later an editorial appeared in *Gold Eagle*, the magazine promoting the eponymous American gold coin and sponsored by the WGC, in which the Murabitun's Islamic Dinar was described as a potential "Islamic Bomb"—but a good one—on the level of Pakistan's recently detonated nuclear device. With the potential to "pose an even bigger threat to our existing financial system" than a real bomb, this currency bomb would at the same time "be enormously bullish for gold" (Taylor 1998:1). Opting for "real money rather than the fake stuff," the editorial contends, Muslims "acknowledge man's true need to live by a higher order," and, more importantly, are developing products that "portend well for the price of gold in the near future" (p. 6).

Curiously enough, the article from *Gold Eagle* found new life in an Internet discussion group dedicated to LETS, where it generated heated debate.[2] One contributor had summarized Taylor's article and Vadillo's treatise. Another contributor, noting that using a gold coin as an alternative currency would put the system "at the mercy of the gold bullion brokers," argued that units of currency in LETS are based on "the true substance of value," namely, "human work." Challenging the idea put forward by Vadillo that credit in itself is usurious because it "artificially" increases the money supply, he argued that "credit is actually the perfect substanceless medium of exchange." He also took issue with the profit-and-loss sharing mechanisms through which Islamic finance conventionally avoids interest-bearing debt. "[W]hen you lend to someone in an interest-free system, you are doing it *not* for a share of what he made by accepting a share of what he may lose" (emphasis added). Rather, you are "helping your neighbor become rich" so that he can help you with his riches later on in your time of need. Here, the contributor to this debate cited Paul's second letter to the Corinthians.[3] He also made note of the fact that the Islamic Party of Britain has not "been fooled" by "such 'substance' enticements" like that offered by a gold-based alternative currency but has instead "officially endorsed LETS currencies," those substanceless tokens of credit: wiseman's, not fool's, gold.[4]

INDONESIAN GOLD

During the same period that this international debate among alternative currency proponents was taking place, international gold markets hit turbulence because of the Asian financial crisis. Demand worldwide fell by 55 percent.[5] Two countries were responsible for most of the damage. In South Korea, a "Save the Nation" campaign encouraged citizens to sell their gold for won in order to help the country pay its debts to the International Monetary Fund. This resulted in net sales of 250 tons. In Indonesia, people began selling their gold to meet basic needs as the rupiah's value fell by more than 80 percent (*Business Day Bangkok*, July 3, 1998). The government-run pawnshop, Pegadaian, faced a liquidity crisis as a result of this sell-off, having no more cash to provide those who sought to sell their valuables to make ends meet (*China Daily*, Sept. 18 1998). The effects of the Asian crisis redounded into other gold markets, especially Saudi Arabia's "pilgrim" market, as fewer Malaysian and Indonesian Muslims made their religiously mandated voyage to Mecca (WGC, "Gold Demand Trends," no. 24).

By August 1998, demand had picked up again, but was still 14 percent lower than the same period of the previous year (WGC, "Gold Demand Trends," no. 24). In Indonesia, however, two contradictory trends developed: people were both "dishoarding" their gold, selling it back into the market for cash to make ends meet, and buying at record levels. The WGC surmised that the currency crisis had prompted "a growing public awareness of gold's role as a monetary asset" (WGC, "Gold Demand Trends," no. 24). The situation was highly unstable. By January 1999, the WGC's country manager for Indonesia, Leo Hadi Loe, reported a large increase in Indonesia's gold jewelry exports as more gold flooded Indonesian markets and jewelry sales within the country fell (*Bernama*, Jan. 16, 1999). These exports resulted in a "net increase in wealth in rural areas," according to the WGC's August 1999 report, and accordingly, rural gold purchases recovered quickly and dramatically, "reaching 80% of pre-crisis levels": those who had sold gold in the first quarter of 1998 began to repurchase it in the second quarter (WGC, "Gold Demand Trends," no. 28).The East Asia regional director of the WGC concluded his August 1999 report with an anecdote about an Indonesian woman who had sold her gold jewelry to buy "coconut oil, soap and a paddy field" and who hoped soon to buy back her gold with her profits. This woman, "and anyone who has heard her story," he remarked, "will not forget this powerful demonstration of gold's traditional role as a store of value and an asset of last resort" (WGC, "Gold Demand Trends," no. 28).

The World Gold Council saw great potential in Indonesia around the time of the crisis. In a proposal drafted in the summer of 1999 for creating a new product to boost the Indonesian gold market, it identified only two potential obstacles. Muslim men are forbidden to wear gold. Hence, the new product could not be in the form of jewelry or other personal adornment. Furthermore, in Indonesia gold shops are associated with the country's ethnic Chinese community, a target of violence throughout Indonesia's history, especially during times of economic crisis, and generally (although not accurately) perceived as non- or even anti-Muslim. The design of the new product thus had to be somehow explicitly "Islamic." The product would have the ancillary benefit, too, of changing the "image of gold retailers from [a] traditional Chinese look into [a] more Islamic nuance to attract consumers" (WGC 1999, p. 5). Despite those problems, the proposal laid out two hopeful signs. First, as the WGC had already noticed, the economic crisis had had the ironic effect of facilitating gold purchases among the more rural and poor sectors of society, while urban and wealthy people suffered as their rupiah in the bank lost value. Second, Indonesia represents a huge market for gold. If only 5 percent of the population bought just two grams a year, the net result would be twenty tons per year (WGC 1999, p. 2).

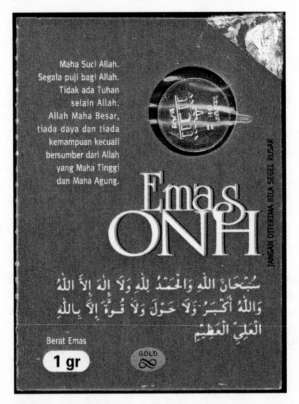

Figure 5.1 The Koin Emas ONH. Note the counterfeit-protection holographic sticker in the upper right corner of the packaging, itself secured with cellophane tape

In August 1999, then, the World Gold Council, in collaboration with the Indonesian pawnshop Pagadaian, launched a new product: the Koin Emas ONH (Ongkos Naik Haj), or Gold Coin for Pilgrimage Expenses (fig. 5.1). The cost of the pilgrimage in 1997 stood at around Rp 7 million; by 1998, it was Rp 21 million. People who had been saving rupiah for years suddenly found their goal virtually unreachable. The cost of the pilgrimage in gold, however, had actually decreased, from 233g in 1997 to 220g in 1998 (WGC 1999, p. 2). People with gold in their pockets before the crisis hit found themselves in a much better position than their compatriots with bank accounts. Indeed, in South Sulawesi, which benefited from the effect of the economic crisis on export commodity prices, the number of pilgrims leaving Makassar for Mecca doubled, from a steady flow of around 16,000 individuals per year from 1995 to 1999 to 30,475 in 2000 (RI Dep. Agama 2000).

Made of twenty-four-karat gold and in six different weights (1g, 2g, 3g, 5g, 10g, 20g), struck with images of famous mosques and holy sites on each side, the Koins were to be distributed by Pegadaian and gold shops around the country as an investment and saving vehicle for Muslims wanting to make the pilgrimage to Mecca (*Suara Pembaruan Daily*, Aug. 27, 1999). In just two weeks, Pegadaian sold 7.5 kilograms worth Rp 500 million, providing a substantial shot in the arm to its other credit and lending programs (*Bisnis Indonesia*, Sept. 9, 1999) The September 12 issue of the national newsmagazine, *Tempo*, contained an article on the Koin that placed it in the context of other *tabungan haji* or pilgrim savings accounts offered by some of the major banks. Such accounts generally accrue revenue in the form of payments derived from profit-and-loss-sharing contracts instead of interest, and the returns can fluctuate widely. In addition, they are denominated in rupiah. The Koin's advantage relative to these products, *Tempo* reported, is that its value is incredibly stable relative to the U.S. dollar and has a very high degree of religious "purity" (*kebersihan*) (*Tempo*, Sept. 12, 1999, p.78). By the end of 2000 it was being sold in at least 400 outlets across the country (*Surabaya Post*, Oct. 16, 2000). And by January 2001, after around 250,000 individual coins had been minted and distributed, Pegadaian reported that only 5.6 percent of the Koins they had sold had been resold for cash, leading the company to conclude that most purchasers of the Koin were indeed accumulating them as a means of financing the holy pilgrimage (*Suara Merdeka*, Jan. 22, 2001).

BAD CHOICES: TOKEN OR COMMODITY?

The Koin Emas ONH can be understood in terms of the large variety of formal and informal credit and savings options at Indonesians' disposal (see, e.g., Alexander 1987; Sullivan 1994; Znoj 1998). At one end are bank accounts, credit cards, and life insurance policies, even stock market portfolios. At the other end are informal mutual assistance organizations and rotating credit associations, including supposedly traditional associations such as *arisan* and the labor-sharing *gotong royong*. Somewhere in between are organized, bureaucratized cooperatives (*koperasi*), an explicit element of Indonesian development policy instituted at the founding of the Republic by the Constitution of 1945, and less organized, more informal cooperatives. The pattern of using pawnshops as one of a set of credit organizations rather than as a last resort in times of dire need seems long-standing. Laanen (1990:263) notes that during the colonial period the use of government-created pawnshops supplemented other forms of savings and credit and "facilitated the monetisation of the indigenous community."

Furthermore, as John Bowen (1986) has argued, the mundane credit and savings associations and mutual assistance schemes in which many Indonesians are involved were either actually instituted or promoted by the state apparatus. J. S. Furnivall's classic texts on Netherlands India's "plural economy" demonstrate that the same was true in the colonial era. Furnivall documents Dutch efforts, especially on the part of de Wolff van Westerrode, a student of European cooperative societies, to link village cooperatives into banks and larger credit organizations, as well as to create state pawnshops and agricultural credit banks as parts of a unified whole (1939:357). De Wolff's visions were implemented by the colonial government, much to the credit of the state itself, which earned a profit off of such schemes of 12 million guilders a year, and a total of nearly 150 million guilders from the start of their implementation (Furnivall 1939:359). Furnivall noted certain structural weaknesses in the system, however, due, he thought, to their limited reach—they mainly served civil servants—and the "non-cooperation movement," which had "stimulated the foundation of numerous 'wild' co-operative societies, free of Government control" (about which "little information is available"; pp. 359–60). He concluded that the existence of these societies indicated that "past neglect of co-operative credit by the State may lead to the growth of a co-operative movement among the people with a greater vitality than a movement depending on the support of the Government" (p. 361). In effect, such independent cooperatives took the state's forms and put them to "wild" uses, uses that Furnivall feared might erode state authority.

The Koin Emas ONH can also be understood in terms of World Gold Council strategies for increasing demand in developing countries. In a research report on gold banking released in June 1998, just as "dishoarding" was decreasing and demand picking up in the Southeast Asian markets, a consultant to the WGC happily remarked that gold had become "just another currency" through innovative "gold banking" products (Doran 1998:10). Explicitly countering the notion that savings held in gold constitutes "hoarding" and is "linked to the black economy" (p. 33), the report shows how consumers' everyday activities can point the way toward new investment products. Exemplary is the case of Turkey, where "traditionally" gold items of all sorts have served as a "key savings medium," especially for weddings and gifts to the parents of betrothed women (p. 18). In addition, the report cites the Turkish "tradition of rotational [sic] savings schemes" among groups of friends, neighbors, and coworkers (p. 19). In such schemes, members make monthly contributions toward the purchase of gold coins "with the coin allocated to each member of the group in turn" (p. 19). The Turkish Toprak Bank used these as models for developing several new products, including a "gold accumulation plan" through which consumers agree to make small monthly purchases of gold per month (which are deposited into a gold-interest-earning gold account), in addition to a gold savings account that returns 106 gold coins per annum for every

100 deposited, and another type of account in which gold objects can be assayed and converted into a pure-gold equivalent (p. 19).

The World Gold Council's mission of promoting the use of gold, especially its use as a currency, exemplifies what Keith Hart (1986) has called commodity theories of money. The WGC is reminiscent of the Goldbugs of the American nineteenth century, who demanded a national currency backed by specie, not government promises, and who not only engaged in vociferous debate against the fiat-money-supporting Greenbackers but also spurred artistic and literary figures to contemplate the money-form itself, its putative signifying capacity (Ritter 1997; Michaels 1987; Shell 1982; Foster 1999). If governments could create money by fiat, Goldbugs worried, "arbitrary signifiers could displace natural signifieds" (Foster 1999:214), and we would live in a world created by whim out of insubstantial paper and straw, the subject of Thomas Nast's oft-reproduced political cartoons. Commodity theories of money treat it as a substantial thing with value in itself that relies on nothing other than itself, its brute materiality, for that value. Commodity theories, like World Gold Council texts, fetishize specie in familiar ways. "Gold is back," says the chief executive officer of the WGC, "with its customary charisma; . . . it outshines all else for its universal acceptability. . . . Arousing always human passions, its mystique will never fade" (Fukuda 1999). Indeed, the main political and economic work of the WGC is to ensure that nothing hinders the "natural" and "universal" acceptability of gold. Removing trade barriers and tariffs, encouraging mining interests, and promoting new uses for the metal does not demystify it by revealing the network of social and political relations required for its production as a valuable commodity. Rather, like burnishing, such work permits its charismatic appeal to shine forth. Much like the Murabitun movement, the WGC sees gold as money of a natural kind. Its importance is its substance, a substance that stands for itself. Indeed, like a fetish object, it encompasses those relations that make it, simultaneously embodying "religious, commercial, aesthetic and sexual values" from heterogenous and discontinuous social fields (Pietz 1985:7). Its materiality matters, as "a material space gathering an otherwise unconnected multiplicity into the unity of its enduring singularity" (p. 15).

In contrast, LETS proponents and the Islamic Party of Britain, arguing that a gold-based currency would only place itself at the mercy of the gold markets (indeed, the WGC), promote what Hart called "token" theories of money. Token theories hold that money is a symbol of a relation: a relation between people based on trust and credit, a relation to a nation imagined as a set of popular institutions that reflect, embody and promote the national will, or a relation to a state that defines money by law and the power of the sovereign (Hart 1986:644, 646). For LETS proponents, their money is a token of personal relationships and credit extended to others.

This is money's "substance," and it is the "perfect substanceless" substance. In fact, in LETS systems, money is utterly immaterial except for the traces of ink in a ledger or pixels on a screen running a LETS database program. It is a "signifier referring beyond itself" to human labor (Foster 1998:66). It is an effect of labor and trust, not a substance in itself.

In interviews conducted in Makassar, South Sulawesi, I found that the Koin Emas ONH muddles the neat distinction between commodity and token, substance and effect, just as Furnivall's "wild cooperatives" blur the line between state-promoted credit and "local" credit that takes the state's forms and puts them to other ends. People bought the Koins because of gold's commodity status. Gold is valuable in itself. People said they buy gold because they like it [suka]. At one gold shop, five or six women clerks in uniform crowded around as their boss took some Koins out of a hidden, locked case for me to take a closer look. Fascinated by the objects, they passed them around as if they rarely had a chance to look at them up close. Indeed, the owner told me that only a few a month were sold there, and that most people bought the larger weight (especially 10g) Koins. She thought a lot were being sold, just not from her shop, and that people bought them from other places like Pegadaian. As the young women passed the Koins around, I asked whether they liked them. They replied, "Of course; it's gold, isn't it?" At another shop, bedecked with numerous green and gold Pegadaian posters and hanging displays advertising the Koins, and displaying them in its most prominent jewelry case, the shop clerk asserted that the real interest in the item was that it was gold, not necessarily that it served the purpose of helping people make the pilgrimage to Mecca.

At the same time, gold was understood to be a symbol like any other currency symbol, be it the rupiah or the U.S. dollar, and to be freely convertible. People were drawn to it not merely because they "liked" it but because of a crisis in the symbolic status of the rupiah. People had few illusions about the nature of value or the origin of price in their current predicament. They thought value and price were less about the supply and demand of commodities, and more about international investors' faith and trust (or lack thereof) in the current Indonesian government. In the context of a discussion about the value of gold and the religious obligation of pilgrimage, one interviewee explained to me the nature of agricultural profit: "in this time of monetary crisis, . . . profits from the land [hasil bumi] have been very good. Agricultural products have been very good, such as chocolate—it follows the dollar [ikut dolar juga] and if the dollar goes up [relative to the rupiah] than we get a lot of profit. So for going on the haj . . . very many can go. Because the agricultural profits have been great." For him, gold indexed the dollar and existed not as a root signified but as a sign in a chain of signifiers that included itself, the dollar, and export commodities like chocolate. Gold's chief difference from the dollar is that, for everyday

Indonesians without bank accounts, it is easier to obtain than dollars. But here its chief characteristic is not as substance, but as effect. When I asked a representative of Pegadaian why gold was chosen as the material from which the Koins were struck, he replied, "Because gold is flexible [*fleksibel*]. Its characteristic [*sifat*] is that it's flexible." Another person added that it is easy to sell and that it always follows the dollar [*mengacu ke dolar*]. "If the dollar goes up, gold goes up too. If the dollar goes down, gold also goes down. It's flexible [*fleksibel*]; what's the English word for that?" The gold of the Koin Emas ONH exists as substance and as insubstantial flexibility, commensurability between different sign systems. The Koins are both signs-in-themselves and a transnational value derived from their referencing of other signs (dollars, other commodities).

They are also signs of a different value: the moral value of the pilgrimage to Mecca. Potential pilgrims do purchase the Koins, and see them as cleaner or more pure than other forms of saving, especially interest-based forms. Some were familiar with the *hadith*, frequently cited in international Islamic banking circles, that relates that the Prophet once said, "Trade gold for gold, silver for silver, wheat for wheat, barley for barley, dates for dates, salt for salt, measure for measure and hand-to-hand" (quoted in Saleh 1986:43) as an injunction against *riba* or speculative increase. Pegadaian Makassar was selling about 300g per month in the summer of 2000, and five customers had already cashed in their Koins and made the pilgrimage.

In its capacity as moral marker, however, the Koin seems to be as worrying as chrysographic writing. Just as it blurs the distinction between token and commodity, it also troubles the line between the holy and the unholy. But it is unclear whether or in what sense this matters. In newspaper stories the Koin teeters on the edge between the legitimate and forbidden in Islam. It does not do so around the issue of currency trading (for instance, exchanging gold for rupiah or dollars), as some interpretations of the "measure for measure" *hadith* might suggest (see Saleh 1986). Rather, it does so around the issue of gambling. Company concerns about advertising the product (*mensosialisasikan*, *Suara Merdeka*, Jan. 22, 2001; *Info Iklan*, 19 June 2001) resulted in promotional gimmicks like lotteries and prize drawings. One such lottery attracted almost nineteen thousand participants from around the archipelago. Eight lucky winners received the grand prize of a free trip to Mecca for the *umrah* (the lesser pilgrimage with fewer ritual obligations that is not undertaken during the haj season). One hundred other winners each received a 2g Koin Emas ONH. The lottery was meant to teach the virtues of saving, as well as to promote the Koin product (*Suara Merdeka*, January 26, 2001).

Apparently, however, the Majelis Ulama Indonesia (MUI, the national Indonesian Council of Religious Scholars) does not view the practice of holding such lotteries to be a form of forbidden gambling (*judi*).[6] The

MUI's judgment was related by way of a representative of Pegadaian, as reported in the East Kalimantan newspaper, *Kaltim Post*, which wrote that the MUI has held that such lotteries are fine so long as they do not have a negative impact (*dampak negatif*) on society. In Islamic law, the scholars are reported to have concluded, the practice of holding such lotteries falls into the *fiqh* juridical category *mubah*, placed in parenthesis in the article after the Indonesian term *boleh*, permissible (*Kaltim Post*, May 4, 2001). The chain of authority for this conclusion, whether from the *hadith* or the MUI, clearly did not follow a straightforward route. Furthermore, *mubah* is in fact a neutral term, referring to acts that are neither forbidden nor required.

By mid-2001, incidentally, the product did seem to have been rather successfully "socialized." The magazine *Investasiku*, in an article on the pluses and minuses of investing in gold, listed four main ways of doing so: gold bars, jewelry, the Koin Emas ONH—and gold futures trading.

The Koin Emas ONH both does and does not refer only to itself. It is a naturalized commodity, and at the same time it always references other monetary and moral signs. But it also never refers only to that of which it ostensibly is a token: religious faith. For coins bearing images of the Dome of the Rock and the Kaaba, the most holy sites in Islam, became tokens in games of chance, the runner-up prizes in a lottery, a company's gamble on its future, and a speculative technique for making money out of money.

THE APPEAL OF THE COUNTERFEIT IMITATION

In a speech to the World Gold Council in 1997, before the explosion of the economic crisis, the Indonesian Country Manager of the WGC, Leo Hadi Loe, mentioned in passing but said he would not discuss further "the fool's gold" of the Busang scandal (Loe 1997). A Canadian company, Bre-X, had created a flurry of excitement and investment activity upon news that it found "the biggest gold strike in the world" in Busang, East Kalimantan (Tsing 2000:116), when, in fact, "[t]here was nothing there" (p. 117). Contrasting this "fool's gold" with what he characterized as "the wiseman's gold" that the WGC had been promoting in Indonesia, Loe emphasized the impact of the WGC's successful lobbying to remove the 10 percent VAT (value added tax) on gold, its promotion of gold expos, and its progress toward a target of one gram per capita gold consumption (Loe 1997).

Loe's careful circumlocution around the fool's gold of Busang highlights the false fixity of both the wiseman's gold and the relation between the fool and the wiseman. James Siegel (1998) offers remarkable reflections on counterfeiting and the Indonesian neologism, *aspal*. Derived from the terms *asli* (authentic) and *palsu* (false, borrowed from English), it also means "asphalt," that imitation stone that provides routes, direction, and other lines of flight. The term captures the sense that even what is genuine is not necessarily authentic. *Palsu* itself already has the sense of "almost valid," not simply "counterfeit" (p. 57). Like Loe's fool's gold, absent yet present and indeed structuring the entire text of his speech, *palsu* and *aspal* do not replace the real with the fake but rather put the real, the fake, and the relation between the two under erasure.

As Siegel shows, the Indonesian media is replete with reports of the *palsu*. Stories about the Koin Emas like those cited above are cases in point. When a Koin is a prize in a gambling game, the line between the item *tossed for* as a trophy can become confused with the item *tossed in* as a token in the game (after Shell 1982:194), especially because the trophy is both a token in another game—not only fealty to God but the social status that accrues to a *haji*—and a fungible, flexible commodity money.

Take the case of the swindling pilgrim. As reported in the *Surabaya Post*, this individual had acquired more than Rp 2 billion from various unsuspecting potential pilgrims seeking a holy means of saving for the *haj*. Each had contributed between Rp 100,000 and 5 million. The man invested the money in two bank accounts, his own personal cash box, and seven Koin Emas ONH. Was the swindling pilgrim an authentic pilgrim or not? It is impossible to know, although he did arrive in court in the full white robes and hat of a *haji*. But would, or could, a true *haji* undertake such an act? Moreover, why did he buy the seven Koins? Because of the stability of gold as a commodity or because of the cleanliness of gold as a token of faith? The article leaves these questions unasked. Instead, the interest in the article is drawn to the means by which this *aspal* pilgrim carried it out this *aspal* pilgrimage savings scheme (*Surabaya Post*, May 1, 2001). "It is not the illicit nature of this activity that is stressed," Siegel writes, about an analogous case, "it is, again, the manufacturing of something: a scheme, a form, and so on" (1998:56). The *aspal* pilgrim did, after all, raise a considerable sum of money, which was the stated purpose of the scheme in the first place, and the article makes no insinuation that he was about to abscond with it. Indeed, the whole thing probably would have worked like any other rotating savings association. The real crime was that it was an unregistered and unlicensed affair without the proper authority of the government's central bank, the Bank Indonesia—itself something of an *aspal* operation given the economic crisis. The man had crafted an "almost valid," genuine but not authentic, pilgrimage savings scheme.

Busang, too, was almost valid in the sense that, like any other transnational investment venture promoted far from the actual site of production, it generated a huge amount of capital through the self-same mechanisms that any other enterprise would. As Anna Tsing cogently remarks, "deregulation and cronyism" might "sometimes name the same thing," and require of analysts a "less pious attitude toward the market" (2000:115). Here, however, I want to suggest that a more pious attitude might be more appropriate—not toward the market, but toward its chrysographic traces. Those traces may not be identical to either the market's self-referentiality, mirrored in commodity theories of money, or the self-referential relations presumed in token theories.

CHRYSOGRAPHIC TRACES

Keith Hart chastises economists and anthropologists for being at theoretical extremes, either emphasizing money as commodity or money as token. "It is surely the case," he writes, that money "has two sides and that what matters is their relationship, the mutual constitution of politics and markets in a moving social whole" (1986:647). Recuperations of Georg Simmel (1907) have sharpened the analytical focus on relations between persons and things, subjects and objects, in systems of exchange and social reproduction (see Rutherford 2001; Allen and Pryke 1999). Some alternative currency systems unwittingly reflect in social practice Simmel's monetary theories. My hesitation, however, comes from my encounters with objects like the Koin Emas ONH that throw into relief the problem of adequation pinpointed by Shell in his discussion of chrysography and the philosophy of the limit (1982:191–95). First, what do imitations that approach the real do to the imitation, the real, and the relation between the two? The uses to which Koins have been put can be summarized easily enough in table 5.1. It is a token of the faith, bought because it is religiously clean, a wiseman's coin for making the pilgrimage to Mecca; it is also a counterfeit when won in a game of chance for an unholy *haj*; it is a solid commodity for a life-saving exchange in a time of crisis, and a fetishized commodity whose attraction is its likeness and likeability.

Second, however, what of the Koin as a fake imitation in relation to a nonoriginary real, as *palsu* or *aspal*? It was, after all, a marketing ploy of a transnational organization to boost gold consumption. But it was also purchased by a possibly counterfeit *haji* as part of a possibly real pilgrimage savings scheme. The core difficulty lies in the relations among the cells in table 5.1 when the irreducibility of *aspal* is taken into account. The swindling *haji* was both and neither counterfeit and genuine. The Muslim scholars' decision came down by way of a twisting and indirect route, and it was a decision to permit gambling as neither required nor forbidden of the faithful. Where in table 5.1 would one place the seven Koin Emas OHN found in the possession of the *aspal* pilgrim? Indeed, where would one place the Koins used for their advertised purpose, cashed in at Pega-

TABLE 5.1
Wiseman's or Fool's Gold?

	Fool's	Wiseman's
Commodity	Fetish, object of "like"	Paddy fields, object of production
Token	Unholy haj, gambling prize	Fealty to God

daian for rupiah so that a person can go to Mecca? For the Prophet is reported to have said "trade gold for gold" in a *hadith* that has been interpreted in ways that, if it does not outright throw it into question, at least opens up the very status of paper currencies' and gold's exchangeability as commodities of the same genus and efficient cause (see Saleh 1986:16–24).

Is the Koin Emas ONH representationally flawed in the manner Robert Foster has suggested? Perhaps not. Perhaps money here is neither representationally flawed nor an index of representation's failure. Perhaps it is simply *aspal*, neither flawed nor perfect, pure nor impure, but both and neither. And productively so: it does not suggest ambiguity or confusion but instead fascination—interest, of the intellectual and usurious kind—*at the manner in which it became and remains efficacious*, for gambling, making a pilgrimage, buying a rice field, making ends meet in a time of crisis, or anything else. The Koin does not provoke the kind of either/or debates that have vexed alternative currency proponents, gold standard adherents, or twelfth-century monks. Instead, it became and remains efficacious not to the extent that it is still circulated but to the extent that the revelation of the representational and theological conundrums that are *possibly* behind it does nothing to displace its functioning or to clarify, as it were, the *aspal* over which it travels.

Here, then, is it not a matter of either commodity theories or token theories being inadequate. It is a matter of their *relation* as an analytic device not suiting the case at hand. The rubric of "mutual constitution" and relationality displaces the efficacy of the Koin as a commodity and token that places its commodity-ness and token-ness under erasure. The Koin instead journeys through a terrain crisscrossed by pilgrimage routes written in gold and *aspal*.

CHAPTER 6

Mutual Life, Limited: Insurance, Moral Value, and Bureaucratic Form

> *Salarino*: . . . I know Antonio
> Is sad to think upon his merchandise.
> *Antonio*: Believe me, no. I thank my fortune for it,
> My ventures are not to one bottom trusted,
> Nor to one place; nor is my whole estate
> Upon the fortune of this present year:
> Therefore my merchandise makes me not sad.
> —William Shakespeare, *Merchant of Venice*, I.i

IN THE WAKE OF the U.S. stock market crash of 1929, economist Frank Knight's *Risk, Uncertainty, and Profit* (1933) spelled out a distinction between objectifiable risk and subjective uncertainty that was to remain intrinsic to twentieth-century market logic and gain a foothold in the new techniques of governance based on actuarial practices. Such techniques of governance emerged from the social statistics of the nineteenth century, and are generally held to decompose the subjects of liberal democracy into disaggregated individual biologies and histories, only to reaggregate them again into populations and risk profiles (Simon 1988; Hacking 1990; Foucault 1991; O'Malley 2000; Rose 1996). Uncertainty, Knight asserted, was a subjective condition resting on belief, and concerned those features of the universe not amenable to rational calculation. Risk, on the other hand, represented the mastery of uncertainty—and with it, the future—through probabilistic measurement of alternative outcomes over time.

Imaginings of risk as the rational calculation of future possibilities have been central to insurance (Defert 1991; Ewald 1991; Knights and Vurdubakis 1993). Antonio's speech quoted above attests to the rise of certain insurance practices with the expansion of European transatlantic trade in the Renaissance and early modern periods. As Kindleberger and Braudel note, before the advent of marine insurance, it was common practice in Renaissance Venice to transport goods in "little ships to divide the risk" (Kindleberger 1984:179; see Braudel [1949] 1995:306). Antonio's strategy of spreading his investments among various ship bottoms rather than trusting them to a single hold represents just one of many practices of marine insurance (Kindleberger 1984:179). This form of security interests in ships and cargoes facilitated financial insurance against losses, and even permitted a trade in security interests and insurance shares, contributing to the rise of such institutions as Lloyd's Coffee House of London. Life insurance followed, to protect a lender's capital in the event of a borrower's early death (Kindleberger 1984:180), and, in effect, to turn the lender's risk that the borrower might die into a kind of capital in itself (Ewald 1991). "In the eighteenth century, too, insurance was taken on the lives of public figures as a wager with long odds," Kindleberger writes, and "[b]y the middle of the century actuarial tables had been produced and premiums for life insurance based on age came into existence" (Kindleberger 1984: 179).

As wagers on public officials' lives made apparent, early-modern insurance and actuarial practice contained a troubling similarity to gambling.[1] Insurance, and the conception of risk it depended upon and simultaneously empowered, only gradually became distinct from gambling, as the result of ideological and material practices that transformed the epistemological weight and ontological status of chance and mathematical means of representing it. Gambling had been morally troubling because the "erratic and fluctuating character of the gamblers' passion eroded self-control, eclipsing past commitments and future duties" (Knights and Vurdubakis 1993:739). Insurance only became distinct from gambling with the "social, moral and knowledge practices" that made risk calculation a practice of rationalization and normalization (p. 738). The interests had to overcome the passions, and a new vision of number and probability that animated statistical and rational calculations of risk allowed them, in theory at least, to do so (Daston 1988; Hacking 1990). In England, the 1774 Life Assurance Act effected this dominance of interests over passions by forbidding insurers to cover "people or events where the insurer could not prove an 'interest' in the person or event insured against" (Knights and Vurdubakis, 1993:739). Thus, economic "interest" became the legal and moral "principle of differentiation between the risks of insurance and the risks of gambling" (p. 739). Risk was thereby redefined as a "quantifiable state of uncertainty which was morally tenable" (Leyshon and Thrift 1997:17). Nonetheless, the troublesome link between insurance and gambling, as well as the rejection of the apparent profanation of human life through its commodification in life insurance, preoccupied social theorists, social reformers, and nascent consumers throughout nineteenth-century Europe and the United States (Zelizer 1978, 1979).

In the wake of the Asian financial crisis of 1998, contemporary Muslim Indonesians have been exposed to life and other forms of insurance for the first time, although not necessarily as a casual outsider (or itinerant anthropologist) might have at first predicted. In the Muslim world in general, and in the academic discipline and institutional practice of Islamic banking and finance, ongoing intellectual and popular debate continues over the distinction between insurance and gambling (Siddiqi 1985; Muslehuddin 1995; Hasan 1996; Husein 1997; Lupiyoadi 1997; Antonio 1997), since gambling is prohibited in Islam.[2] As an index of this broad debate, Browne and Kim's (1993) survey of factors influencing international consumer demand for life insurance products found a determining factor to be whether a country has a majority Muslim population. In Indonesia, the world's largest Muslim state, however, that concern is less important than other motives people have for exploring insurance, motives that are both more materialistic, and more pious, than gambling or its avoidance.

During my fieldwork in Indonesia, the issue of gambling came up only in conversations with professionals in the banking, insurance, and investing business, and never with people without such expert knowledge. One insurance salesman casually dismissed the gambling debate by stating that it is a simple "difference of opinion" (*perbedaan pendapat*) and reduced the problem to one of personal opinions cum market preferences: Some people say insurance is gambling, others say it is not. "For instance, I fly Garuda; you fly Merpati" (two Indonesian airlines).[3] However, he stressed that he made sure his clients had a good understanding of the insurance product before they signed on the dotted line, in accordance with the widely held doctrine in Islamic banking that a risk entered into with eyes open as to its possible benefits and costs is permissible in Islam. The only financial services professional I met who immediately and without prompting raised the issue of gambling was a representative of the Makassar branch of the Jakarta Stock Exchange, who began our interview by stating that Indonesians are afraid (*takut*) of the stock market because they fear it is a form of gambling (*main judi*). Her mission, as she sees it, is to educate people, to make them more brave (*berani*), and thus "socialize" (*bersosialisasi*) the concept of stock market investing in Indonesia. This was a tall order in the wake of the financial crisis, and became more so after the bombing of the Jakarta Stock Exchange building itself just a few weeks later.

Despite the lack of awareness of the possible connection between insurance and gambling, except among financial professionals, Muslims in Indonesia have access to an Islamic alternative to conventional insurance, *takaful*, a scheme originally devised by international IBF professionals to serve Muslims' insurance needs without violating the letter or the spirit of Islamic law. To most Indonesians insurance of any kind is a foreign concept. Several told me they were confused (*binung*) by it or failed to see the point or the use (*guna*) of it, some even seeing it as similar to tax: paying money for something of an obscure payoff. But for others *takaful*, used as a savings account more than a life insurance policy, fulfils a very important metaphysical and mundane desire: the desire to make the pilgrimage to Mecca, the *haj*, and thereby to establish a closer relationship with God by demonstrating one's fealty and to increase one's standing in the local community. It is these desires, and the manner in which they are arrived at, that originally motivated this chapter. In attending to them, however, I became less interested in the way life insurance might function to insure the soul or one's standing in the community, and more interested in the moral valences of the insurance technologies themselves, their bureaucratic instantiation, and the implications they held for anthropology's disciplinary claims to knowledge.

Takaful in Indonesia fits into a network of credit alternatives, some of which date from the colonial period and most of which have their origins in colonial or national state planning. These bureaucratic inventions attempted to "fix" Indonesians and the Indonesian economy within a particular frame and toward specific productive ends. Bureaucratic means of visually representing "the economy" rendered it a whole, total system and placed Indonesians in confined boxes on the diagram in the name of economic development and in accordance with nationalist concepts of mutuality and togetherness. At the same time that *takaful* taps into those same representations and nationalist concepts, it opens them up, renders them incomplete and prevents their closure, leaving them vulnerable to risks. That vulnerability is not, however, a negative value.

This chapter ultimately is concerned with risk as a mode of governance, an ethical code, and a characteristic of anthropological analysis. It emphasizes the status of the technical and the moral in Islamic insurance practices as well as anthropological knowledge production. The bureaucratic forms of Islamic insurance and the analytical forms of anthropology, I argue, have a lot in common. This is for a variety of reasons. For one thing, transnational Islamic banking and finance knowledge practices link up with the academic social sciences in which anthropology is often located. Both Indonesian and IBF academic and professional trajectories, either jet trails or citation trails, often pass through or point toward the Western academy. In this chapter, however, I focus on a shared past of the representational techniques of modern, bureaucratic state planning, and a shared present of trucking in trust and in risk.

TAKAFUL, THE *HAJ*, AND ECONOMIC AND EPISTEMOLOGICAL CRISIS

For regions of the country like South Sulawesi province that are dependent on export commodity production, the *krismon*, or monetary and economic crisis of 1998, was a blessing in disguise. When the value of the rupiah fell by 600 percent against the U.S. dollar in a period of six months, South Sulawesi experienced a mini–economic boom as its shrimp, squid, chocolate, and coffee became bargains on the world market, and hard currency in the form of the U.S. dollar and Japanese yen flowed into the province. Makassar, the capital city, witnessed construction of several upscale shopping malls, complete with McDonald's and Hugo Boss. And the number of pilgrims leaving Makassar for Mecca doubled, from a steady flow of around 16,000 individuals per year from 1995 to 1999 to 30,475 in 2000. Disaggregated data at the district (*kabupatan*) level indicate that between 60 and 74 percent of the pilgrims in 2000 were women (RI Departemen Agama 2000).

The miniboom in South Sulawesi led the banks that had not failed during the crisis to develop various financial products to help Muslims save money for the *haj*. These *tabungan haj*, or "pilgrimage savings accounts," often do not accrue interest (although some do) and can be seen as a cleaner or more pure method of saving than an interest-bearing account.[4] The real marketing gimmick and attraction, however, is that they also were linked into the national computer network through which the Department of Religion organizes and controls Indonesia's religious pilgrims. This computer network, SISKOHAT, or *Sistem Komputer Haji Terpadu* (Integrated Pilgrim Computer System) is a centralized network that connects the Department of Religion with all the banks that offer *haj* savings accounts as well as with Garuda Indonesia, the national airline. When a potential pilgrim opens an account, the Department of Religion and Garuda know immediately that she is intending to go on the *haj*. Garuda does not handle all the flights due to their limited capacity (especially after the *krismon*, when Garuda had to return several long-haul aircraft leased from Airbus in European currencies), but, through SISKOHAT, it can reserve seats with British Airways and other airlines. Without a *haj* account, and an entry in SISKOHAT's database of potential pilgrims, one could find oneself with the money but not the seat for the voyage. Bank managers informed me that most customers seeking *haj* accounts would have already saved enough money for the journey before they opened the account; their real motivation in opening one is acquiring a guaranteed reservation on an airplane.

People saving for the pilgrimage do so in all manner of ways. Some use conventional savings accounts. Some use the new *haj* accounts. As discussed in the previous chapter, the national Indonesian pawnbroker, Pegadaian, even began minting small gold coins of various weights and promoting them as a safe, stable, and Islamically pure method of saving for the pilgrimage, complete with graphs and charts demonstrating the relative stability of the price of gold compared to the wild fluctuations of the rupiah. Islamic life insurance, *takaful*, entered this scene as another popular means of financing one's pilgrimage.

Being relatively unfamiliar with life insurance and its marketing before beginning research into global Islamic banking and finance, I admit that I felt a good deal of confusion after an employee of one of Makassar's Islamic life insurance companies presented me with scores of marketing brochures and photocopied handouts explaining the *takaful* system. This confusion was not merely due to linguistic barriers; some of the material was in English. But most of it just seemed not to parse, even with the aid of a dictionary, a fluent speaker, and many native speakers of Indonesian whose introduction to *takaful* came through my brochures and questions. In advance of my subsequent meetings with employees of this life insurance company I began writing questions on self-adhesive notepaper and attaching them directly to the brochures.

A brochure titled *Takaful Asuransi Syriah* contains information on three types of insurance: *Takaful dana siswa*, *Takaful dana haji*, and *Takaful dana investasi*. These translate to *takaful* student fund, pilgrim fund and investment fund, respectively. Helpful charts demonstrate how Ali, age thirty, can pay his premium of Rp. 1 million a year for seventeen years and fund his children's education; how Umar, also age 30, can pay his premium for ten years and fund his pilgrimage; and how Usman, 30, can after twenty years double his money and accumulate nearly Rp. 42 million. Off to one side, for each example, the brochure notes what would happen should Ali, Umar, or Usman die five years after taking out their insurance policies; in each case, their beneficiaries would receive between Rp. 10 million and Rp. 20 million. But these explanations are marginal. The text heading "Manfaat 1" (Use or Benefit 1) for each policy, explaining how the policy works to fund education, pilgrimage, or investment, is in bold-faced type. An unbolded and unlabeled "2" notes, "If Ali dies during the term of the policy (say in the fifth year)," and proceeds to note the benefit to spouses and children.

The self-adhesive note I attached to this brochure, written just hours after I had received it, asks, "Are these more like investment accts? I don't understand . . . " It seemed to me at the time that the life insurance aspect of these policies was beside the point. They were investment funds. Upon e-mailing a colleague in the United States whose father had been a door-to-door insurance salesman, I learned that her father's most effective marketing ploy had been to sell life insurance policies as a form of savings account, and not as a means of providing for the comfort and well-being of widows and children after a male breadwinner's demise (or speculating on a hated spouse's untimely and arranged passing, as Barbara Stanwyck's character does in *Double Indemnity*!).[5]

This was the draw of *takaful* for middle-class Muslim women in Makassar. The use and explicit promotion of life insurance as a savings mechanism was, then, essentially the same as for some people in the United States, and a feature of bureaucratic rationality and capitalist modernity that goes without saying for everyone (except me, apparently) because so self-evidently obvious. Anthropologists drawn to the study of bureaucratic forms and structures point out the apparent failure of knowledge that occurs when the "other's" bureaucracy looks like so much indigenous sociology or anthropology, indistinguishable from our knowledge practices and commonsense (Riles 2000; Strathern 1999; see also Shore and Wright 1999; Herzfeld 1992). There seems to be nothing to say, no hidden meaning to discover, since bureaucratic practice and its auto-documentation is so transparent, rational, and familiar. Anthropology, faced with the mundane, is left in an epistemological quandary: what is there left for it to do (Riles 2000)?

Mundane Credit and Savings Associations

In a sense, *takaful* as a means of saving for the *haj*, although probably relatively unfamiliar to most and only recently on the scene in South Sulawesi, can be mundane for Indonesians, as well. It fits into the large palette of formal and informal credit and savings options at people's disposal reviewed in chapter 5. At one end are bank accounts, credit cards, and life insurance policies, even stock market portfolios. At the other end are informal mutual assistance organizations and rotating credit associations, including supposedly traditional associations such as *arisan* and labor-sharing *gotong royong*. Somewhere in between are organized, bureaucratized cooperatives (*koperasi*), an explicit element of Indonesian development policy instituted at the founding of the Republic by the Constitution of 1945, and less organized, more informal *koperasi*. There are about eight hundred official cooperatives in South Sulawesi province.

Rudi was a thirty-two-year-old man from Makassar who worked for a government-supported cooperative. At the beginning of June 2000 with a small group of friends (initially, four) and an initial pooled investment of Rp. 3 million, he started an informal *koperasi* to provide small loans and generate revenue for a performance group he and some other members of the *koperasi* are involved with, as well as for the *koperasi* members themselves. Charging 10 percent interest for friends and 15 for others who joined the *koperasi* during the month of June, the *koperasi*'s capital stood at Rp. 3.76 million in just one month.[6]

In addition to his own *koperasi*, Rudi is a member of the cooperative that employs him and an *arisan* made up of a circle of friends who also work at that cooperative. During the same month in which he established his informal *koperasi*, Rudi pawned his motorcycle for cash to help his parents in the countryside make repairs to their house. He did so with the knowledge that he was next in line to receive a payment from his *arisan* and that, given the health of his informal *koperasi*, he would be able to make up the difference with a small loan to himself and repurchase his motorcycle within the month. All of these credit and savings alternatives articulate and work together, and, thanks to the pawnshop, work together with whatever relatively valuable items a person might have at his disposal to convert into ready cash. For those who have them, *takaful*, bank accounts, bank loans, credit cards, and the like can operate as other such credit and savings alternatives.[7]

There is a crucial difference, however, between *takaful*, Islamic banks and credit associations like cooperatives and *arisan*, on the one hand, and conventional banking and credit, on the other. Indonesians I spoke with objectified the former in the same manner, using the same terms and even the same or very similar diagrams to explain them to me. They did not do so for the latter. They also objectified the former in terms that occupy an important place in nationalist discourse, and, in particular, Old Order, Sukarno-era discourse. As I discuss further below, this objectification is a kind of indigenous economics (after Riles's [2000] indigenous sociology) that turns the knowledge practices of social science to ends that are perfectly legible within its terms but unanticipated by them.

Thinking to further develop his *koperasi* to provide more funding for his performance group, Rudi decided to write a grant proposal to an international nongovernmental organization interested in microcredit. He showed me a draft, which included a list of goals (*tujuan*) for the cooperative. These included "freeing the target group from usurers," "developing the economy of Indonesia," and "creating a field of employment."[8] To me, these seemed rather grand goals for a cooperative that, at the time, had fewer than twenty members (when in reality they are no grander than any act of social-scientific analysis). When I asked him to explain how a cooperative would further those goals, Rudi stated that it would strengthen cooperative spirit, mutual help, and togetherness. The terms he used were *semangat berkoperasi*, *tolong-menolong*, and *bersama-sama*.

After my very first visit to the Islamic life insurance company, I asked an Indonesian friend, who had been my most patient language instructor, to explain to me why life insurance was *asuransi jiwa* (lit., soul or spirit insurance) and not something like *asuransi pribadi* (personal or individual insurance). The very idea of there being an *asuransi pribadi* puzzled him. In trying to explain *jiwa*, he used his right hand to gesture toward his heart or liver (the same place on the torso that people gesture toward or touch after shaking hands with someone) and waved his hand up and down, fingers pointing inward to that spot on the torso. He said "everybody has it," and "it's like *semangat*" (*seperti semangat*). *Pribadi*, in contrast, is not something shared by everyone, but refers rather to a specific characteristic of someone.

Given his definitions, and in a fit of frustration with the language and apologia for the insurance industry, I came away grumbling that *pribadi* should be the best term after all, since life insurance *needs* to be overwhelmingly concerned with highly specific characteristics of an individual in order for it to be profitable in the long run. Persons *need* to be disaggregated into characteristics and behaviors so that risk profiles, actuarial tables, and the law of large numbers can enable the insurer to set premiums, manage risks, and make a profit. *Jiwa*, to me, resonated more with concepts like *bersama-sama* or *tolong menolong* (togetherness and mutual assistance) than profiling or actuarial practice. And yet the whole point of *asuransi jiwa* is to deal with risk. Yet, again, maybe not: after all, the real motive behind people's choice of *takaful* over other forms of insurance is in fact the promise of a rate of return, because *takaful* is an investment fund: people earn a return from their life insurance account, and do not actually see their money disappear into never-never land "like a tax," as some said was the case with conventional life insurance.

The actual mechanics of *takaful*, the way it generates a return for its clients, do suggest that it serves the purpose of togetherness and mutual assistance more than it does individualizing, profiling, or the disaggregation of the person into constituent risks, and that the term *jiwa* is appropriate after all. *Takaful* functions through a particular kind of contract popular internationally in Islamic banking and finance called *mudarabah*.

A *mudarabah* contract is a profit-and-loss sharing equity partnership agreement that provides a means for financing business activity without the use of interest-bearing loans. Investors provide funds to a business enterprise and receive a predetermined proportion of the profits of that enterprise together with the return, over time, of their initial investment. They also absorb a predetermined share of any losses. *Mudarabah* thus spreads the risk of business among investors and enterprises and is deemed a just and fair financing mechanism for this reason. The Indonesian term for profit sharing of this kind is *bagi hasil*, and the term is ubiquitous in discussions of Islamic finance (and one that hides the fact that *mudarabah* is also loss sharing). Most people I interviewed, when asked if they knew anything at all about Islamic banking and insurance, replied, "Oh yeah, *bagi hasil!*"

A diagram in the Islamic life insurance company's packet of information renders visible the profit-sharing mechanism at work (fig. 6.1).[9] Clients' premiums are invested with businesses and banks in a profit-and-loss-sharing system. Returns on the investments are added into the general fund. The operating costs of the insurance company are deducted from the fund. Of the surplus, 70 percent becomes company profit. Thirty percent is placed into another *mudarabah* fund, managed by the insurance company and financing business enterprises. The profits by the clients are based on their contributions in the form of their premiums, and recirculated into the *mudarabah* fund. The recirculation is interrupted only if a client withdraws from the system or files a claim. As the diagram makes clear, there is thus a profit-sharing relationship between the clients and the shareholders in the insurance company, and among the clients themselves. The net result: the spirit of mutual assistance.

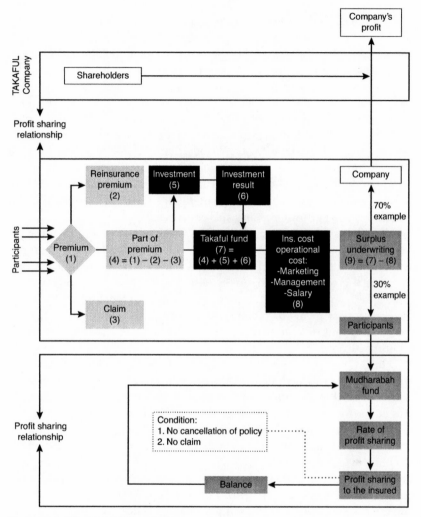

Figure 6.1 The *Takaful* Mechanism

NATIONAL ECONOMIC KNOWLEDGE AND FIXED OPEN-ENDED CONCEPTS

Indonesian terms like *koperasi*, *gotong royong*, and *tolong-menolong* became central to state power and state reorganization of the rural countryside during the postindependence period (Bowen 1986).[10] Their use in political and nationalist rhetoric and economic planning can be traced to the speeches of Mohammad Hatta, the first vice president of Indonesia. Indeed, my first exposure to the terms was during language study, when I turned the page of my textbook and found myself reading a short passage by Hatta himself. During the Japanese occupation, Hatta's speeches invoked *tolong-menolong*, mutual assistance, a term I found much more widespread than *gotong royong*. The latter term came to prominence in his postindependence lectures on creating "indigenous democracy" based on traditional "uncorrupted" village lifeways (see p. 549), and achieved national significance in Sukarno's "Birth of Pancasila" speech delivered on June 1, 1945: "The Indonesian State that we erect must be a *gotong royong* State! How splendid! A *Gotong Royong* State!" (quoted on p. 551). As Bowen summarizes, for Sukarno-style nationalism, *gotong royong* would "bring together Christians and Muslims, rich and poor, and native Indonesians and naturalized citizens in a mutually tolerant struggle against the enemy" (p. 551). Bowen charts subsequent shifts in the term's fortunes, as the 1965 attempted coup led to the rise of Suharto and the recently dissolved New Order. There, *gotong royong* came to stand for "state intervention in village life" rather than "the horizontal interaction between functional groups that make up the nation" (p. 552). And its new versions led to fresh and sometimes resistant responses (p. 555). Ultimately a misrecognition of forms of reciprocity, it became a polyvalent vehicle for national aspirations and national consolidation throughout the twentieth century (p. 555).[11]

Thus, the mundane credit and savings associations and mutual assistance schemes in which many Indonesians are involved were either actually instituted and promoted by, or, minimally, touch on, the state apparatus and state economic planning, as noted in chapter 5. J. S. Furnivall's classic texts on Netherlands India's "plural economy" demonstrate that the same was true in the colonial era. Furnivall documents Dutch efforts to link village cooperatives into banks and larger credit organizations, as well as to create state pawn shops and agricultural credit banks (1939:357; see Furnivall 1934a and 1934b). De Wolff's visions were implemented by the colonial government, and garnered considerable profit (Furnivall 1939:359). Furnivall noted certain structural weaknesses in the system, however, due, he thought, to their limited reach—they mainly served civil servants—and the "non-cooperation movement," which had "stimulated the foundation of numerous 'wild' co-operative societies, free of Government control" (about which "little information is available," he wrote; 1939:359–60). As previously noted, Furnivall worried that the existence of these "wild" societies indicated that "past neglect of co-operative credit by the State may lead to the growth of a co-operative movement among the people with a greater vitality than a movement depending on the support of the Government" (p. 361).

Subsequent nationalist political economic planning ironically warranted Furnivall's prediction, and in two senses. First, Sukarno and Hatta's anticolonial vision of mutual assistance and cooperation signaled in terms like *gotong royong* was just such a cooperative movement from among "the people" (read: non-Dutch) with incredible—stifling, even!—vitality. That it would succeed in achieving the tight centralization of the state that both Old Order and New Order Indonesia are famous for is testament to that success. Second, at the same time and running parallel to Old and New Order attempts to enforce cooperation, all the mundane credit and savings associations people use for their everyday needs trundled along, with a popular vitality that exceeded their putative state control and organization. There are still, after all, "wild" cooperatives like Rudi's. Using state forms and guidelines for how cooperatives should work, and using standardized double-entry accounting ledgers to record credits and debits (fig. 6.2), they do not touch on the state in any other way (except through the use of the national currency) but reach instead toward international NGOs for funding and legitimacy.

Furthermore, there are Islamic systems of savings and credit that also escape the state, even though they have been partially instantiated by it. As Robert Hefner has documented, Islamic banking in Indonesia grew from efforts of Muslim intellectuals to benefit the country's poor Muslims against perceived economic domination by ethnic Chinese, to carve a place for themselves in Indonesia's New Order power structure, and to create a client base of their own for political purposes (Hefner 1996, 1998). Indonesia's national Islamic bank, Bank Muamalat Indonesia, was established with the assistance of ICMI (Ikatan Cendekiawan Muslim se-Indonesia), the government-sponsored Muslim intellectual organization established in 1993, as were numerous Islamic credit cooperatives (Bitul Maal wa Tamwil, or BMT, which function like cooperative societies but use *mudarabah*). In my interviews and informal conversations with people, even professionals and academics interested in Islamic banking and finance, I found that many believed ICMI-sponsored activities to be an effort to create patronage relationships with the poor and to create, in the words of one, "a new economic dependency" (and he used English for this phrase). Some saw ICMI's efforts as a crass attempt to maintain relevance in a post-Suharto Indonesia by focusing less on political power and more on economic power. For many, however, the ICMI-inspired architecture of Islamic banking in Indonesia was simply *tidak jelas*, unclear or confusing. What was clear, and did make sense, was the principle of *bagi hasil* and the spirit of cooperation and mutual assistance they thought Islamic banking facilitated—principles taken from the toolkit of Sukarno-era economic planning but set in motion for new tasks.

TGL.	KO TP	KETERANGAN		DEBIT	KREDIT	SALDO
6 JUN 00	01	Mada Ayal	Rp	1.300.000		Rp. 1.300.000
6 JUN 00	02	Kreditur Sdr Arif R	Rp	600.000	Rp 500.000	Rp 800.000
8 JUN 00	02	Kreditur Sdr Erni	Rp	300.000	Rp 300.000	Rp 500.000
8 JUN 00	02	Kreditur Sdr Hj ATi	Rp		Rp 500.000	—
9 JUN 00	03	Angsuran Hj ATi	Rp	19.000		19.000,-
9 JUN 00	01	Tambahan Rahl dirfg	Rp	1.700.000		1.719.000
9 JUNI 00	02	Kreditur Oudy			50.000,-	1.669.000
10 JUN 00	02	Kreditur Nasir			100.000	1.569.000
10 JUN 00	02	Kreditur Alam			60.000	1.509.000
12 JUN 00	03	Angsuran Kred Erni	Rp	30.000		1.539.000
12 JUN 00	02	Kreditur Ani			600.000	939.000
12 JUN 00	03	Angsuran Kred Hj ATi		38.000 ✓		977.000
12 JUN 00	03	Angsuran Kred Nasir		4.000		981.000
13 JUN 00	03	Angsuran Kred Hj ATi	Rp	19.000		1.000.000
13 JUN 00	03	Angsuran Kred Erni		20.000		1.020.000
	03	Angsuran Kred Ani		40.000		1.060.000
	03	Angsuran Kred Nasir		4.000		1.064.000
14/6/00	03	Angsuran Kred Nasir		4.000		1.068.000
15/6/00	03	Angsuran Kred Ani		40.000		1.108.000
	03	Angsuran Kred Erni		20.000		1.128.000
16/6/00	03	Angsuran Kred Nasir		4.000		1.132.000
16/6/00	03	Angsuran Kred Hj ATi		38.000		1.170.000
JUMLAH:						⟹

Figure 6.2 A page from the *koperasi* ledger

Let me spell this out further. On the one hand, nearly everyone I talked to identified Islamic banking as *bagi hasil* and as a good thing. At the same time, almost all also commented that Islamic banking was *tidak jelas*, unclear, generally spoken to indicate a negative value. Similarly, in this post-Suharto moment of freer speech and exciting and dangerous possibilities, and in the wake of the economic crisis (which for Makassar was a mini-boom), while many expressed dissatisfaction with all things having to do with the central state apparatus, all agreed that they trusted state banks more than private banks. A volunteer worker for ICMI itself said he found

Islamic banking not merely unclear but boring (*bosan*). He complained that not only was it identical (*sama*) with conventional banking, but it was also insincere (*tidak ikhlas*), possessing the name and nuance of Islam only (*hanya nama Islam dan nuansa Islam saja*).

The apparently paradoxical nature of people's relation to the state and state institutions, discourses, and vocabularies is a clue to the apparent paradox in their embrace of Islamic banking as *bagi hasil* and simultaneous assessment of it as *tidak jelas*. Just as in Furnivall's day of the "wild" cooperatives flourishing alongside colonial cooperative institutions, the subjects of state planning exceed their emplotment or enframing in bureaucratic forms. As they do so, they take along the tools of the trade— double-entry books, the principles of *tolong-menolong* and *bagi hasil*, and the organizational forms that enable and instantiate them. So, although Islamic financial products like insurance may be considered unclear or confusing, as *bagi hasil* they articulate neatly to the mundane credit and savings associations of Indonesian nationalist thought and its hegemonic transformations in popular life. *Bagi hasil* conjoins Islamic insurance and cooperative credit the way *koperasi* (an ambiguous cognate) suggests both corporate and cooperate.[12]

Returning to life insurance, what is striking about it is that is insures the *jiwa*, the life-force, and participates in the spirit of cooperation or *semangat berkoperasi* that characterizes other credit and savings systems. Unlike conventional insurance, which is like a "tax," *takaful* carries a promise of return through *bagi hasil*, the same *bagi hasil* that mutually reinforces *jiwa* and *semangat*. Conventional insurance is closed; one gets a return only when the policyholder dies. *Takaful* is open; one continuously gets a return, even as that return is cycled back into mutual investments in nested profit-and-loss sharing contracts. Note that the only dotted lines on the diagram (fig. 6.1) indicate the possibility of that closure. Even the closure of death is represented as a tentative potentiality, not a certainty.

Consider Susan Buck-Morss's (1995) discussion of the manner in which the economy has been made visible in European and American world-orderings. Since the economy is "not found as an empirical object" it must, "in order to be 'seen' by the human perceptual apparatus . . . undergo a process . . . of representational mapping. . . . The map shifts the point of view so that viewers can see the whole as if from the outside, in a way that allows them, from the inside, to find their bearings" (Buck-Morss 1995:144; see also Castree 1999; Bloomfield and Vurdubakis 1997; Mitchell 1998). She contrasts messier representations of the economy with the minimalist visual displays of neoclassical economics like the classic supply-demand curve that fixed economics as a science, a science that measured observable facts and postulated universal laws. Economics' minimalist envisionings of the economy represent for Buck-Morss the impoverishing of

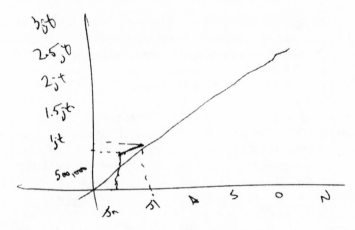

Figure 6.3 Rudi's sketch of the projected yield (*hasil*) of his *koperasi*

political economy's philosophy to the point where "it appears to make no metaphysical claims" at all (1995:465)—the point where it simply reflects the real at the end of ideology and analysis.

Even more minimalist, however, is Rudi's drawing of the *hasil* of his new *koperasi* (fig. 6.3). Looking for all the world like an econometric graph, the line itself is not identical to the lines of similar, more familiar projections of profit. This *hasil*, after all, this yield of investment and inventiveness (for the term *hasil* refers to products of the mind as well as products of the field) will be *dibagi-bagikan*, divided, shared, separated into parts. The line is not contained within itself for it already bundles together intrinsic parts (like the sections of an orange, or corns on a cob, or the word *dibagi-bagikan*), themselves effects that enable him to discern the *semangat berkoperasi*, the corporate/cooperative spirit. It is not a line with an origin point and a destination. One might name it a line of continual becoming (Deleuze and Guattari 1987:293); but doing so might undo its lateralizations with other forms by forcing it under one universal cover of law.

Now, consider Shelly Errington's discussion of *semangat* (or *sumange'*) in South Sulawesi: "intangible, . . . it cannot be seen, heard, touched, tasted or smelled. The fact that it cannot be perceived by the senses means that its presence can be discerned only by its effects" (Errington 1983:555). *Semangat* also both unites and divides, she writes (p. 568), and resonates with Geertz's Javanese "conception of the cosmos being suffused by a formless, constantly creative energy" (Geertz 1972:7). Errington's *semangat* also strangely prefigures Moise Postone's (1993) riff on Marx's "abstract labor," which is also made visible only through its effects, like the commodity form, money, and capitalist time. Here, perhaps, *semangat* is made visible through *takaful* and *haj* savings accounts, gold coins from Pegadaian, and the cosmological and national time of Islam and Indonesia.

Finally, consider again the *takaful* diagram (fig. 6.1). Similarly minimalist, it only exhausts itself for *our* analytical metaphysics; it is not self-identical to those metaphysics but, like the concepts of the state when they appear in mundane credit and savings associations, a tool that becomes a means to another end. Only this end is open, not final. Bureaucratic representations of the *takaful* system represent this openness in the two spaces of *bagi hasil*, labeled "Profit Sharing Relationship" on figure 6.1. The flow chart only dead-ends if the policyholder dies or cancels his or her policy. Otherwise, the system remains open-ended, a continuous means, as it were, and not a means to an end.[13] It remains unstable, too, because that relationship is also a loss-sharing relationship. But that is the nature of the risks of trust and insurance, the instability of fixed yet open concepts.

Mutual Anthropological Life Insurance, Limited

Sociologists and others influenced by the literature on governmentality (Foucault 1991; Ewald 1991; Defert 1991; Simon 1988) and Ulrich Beck's (1992) conception of "risk society" describe insurance's rationalizing effects and speculate on its consequences for democratic personhood and community. This position has been criticized for unwittingly accepting the "actuarial standpoint" of its object of study (Baker 2000:559; O'Malley 1999). Tom Baker's (2000) excavation of the moral discourses of insurance suggests that actuarial practices do not merely disaggregate the person into measurable, quantifiable risk factors but morally evaluate the person—does she have bad habits?—and morally entrusts the person, as well: will he stage an accident to make a claim, or will he be killed by his wife for the insurance money? The measure of the man taken by the actuary is always-already both statistical and moral (and gendered), as the dramatic conclusion to the classic film noir *Double Indemnity* made clear. Baker demonstrates how insurance also involves moral assessments of institutional arrangements and bureaucratic systems ("efficiency," "social welfare"; see also Bennett 1999, 2000). The case of Islamic insurance makes this even more apparent. Self-consciously positioned as a moral and ethical alternative to conventional insurance, it employs the same actuarial tables and statistical conventions while serving the perceived needs of the faithful, whether those needs be to provide for family after death or save money for the holy pilgrimage. Indeed, Islamic insurance merely makes explicit what was implicit in the actuarial technique of insurance, and what critical analysis of insurance needed to bring out into the open to fulfil its own critical desires—that it is a form of moral or ethical evaluation, that its facts are always-already values.

Viviana Zelizer argued, for instance, that nineteenth-century Americans viewed life insurance as dangerously commensurating incommensurables: a human life (or death) and economic, monetary value (Zelizer 1978, 1979; see also Espeland and Stevens 1998). Ritualizing life insurance as an ethical responsibility toward one's kin and a means of remembrance of the departed solved this moral problem. The ritualization reconciled "human values" with "market values" (Zelizer 1978:591, 1979; see also Beito 1999; Whaples and Buffum 1991; Jureidini and White 2000). No such ritualization is needed for Islamic insurance: the life insurance product, explicitly figured through Islam, is already a moral technology: purchasing Islamic life insurance over conventional life insurance is by definition the ethical choice. Islamic insurance, by its very nature, recognizes the inseparability of the moral from the technical. And if insurance poses any moral problem at all, it is not commensuration. Rather, at least for IBF professionals and intellectuals, if not for actual clients, moral and mortal dangers lie in conventional life insurance products that seem to verge on gambling or speculation, or that touch other financial products or relationships involving interest-bearing debt.

If some analyses of insurance have unwittingly reproduced the calculative, rationalizing actuarial standpoint, does it matter when other analyses of insurance adopt its *moral* standpoints? Can either form of theoretical reflection help but to do what it does, especially when the people one studies move simultaneously within various technical discourses of calculability, rationality, and actuary as well as moral discourses of character, social welfare, and even faith?[14] This is not just an issue for explicitly religious financial forms (or their "secular" counterpart, socially responsible ones). With the dominance of neoliberal formulations of governance and free markets, sold not only as the only possibility for being-in-the-world but also the only morally correct one—where government intervention in the private domains of the economy or the person is not only inefficient, but morally suspect if not evil—it should come as no surprise to find moral and technical articulated together in a seemingly indissoluable relationship. And this lack of surprise is strangely comforting and familiar to an anthropology that puts its faith in a holism content to relate parts to other parts in complex wholes in which elements from one cultural domain inform and intertwine with elements from others, or in which hybrid or blurry objects demand perspective-shifting, blurred, and hybrid analysis (Strathern 1992a, 1999).

Where does that actually leave analysis? In other words, what are the implications for anthropological knowledge when the theoretical form of analysis (anthropological holism, showing how the moral is technical and the technical is moral), the bureaucratic form of the object (Islamic insurance, always-already a moral-technical whole, a hybrid), and the cultural form of people's social interactions and beliefs (using insurance for one's metaphysical and mundane desires and hybridizing state and popular forms of credit and savings) all seem uncannily to converge (Riles 2000)?

It is not at all clear, however, that the bureaucratic form of the object in this case stitches together the kind of *complex* or *hybrid* wholes anthropologists like to see and social practice seems always to entail. If anything it is straightforwardly minimalist, especially in its visual representations. If in this chapter I have emphasized the way bureaucratic practice envisions its activities and its objects, it is with the aim of devisioning anthropology from its commitment to seeing things through others' eyes and thereby distancing our knowledges from theirs. This might be taken as an abandonment of the discipline's relativist stance, its own grounding as not merely an academic discipline but a moral mission. It could also be taken as an abandonment of analysis altogether. Like Shakespeare's Antonio, however, I mean it rather as an exhortation not to entrust our ventures to one bottom or place, to the comforts of anthropological holism, or to the fortunes of the past or present. The strategy is open-ended, but limited—in other words, a spirit of mutuality, and a form of insurance.

Restaging Abstraction and Adequation

> The word God is the algebraic x in morals, and the Hebrews
> with right philosophy made it unspeakable. But the stupid
> world, finding a word, assumes this scientific for a baptismal
> name, and talks of him as easily as Captain Gulliver.
> —Ralph Waldo Emerson, *Journals* (1849) 8:4

> It appears to me that this mystery is considered insoluble for the
> very reason which should cause it to be regarded as easy of
> solution. I mean the outré character of its features.
> —Edgar Allen Poe, "Murders in the Rue Morgue" (1841)

To THE ISLAMIC BANKING professional who contrasted "Mickey Mouse Islamic banking" with that "which calls things by their names," I ask: what
does it mean to call things by their names? How can we understand the
momentary invocation of the name—or the line on a page tracing a projected profit, as in Rudi's drawings of the yield of his *koperasi*; or the inscription of a local landscape on the Ithaca HOUR; or the oscillation of the "I"
that sometimes distinguishes Islamic banking from conventional banking
as an utter difference in kind and other times merely demarcates a niche
product, when Islamic banking professionals and their clients abbreviate
the field "I-banking"; or the slippage from hour to HOUR and back again,
even as back-calculations render the equivalence suspect if not outright
false? How does an instance of the letters "m-u-d-a-r-a-b-a-h" on the page
of a contract function in an Islamic banking endeavor that in all other
respects iconically re-presents a conventional contract, word for word,
form for form, line for line on the physical piece of paper, except for the
interjection of those nine Roman letters signifying—what? An Arabic
word? A word as English as burrito? A divine call to virtue? An effort?

Money, after all, is the copula, the "is," the grammatical element structuring a proposition of adequation between different commodities and between a commodity and the coin. It is also a statement of the implication
of a quality (value) in a substance or service (commodity). It is a statement
of formal equivalence as it triangulates between different commodities and
between commodities and itself. And it is a statement of actual identity, in
so far as substances and services "are" what their value is. It is all these

things at once, and it is also the supplement, the "and," that connects them and undermines the relationship between word and thing, signifier and signified, sign and logos. Hence its unavoidability in theory that is after an account of the fall of the sign from logos, and after the fall of the currencies of thought from transcendental, abstract value.[1] What stands as a mere assertion here has functioned as the open-ended argument of this book and has put into circulation the alternative currencies it restages and accelerates.

Yet the monetary metaphor is a trap, indeed, a mousetrap that restages semiotic and philosophical problems even as we try to accelerate past them. Western theories of signification have often resorted to monetary metaphor and monetary reason to establish their claims to speak meaningfully about the world of signs. Can money be rendered intelligible in terms other than its own if money itself is internal to semiotics? Or, as Moishe Postone (1993) would have it, is such an effort a fruitless and indeed misguided project, since it presumes the very outside that capitalist abstraction postulates and maintains as its structuring dynamic? Marc Shell argues that "[t]he monetary information of thought, unlike its content, cannot be eradicated from discourse without changing thought itself" (1982:180–81).

Cultural critics generally turn to semiotics and when faced with questions about the relationship between cultural and linguistic expressions and cultural or physical materiality. They do so in two modes: as attempts to interpret material signs as part of the fabric of the cultural world, and as attempts to assess their own theories' adequacy to the cultural materials they purport to explain. The first mode is familiar to ethnographic description and analysis, following upon Ricoeur's "culture-as-text" metaphor and especially Geertz's aphorism that "culture is a system of meaning embodied in symbols." Whether or not they identify with or remain wedded to structuralist or symbolic traditions in anthropology, ethnographers in the field and in their writings find the classification, identification, and analysis of signs good to think and good for their practice.

The second mode is familiar to theoretical critique in anthropology. It is often the foundation of theoretical innovation and collaboration across area-bound "fields." And it is, I believe, the most difficult to dislodge. I might not know anything about an Amazonian village except what I learn in a well-crafted ethnography, but I can discuss and criticize the ethnography's theoretical framework with reference to implicit and explicit theories of signs, signification, and adequation. Such a critique would probably take the form of statements following the formula, "The ethnographer claims X is an example of Y and means Z, but I think X is actually an example of A and means B." Such a critique would be considerably strengthened by deducing meanings and sign functions "missed" by the ethnographer: "Indeed, we can know that X is an example of A because we can notice certain metaphorical, iconic, indexical, or analogical associations that the ethnographer, for whatever reason, did not." Reading ethnography in this manner depends on particular, and not always competing, theories of signs, and is itself, of course, a signifying practice interesting in its own right. Money, as a sign and as formative in theories of signs and of adequation, foregrounds the link between these two modalities of anthropological reason. Anthropological reasoning about money—and anthropological reason itself—have been set in motion by this money form. That is why this book has sought lateral reasons, athwart the money forms and operations of adequation that animate anthropology, that sit beside the claims of semiotics.

The materiality of the word, its transubstantiation, has been of interest to anthropologists looking for ways of minting theories of signification/materialization that obviate the division between word and world. Nancy Munn (1986), Webb Keane (2003a), Michael Silverstein (1976), Alfred Gell (1998), and many others have sought modalities of inquiry astride linguistic referentiality or logical or cognitive rules. These authors have found C. S. Peirce's taxonomy of signs helpful for specifying the potentiality of an object's qualities to matter forth into language, or the multiple appearances of deposits of ink on a page to operate under a governing principle that transforms them into instances of the same thing (e.g., the "the"s on this page all magically become instances of the "same word"; see Keane 2003a).

I am less interested in Peirce's taxonomy than I am his coinages. To Peirce, word coinage was an ethical responsibility of philosophy and science. New words minted in the service of science should be so unusual as to be rendered distinct from words in common circulation. "It is good economy," he wrote, "for philosophy to provide itself with a vocabulary so outlandish that loose thinkers shall not be tempted to borrow its words" (2.223).[2] It is also an ethical "duty" (2.222).

Two of Peirce's contributions to the *Nation* specifically reference currency and stress efficacy and human commensal weldings over any thing-in-itself-ness of gold or money. In a review of a book on ancient weights and measures, Peirce complained that internecine disputes among scholars of the topic had failed to appreciate that "language[s] of quantity," like "dialects of speech," achieve a "unification of units" only through "commerce, extensive, pervasive, and voluminous."[3] Exchanges of signs create signs' values, values that can increase over time as they approach a (golden) mean.[4] In another of Peirce's book reviews, he speculated that even gold itself could be created by such voluminous human transaction, rendering that metal an effect of human signification rather than its cause: Peirce found it not at all far-fetched to suppose that Madame Curie's experiments with radioactivity would soon fulfill the wishes of the alchemists' dreams by transmuting lead into gold.[5] As this would in effect render gold the product of human activity, that substance would also transmute from a natural essence whose names are always inadequate, to the product of human activity and the human welding of meanings to other meanings to create new ideas. Recalling the citation of Qur'anic verse on Adam's knowledge of the true names of things, this would render gold more akin to the flux and flow of the praxis of Islamic banking where the effort, not the arrival, is what counts, or the figuring of labor hours into value by the seizing and democratizing of the money-form in Ithaca HOURS. Or, at least, it would do so momentarily, before the reassertion of gold's and Islam's and labor's purity, unity, abstraction, or transcendence.

On the topic of naming, Peirce argued for the *necessity* of word coinage. Biology had succeeded in developing a new classificatory scheme,

> Not by appealing to the power of congresses, but by appealing to the power of right and wrong. For only make a man *really see* that a certain line of conduct is wrong, and he *will* make a strong endeavor to do the right thing—be he thief, gambler, or even a logician and moral philosopher. The biologists simply talked to one another, and made one another see that when a man has introduced a conception into science, it naturally becomes both his privilege and *his duty* to assign to that conception suitable scientific expressions; and that when a name has been conferred upon a conception by him to whose labors science is indebted for that conception, it becomes *the duty of all—a duty to the discoverer, and a duty to science*—to accept his name. (2.224, emphasis added)

This passage strongly evokes his earlier text titled "Vitally Important Topics," in which he extolled the virtue of a "conservative sentimentalism" by which one "modestly rate[s] [one's] own reasoning powers at the very mediocre price they would fetch if put up at auction" (1.673).[6] "Then," he wrote:

> . . . the very first command that is laid upon you, your quite highest business and duty, becomes, as everybody knows, to recognize a higher business than your business, *not* merely an avocation after the daily task of your vocation is performed, but *a generalized conception of duty* which completes your personality by melting it into the neighboring parts of the universal cosmos. (1.673)

"'Being' remains barely a sound to us, a threadbare appellation. If nothing is left to us, we must seek at least to grasp this last vestige of a possession." Thus wrote Heidegger, in his *Introduction to Metaphysics* (1961), as quoted by Derrida (1979:118).[7] In drawing attention to this fall from grace, Derrida highlights the predominance of the problem of adequation in Western metaphysics. The problem is irreducibly implicated in the supposed primacy of the word. Yet, Derrida demonstrates, while critics conflate the two grammatical senses of "being" represented by being-as-existence and being-as-adequation, they also reveal that the inaccessibility of being-as-existence depends on the supplement of the copula, the third person singular present indicative of the verb "to be." "The copula function," Derrida writes, "would have invisibly governed the interpretation of the meaning of 'to be,' having, as it were, always worked upon it" (pp. 116–17). It is not, then, that the statement "X is Y," will always remain removed from being-as-existence, always a shadow of it, but that being-as-existence makes sense only under the proposition, "X is Y." Furthermore, the copula is always-already shattered and multiple: in "X is Y," the copula can function as the predicate of a logical proposition; a statement of the implication of a property Y in an entity X; a statement of formal equivalence; or a statement of actual identity.[8]

Bullionist Words and Currencies of the Realm

When speaking of money in the concrete, however, holding in abeyance the fragmentation implicit in the shattering of the monetary copula, it is still difficult to eschew the quest for descriptive adequacy, since monetary theories and practices are already participants in that quest. To anthropomorphize: money is continually trying to prove its adequacy to abstract value (really, I am worthy) and to real material in the world (through deixis: really, I am worth *that*). Recall how Ferdinand de Saussure's linguistics rotates around exchange. The linguistic sign is composed of a "concept" or signified and a "sound-image" or signifier, and the relationship between the two is arbitrary (Saussure 1966:16). The signified is not a real object but a thought object. Language, thus, does not depend on the real world so much as it depends on itself, as a "system of independent terms in which the value of each term results solely from the simultaneous presence of the others" (p. 114). Signifiers stand for signifieds, and signifiers stand in relation to other signifiers. Thus the value of a sign derives from the exchangeability of signifier for signified and of signifiers for each other. Saussure gives the example of French *mouton* and English *sheep*, which do not have the same value because English uses *mutton* for the concept of the meat of the animal while French is content to use *mouton* for the concept of both the animal and its meat. Saussure introduces this principle with a French coin:

> To determine what a five-franc piece is worth one must therefore know: (1) that it can be exchanged for a fixed quantity of a different thing, e.g., bread; and (2) that it can be compared with a similar value of the same system, e.g., a one-franc piece, or with coins of another system (a dollar, etc.). In the same way a word can be exchanged for something dissimilar, an idea; besides, it can be compared with something of the same nature, another word. (p. 115)

Terms in a language "mutually condition each other" (p. 122), and signs function "not through their intrinsic value but through their relative position" (p. 118). Language is a system of differences, and hence *"language is a form and not a substance"* (p. 122, original emphasis)—and not just at the level of the sign but the phoneme itself. Sound does not properly "belong to language" as it is mere "material," "a secondary thing to be put to use" (p. 118). Its value comes from "the differences that separate its sound-image from all others": "Phonemes are characterized not, as one might think, by their own positive quality but simply by the fact that they are distinct" (p. 119). Saussure's monetary analogy makes the point clear: "it is not the metal in a piece of money that fixes its value. A coin nominally worth five francs may contain less than half its worth of silver. Its value will vary according to the amount stamped on it and according to its use inside or outside a political boundary" (p. 118). The coin as material substance, in other words, need not be adequate to its conceptual value. Its conceptual value is independent from its substance and is instead a function of the relations of difference, exactly like price in the equilibrium models of Vil-fredo Pareto and the marginalist economics of the University of Laussane, developed while Saussure was based in Geneva (see Ponzio 1993; Thibault 1997:188). It is also, of course, a profoundly postbullionist position. It is self-evident only in a world where people using base metal coins or fiat currencies treat them as if they had the value of specie, for in such a world the value of specie itself is the product of a self-regulating system of prices.

Consider, in contrast, John Locke's semiotic in *An Essay Concerning Human Understanding*. A work dominated by a book on "ideas" and another on "words," and containing at its center an important chapter "Of Adequate and Inadequate Ideas" (II.xxxi),[9] it is, as Constantine George Caffentzis (1989) has argued, a bullionist text preoccupied with the problem of adequation presented by the English recoinage debate. In late-seventeenth-century England, pirates and others sought to line their pockets with the king's metal by shearing pieces off the coins of the realm. The reduction of the silver content of England's coins jeopardized its ability to fund its wars, maintain its empire, and settle its accounts abroad. In the uncertain context of royal succession, Cromwell's revolution, and the settlement that placed William and Mary on the throne of a country governed by a strengthened Parliament, clipped coins also pointed toward an erosion of the government's authority at home. Should the Crown collect old coins at face value and mint new ones with the same face value but of lesser silver content, thereby producing more coins overall, or should it collect the old coins at weight and mint new ones of the same silver content as the preclipped coins, thereby reducing the supply of coins (see Caffentzis 1989:22–23; Hart 2000:77–78)? Locke supported the latter option. In contrast to Nicholas Barbon's assertion that "money is a value made by law,"[10] Locke, while he accepted the basic premise that the coin of the realm should represent the authority of its maker, worried also that it be *adequate* to that authority. Recoinage did not present an economic problem alone, but a political and moral one connected to language, knowledge, and truth.

Locke's theory of language is a theory of adequation. To explain his theory, Locke relates two origin stories. In the first, Adam, traveling in a strange country, comes upon Lamech, who is "more melancholy than usual."[11] Imagining that this might be because Lamech's wife, Adah, has committed adultery, he relates his suspicion to Eve so that Eve will "take care that Adah commit no folly." In doing so, he creates two wholly new words never before heard in the newly fabricated world: *Kinneah* and *Niouph*, one "standing for suspicion, in a Husband, of his Wife's Disloyalty to him, and the other, for the Act of Committing Disloyalty" (III.vi.44). Later on, Adam learns that the reason for Lamech's melancholy was that he had committed murder. But the new words Adam created did not lose their distinct meanings in spite of the fact that they had no explanatory relevance for Lamech's disposition or Adah's actions.[12] Now, a problem arises as the new terms "by degrees came into common use" (III.vi.45). People come upon the terms as "already established and agreed on" (III.vi.45). Adam's children, however, encountering the words for the first time, might develop inadequate ideas toward them, since they do not understand the complex of ideas the terms bind together. However, "there be usually a remedy at hand, which is, to ask the meaning of any word, we understand not, of him that uses it" (III.vi.45). Certain kinds of ideas (Locke called them "modes") are wholly creations of the mind and are therefore always adequate to their objects, the mental ideas we have formed that they express (II.xxxi.3).

Locke presented a second origin story to explain why some words are not always adequate to ideas or things. Wandering in the mountains, one of Adam's children comes upon a shining, glittery, hard yellow substance "which pleases his eye," and brings it home. After considering its qualities, Adam gives it the name *Zahab*, gold. Locke remarks how very different a process of naming this is from Adam's earlier gesture. In the case of *Kinneah* and *Niouph*, Adam "put ideas together, only by his own imagination" (III.vi.46). In the case of the yellow glittery substance, however, not having encountered anything like it before, and assuming it to be a "distinct species" (III.vi.47), Adam's idea is of an archetype, and the "name *Zahab* [becomes] the mark of the species, and a name belonging to all things partaking in that essence" (III.vi.47). As Adam investigates the substance further, however, he learns that it has an infinite number of properties, such as ductility, fusibility, fixedness, and so forth. The name will never capture all of those properties. The name-idea is hence inadequate to the object-idea (see II.xxxi.6–11). Adam has been presented with "a standard made by nature," rather than, as in the case of adultery and jealousy, a "standard . . . of his own making" (III.vi.46). Furthermore, the name will mean different things to different people, as those people each discover new qualities of the object. Instead of inventing new words for the new ideas they reveal in these different qualities, people proceed *as if* "they have supposed a real essence belonging to every species, from which these properties all flow, and . . . have the name of the species stand for that" (III.vi.49). Because of the limitless qualities of the substance, people will never have any idea of its "real essence." Instead, they place the "name or sound, in the place and stead of the thing having that real essence, without knowing what the real essence is" (III.vi.49). The name, and the idea, thus stands in for the absence of adequate knowledge of true essences of substances.

Despite our inadequate ideas about them, however, substances possess a virtue almost by nature of our circumscribed comprehension. They endure over time and across cultural or linguistic difference. Modes, in contrast, are purely linguistic, and, indeed, *"require a name* to preserve and unify" themselves (Caffentzis 1989:81, original emphases). It is only the naming of the mode-idea that concatenates the various ideas that make it up. "Though therefore it be the mind that makes the collection [of ideas into a mode], it is the name which is as it were the knot that ties them fast together" (III.v.10). Hence, the names of modes, as particularistic bindings, are difficult to translate into other languages, while the names of substance-ideas are easier to translate. There is no essence to a mode in the same sense as there is for a substance. While the idea of a substance might fade or be deemed irrelevant or uninteresting to social affairs over distances of time or space, the essence—which we can never adequately know—endures and could, one imagines, be easily introduced to a new linguistic community (as European mythologies from Locke's day and earlier would have related about encounters with savages in gold-rich lands who were ignorant of gold's "true" value). The substance-idea, according to Locke, has an "inherent continuity" (Caffentzis 1989:87).[13] This is a quality necessary for any sound money, since it will need to be useful outside a state's borders for the prosecution of trade and it will need to be temporally consistent for the fulfillment of contracts. Substances, thus, make a better form of money than modes. While our idea of gold—or silver—will forever be inadequate, the metal itself will always be adequate to any money form that seeks transhistorical and transcultural endurance.[14]

What are we to make of the transcodings of money and meaning in Saussure and Locke? Those of the latter have been analyzed by Caffentzis as an effect of Locke's political outlook in the context of a changing state and emerging market. Those of the former have been analyzed by a range of writers, most of whom simply accept or invert Saussure's linguistic economy. Allying Saussure to Marx, Paul Thibault (1997) tries to explain why signs become commodities under capitalism. Baudrillard (1981) writes a critique of the political economy of the sign. Jean-Joseph Goux (1973) views the monetary form of Saussure's model of language as indicative of an isomorphism and psychic homology between economic exchange and linguistic exchange, both inhering in and animated by the lack of a transcendental signified (the general equivalent in Marx, the murdered father in Freud, the phallus in Lacan). "Between money and language," he writes, "one finds in the history of western philosophy the insistence of a comparison that is not exterior . . . but is the local, fragmentary perception of a real, historical-social coherence" (Goux 1973:183, my translation). This coherence, or "correspondence between the mode of economic exchange and the mode of linguistic exchange" (p. 183), indicates a psyche composed of accretions of past and now repressed political economic moments which, in their return as symptom, explain current psychic and economic investments and their accompanying forms of value. Ferruccio Rossi-Landi writes "economics is the study of commodity languages" (1977:62), and is quoted approvingly by Roman Jakobson in his discussion of the relationship between economics and linguistics. Jakobson suggested that money be treated "as a semiotic system with a particular destination" (1990:62). Finally, Umberto Eco (1976), in a grand sweep of human evolutionary time that takes but five pages and two identical diagrams, argues that the signifying process itself operates according to the same principles whether we are talking about the naming of a stone tool by a hypothetical Australopithecine, the formation of commodity money under capitalism, or the so-called exchange of women in Lévi-Strauss's (1969) connubial wonderland.[15] For all of these theorists, the economic analogy is adequate to linguistic phenomena and the linguistic analogy to economic phenomena, regardless of the different methods by which the analogies become effective in their particular arguments. Locke's definition of adequacy would have predicted as much: mixed modes are always adequate to their objects.

Peirce's "word-coinage," however, unsettles these analogies. Eco asserts that "the only difference between a coin and a word is that the word can be reproduced without effort while the coin is an unreproducible item" (Eco 1976). The word-coining metaphor appears in Locke as well: "He that hath new notions, will, perhaps, venture sometimes on the coining new terms to express them: But men think it a boldness, and tis uncertain, whether common use will ever make them pass for currant" (*Essay* III.vi.51). He is echoed by Jakobson: "the speaker, as a rule, is only a word-user, not a word-coiner" (Jakobson 1956:59). The term "only" in Jakobson's phrase is crucial. It sings out in the key of the currencies whose alters animate this book. Presumably, Jakobson's word-users are coin-users, too, and not coin-makers or counterfeiters. Describing speakers as "only" word-users imagines the users as inadequate to the word that precedes them.[16] The phrase itself suggests the problem of adequation of human speakers to transcendent words. It is not so much that this is wrong or bad as it is that this (and its deconstruction) is beside the point if the transcendent word and the bare human are of no particularly huge moment, or if the dichotomy between word and world and the operations of adequation simply lay to one side of other practices going on in the meantime.

If linguistic and capitalist process are homologous (leaving aside Stone Age toolmaking and circulating connubium), do Saussure and Locke differ on the question of the gold standard simply because Locke's doctrine of substances warrants a species of foundationalism Saussure's linguistics, with its play of differences, rejects? Not necessarily. For one thing, Locke's substances are, after all, ideas in the head, not things in the world, and they are ideas that seek to capture the essence of other ideas in the head, the object-ideas that impress themselves on the mind through sense perception.[17] They are always incomplete and inadequate, as well. For another thing, Saussure's play of differences is not quite as free as poststructuralist readings of Saussure might have us believe. Saussure is notoriously unclear on the status of the signified and the degrees of freedom of play that language allows, as it were, to its signifiers.[18] In terms of their theories of language, what is striking to me is their similarities. In terms of their monetary reason, what is striking is that their differences come down on either side of the coin: Saussure implies token theories of money; Locke implies substantive or commodity theories of money (Hart 1986).

Token and commodity are not only two sides of the coin of modern money, as Hart suggests, but two sides of the algebraic equation of adequation, *intellectus* and *res*. We know the problem can be solved by settling sums on each side of the equation to zero. But when solving for x stands in for the production of knowledge, a knowledge locked into the formula of *adequatio intellectus et res*, no new knowledge actually gets produced. Could it be that *this* practical activity, this apparent running in place, is akin to the casuistic arguments of the Islamic bankers and the ethico-calculative quandaries of Ithaca HOURS?

RE-SIGNING MONETARY INFORMATICS

Almost five years after that July screening of *It's a Wonderful Life* with which I opened this book, as I was in the thick of the writing, I received an e-mail from Hugh Raffles, asking whether I had seen the "deception dollars" that were circulating in northern California (figs. 7.1, 7.2). The war on Iraq had not yet begun, and these bills were being distributed at antiwar protests and left on car windshields. Modeled on the U.S. one-dollar bill, these "fraudulent event notes" carry the smirking image of George W. Bush, identified as "Big Brother," and contain scores of references to unsolved questions, mysteries, and conspiracies that may lie behind the events

Figure 7.1 The Deception Dollar, obverse

of September 11, 2001, as well as Web sites devoted to those conspiracy theories. "Bush Knew" and "Cheney Did It" are worked into the design; oil rigs and the names of oil companies are hidden on the front and back. The "Mission Statement" of deception dollars, posted on a Web site, explains that, after the "attempt to redefine the world in an Orwellian manner contingent upon the events of September 11," people had to forge a new theory of knowledge:

> Concerned people sought to build a new map of reality, to understand where we were, and what direction we were suddenly facing. Confusion and disorientation make it difficult to know which way to go: with a good map, a sense of where we have been and where we are heading, people are empowered to change course, and not blindly follow "a leader." The worldwide web facilitated an extraordinary exchange of information, observations, and collaborations in an urgent, spontaneous effort to make sense of what happened.[19]

Deception dollars interested me because they relied on the metaphorical slipperiness limning money and knowledge, as well as the imagination of a worldwide community brought together around and through alternative circuits of information. The deception dollar seemed to function analogously to the alternative currencies I had been researching, from Islamic banking to the Ithaca HOUR. These alternative forms, too, explicitly sought to bring together communities through new articulations of value and information. The fact that those behind the deception dollar took the money-form as their model did not surprise me. In doing so, they were restaging the same problematics of money, community, trust, and truth (as well as counterfeit, totalitarianism, deception, and fraud) rehearsed not only among the people I had been studying for the past several years but also in Western philosophy, economics, and anthropology of money and value.

Figure 7.2 The Deception Dollar, reverse

Keith Hart's (2001) work on the digitalization of money strikes the same chord as the deception dollars, and resonates with the comments I heard at that Islamic banking conference in 1998 about community, trust, and money as well as with other discussions I would have later with participants in Islamic finance and local currency schemes. For Hart, electronic media can facilitate a sort of people's takeover of the money form. New circuits of information offer the possibility for a more profound democratization of the economy than heretofore possible. If money is simply bits of information, there is nothing to stop people from circulating their own forms of it through the Internet with a generalized sense of trust and community to back its value. The printers of deception dollars assumed that the free flow of now-hidden information would allow them to make a new map, to chart a new territory, to move toward a more just society. Those who printed local currencies like the Ithaca HOUR assumed much the same. For them, the information currently hidden is that money is based on nothing but a fiction of its own autonomy and transcendence. Bringing this fiction to light allows people to start imagining money anew, in their own image, away from the state-backed currencies they believe erode trust and toward a money mobilized in the service of community. Similarly, Islamic banking, expressed archetypically by Jimmy Stewart, seeks to hold off the kind of rapacious lending that is only possible when borrowers are denied full information about the terms of their loan or the condition of "the economy": Potter's fifty cents on the dollar looks good only until you realize Potter's not panicking like everyone else in Bedford Falls. As George Bailey explained to the townspeople, "Potter's not selling, Potter's buying!" Islamic banking, opposed to these information asymmetries (as I learned much later), reaches toward a faith in each other that you *can* "feed your kids on."

The assumption here is that Money and Information will not only set you free, they will lead you to the truth, and the truth really is out there. The welded-together entity of money/information has multiple complementary valences, each of which outlines a boundary between good and evil. Those with the money have all the information and are producing false information to enslave the rest of us. Information *is* money, and power, and everything else that goes with them. At the same time, recognizing that money is *only* information, mere words or signs, allows us to seize it and make it in our image, to do good and re-create community and trust. Such recognition, in fact, carries with it the moral obligation to reconstruct and remake. The effect is similar to that attempted by Michael Hardt and Antonio Negri's *Empire*, which calls for recognition that the tools of global capitalism are tools made and used by the billions of people contributing labor and collective product to the global project; becoming aware that these are *our* creations, we have the ability and obligation to seize them for other ends (Hardt and Negri 2001; see Maurer 2004b).[20] Not to do so is to continue with the illusions of the powerful. The truth of money is that it is (simply) a sign, humanly created, not ordained from on high. If it is humanly created, it can be re-created and remade into a moral good. In this sense, as Annelise Riles has suggested regarding information, money is imagined as means, not an end in itself, "one of the given universals whose diverse uses generate the pluralism . . . that anthropological analysis uncovers. The popular treatment of information as a commodity in the global economy . . . furthers the notion that the only issues are its availability, what people do with it, and whose control it should be under" (Riles 2000:93). In the cases at hand, the imagining of money/information as means carries with it the compulsion to seize those means to alternative ends, and the anthropological pluralism Riles identifies is homologous to the monetary/informatic pluralism expounded by Hart, Islamic bankers, and alternative currency proponents alike. It is this homology of form with the analytical impulse that has occupied me in this book.

An Islamic banking professional in London once told me, "[When] there were no *halal* butchers, . . . we had to eat meat that was not killed properly. And we felt bad about it. You feel bad if you do something that goes against your beliefs. You don't need a survey to tell you that. People will choose banking institutions that fit their beliefs if given the opportunity." When participants in alternative financial worlds narrate their pasts in terms of necessity on the one hand and natural tendency on the other, they cite the authority of anthropology, philosophy, and critical social science. They take ready-to-hand forms like Information and Money, mix them up one way, and get Islamic banking; mix them up another way, and get Ithaca HOURS. Mix them up again, and get anthropology. Again, and you get Marxism. Yet again, and the result is neoliberalism. It is as obvious to participants in alternative finance as it is to anthropologists that economics is a social convention. This apparent consensus that "everything is constructed," however, is accompanied by the moral imperative that we can and must construct those worlds at will. This moral corollary unsettles the particular modality of social reference through which moderns configure the distinction between representation and reality, and the modalities of knowledge formation and critique that hinge on that distinction. At the same time that it does so, it also allows people to continue along in the work of the world as if these fabrications are timeless truths; indeed, it makes them out-of-time, like the names of things related by Adam before the angels and God.

Notes

PREFACE

1. See Shell 1978:64. In Plato's *Philebus* (25a), Socrates analogizes "classification and minting: 'We ought to do our best to collect all such kinds as are torn and split apart, and stamp a single *charakter* on them' " (Shell 1978:62n.).

2. The essential Heidegger here is *Being and Time* and "On the Essence of Truth," especially the latter, which begins with and carries its argument forward through a series of propositions about "true coin" and "counterfeit coin." The latter, nonetheless, "is something real . . . [and therefore] the truth of the genuine coin cannot be verified by its reality" (Heidegger 1949:321). Heidegger continues, "What do 'genuine' and 'true' mean here? Genuine coin is that real thing whose reality agrees with . . . what we always and in advance 'really' mean by 'coin.' Conversely, where we suspect false coin we say: 'There is something not quite right here' " (p. 321).

3. See *Critique of Pure Reason*, (2003) trans. Norman Kemp Smith, p. 97. The section of the *Summa* on adequation seeks to demonstrate that truth resides in the intellect, not the senses. Incidentally, Kant's "touchstone" metaphor is monetary in origin; a touchstone is what you use in a money changer's balance to determine whether a coin is true or false.

4. See Altmann and Stern 1958:58–59 and their translation of Isaac's text.

5. In a sense, they return to adequation its motion, its temporality, its unfoldings and infoldings, its "cyclical reversibility," the way that it can involve passing on in a chain, transferring, as well as "drifting, straying and getting lost," and not merely the bringing-into-relation a concept with an object without remainder. The phrases quoted here are from Stefania Pandolfo's gloss on the Berber/Arabic term *mulli* (1997:53).

6. *Exchange* is from the Latin *excambiāre*, the prefix *ex-* denoting expelling, removal, a going out from. Transaction is from *transigĕre*, the prefix *trans-* denoting across, to the side of, or through, and the root *agĕre* meaning to act or to drive. Transaction here is not meant to index the field of transactional analysis in mid-twentieth-century anthropological theory, but rather the critique of exchange initiated in, for example, Strathern 1984.

INTRODUCTION
LATERAL REASONS FOR A POST-REFLEXIVE ANTHROPOLOGY

1. Directed by Frank Capra; screenplay by Frances Goodrich, Albert Hackett, Frank Capra and Jo Swerling; Liberty Film, 1946. Quotations are taken directly from the film.

2. From a passage in the Qur'an, *Surah* 98 ("The Clear Evidence"), *ayah* 7: "(As for) those who believe and do good, surely they are the best of men."

3. In 1997–98, with the onset of the Asian financial crisis, the investment manager and philanthropist George Soros began to sound cautionary notes about unrestrained transnational financial activity, most notably in his 1998 book, *The Crisis of Global Capitalism*.

4. The objective limits of objectivism is Bourdieu's (1977) phrase; that of complicity, Marcus's (1999). On perspectivalism, see Strathern 1991.

5. Stefan Helmreich points out that the project would then be fashioned after abduction, not induction. As C. S. Peirce proposed, "An abduction is a method of forming a general prediction without any positive assurance that it will succeed either in the special case or usually, its justification being that it is the only possible hope of regulating our future conduct rationally, and that induction from past experience gives us strong encouragement to hope that it will be successful in the future" (Peirce, quoted in Doyle 2003:25). As Richard Doyle summarizes, "A missing term—one that may possibly arrive in the future—completes abduction's argument" (p. 25). Doyle uses among other things the contemporary cryonics industry as an example: the dead are frozen as they "wait" for some missing term to complete them and reanimate them in the future.

6. I hesitate to consider repetition, multiplication/replication, and acceleration as three separate analytical options, since, in the worlds this book describes, they were just as often alternative, that is, oscillating options following one another in time.

7. The situation is analogous to the one Strathern has described for models of choice available to late-twentieth-century Euro-Americans: "Individuality without diversity: the customer is pressured into the exercise of choice. . . . Diversity without individuality: the riot of consumer preference collapses all other possibilities, choice becomes consumer choice" (Strathern 1992a:193). Stefan Helmreich reminds me that it is also analogous to that faced by Lévi-Strauss in *Totemism* and Geertz and Geertz re: "kinship" (Lévi-Strauss 1963; Geertz and Geertz 1975).

8. It should be clear that the notion of virtuality deployed here is distinct from that of Miller 1998, which tends to hold steady a set of relations among the real, the virtual, and the abstract that the present endeavor attempts to reenergize, accelerate, and set in motion to other (open) ends.

9. Thus, the veritable torrent of information brought to bear in the analysis engulfs the reader in Timothy Mitchell's (2002) *Rule of Experts* and Donna Haraway's (2003) *Companion Species Manifesto*, the mosquitoes and dogs notwithstanding; these authors demonstrate the difficulties of creating a text in which the natural is simultaneously creative and emergent. I thank Hugh Raffles (and, with a sidelong glance, Webb Keane) for warning me of my own Cartesianism in such instants.

10. On Latour's shifting intellectual trajectories, see Lynch 1993. I am grateful to Hirokazu Miyazaki for directing me to this reference.

11. I have discussed sand dollars in Maurer 2004b, and reviewed some of the scientific literature on their nonhomology there.

12. Nigel Thrift (1996:14) briefly notes the possibility of radial truths.

13. See Mahmood 2001; Hirschkind 2001. I am grateful for conversations with Iris Jean-Klein on these points. I am also grateful to a reading of Alasdair MacIntyre

(1984) encouraged by Saba Mahmood on practices whose unfolding is itself an internal good.

14. The temporal prepositions are after Strathern 1992a.

15. "Articulation takes patience," Thomas Keenan writes, following Marx, and reading "can be no more, and no less, than an effort and a chance" (Keenan 1993:155).

16. This represents one strategy for dealing with the so-called new ethnographic subjects like finance and accounting that resist because they anticipate conventional anthropological analyses. See Maurer 2004a for a review of the finance literature. See also Marcus 1999; Riles 2000, 2004; Miyazaki 2003, 2004; Strathern 1999; Fortun 2001; Fischer 2004. Strategies in those works involve developing parallel knowledges; making theory an ethnographic object; inverting means-ends relations; using hope as a method; and undoing perspectivalism as a knowledge-generating tool.

17 The heading for this section is after T. Keenan 1993.

18. On economic value and moral values, and their separation by traditional forms of social inquiry, see Stark 2002 and, obliquely, Graeber 2001.

19. And the times are indeed mean. Still, this book is offered against "the demand for work/theory/inquiry that will bear immediate fruit and be immediately recognizable as contributing to something already apparent and with a clear trajectory" (Lubiano 1999:14), and against the charge that "if the trajectory of the work . . . isn't clear, then it has no possible progressive political use" (p. 15).

20. From Wiegman 2000:821, writing on the "elusive, unmanageable, and ultimately unable to be guaranteed or owned" future of feminism, and a call for a feminism "in the meantime."

CHAPTER 1
IN THE MATTER OF ISLAMIC BANKING AND LOCAL CURRENCIES

1. In this, they are in a lateral relation with those who debate the delineations of "alternative" and/or "complementary" medicine. See Zhan 2001.

2. I do not mean to overdraw the symmetries, but I do not want to cover them over either. There are tricks of scale involved in any effort to "assess" these phenomena: thus, Islamic banking is "big," "large-scale," "important," and Ithaca HOURS are "small-scale," "unimportant," and so on. Yet many dismiss Islamic banking as a joke despite the billions of dollars involved; and Ithaca HOURS serve as a powerful symbol of the possible for participants and outsiders alike. I take this work of perspective and scale to be data, not just an analytical device.

3. "Issues and Questions: Issues on Zakat, Fitrah," *Pakistan Link*, Friday, January 7, 2000, 19.

4. My account here differs from many other accounts of the origins of Islamic banking in one key respect. Most accounts track early (1960s) experiments with community-based banking in India and Egypt, leading up to the Organization of the Islamic Conference's creation of the Islamic Development Bank (IDB) in 1973, followed by the establishment of a number of national-based commercial Islamic banks during the 1970s and early 1980s (Dubai Islamic Bank, est. 1975; Kuwait

Finance House, 1977; Jordan Islamic Bank, 1978; Bahrain Islamic Bank, 1979; Qatar Islamic Bank, 1984; Bank Islam Malaysia, 1984; see, e.g., Smith 2000:97–98). Prince Mohammed al-Faisal al-Saud, an important benefactor of Islamic banking globally, is also credited with securing the cooperation and support of the Saudi government, and has contributed to Islamic banking debates and congresses (see, e.g., al-Saud 2000). He was instrumental in the creation of Dar al-Maal al-Islami (DMI), one of the largest international Islamic banks, headquartered in Geneva and operating through the Bahamas and Bahrain offshore financial services centers. Yet in my research and interviews I have been continually struck with the extent to which Saudi influence and money competes in origin stories with the intellectual energy of South Asian thinkers like Siddiqi (see below). It seems to me that current invocation of the royal house of Saud has become a sort of ritual obeisance that, once made, is quickly passed by.

5. For example, almost all of the contributions to A. Siddiqi 2000, as well as to the Proceedings of the Harvard University Forums on Islamic Finance (1999, 2000, 2001), begin with some attempt at definition of *riba* before moving on to the specific topic under discussion. Each essay begins as if for a wholly uninitiated reader, despite the fact that these collections are specialist publications mainly for the use of Islamic banking and finance professionals and scholars themselves. The place of definitions of *riba* here is very like that of definitions of *culture* in anthropological publications.

6. There are now numerous certification programs, many of which are associated with economics, business, or finance programs in universities in the United Kingdom, Australia, Malaysia, and elsewhere.

7. The two available on-line credentializing programs were structured very similarly because one had been created by a former student of the other.

8. I am using the term language ideology to refer to "implicit and explicit commentary on and signaling about language-in-use" (Woolard 1998:4; see Silverstein 1998).

9. A citation survey of ten readily available books on Islamic banking in Indonesian reveals the following most cited authors/texts: Mannan (5), Qur'an (official Indonesian Department of Religion translation, not Arabic original) (4), Afazlur Rahman (3), Qureshi (3), Indonesian authors Perwataatmadja and Antonio (3), Ulema Council of Indonesia (MUI, 2), Paul Samuelson (2), Fazlur Rahman (2), Mohamad Hatta (Indonesia's first vice president, 2), M. Umer Chapra (2) and Siddiqi (2). Most were cited in their English original; a few were to the Indonesian translations of Mannan and Siddiqi. The texts consulted are: Muamalat Institute 1999; Fachruddin 1993; Hafidhuddin 1998; Hasan 1996; Kamal 1997; Moehammad 1997; Muhamad 2000; Prawiranegara 1988; Sumitro 1996; Zuhri 1996.

10. Thanks to Kath Weston for keeping the flow charts flowing.

11. This statement tracks Strathern 1992b:188 and Munn 1986:272.

12. This origin story can draw on a long line of Orientalist scholarship that has maintained that Islam is an economic religion, given the "lively interest in matters of trade" one finds in the Qur'an (Torrey 1892:2) and details from Muhammad's biography. Toorey's 1892 dissertation documents the plethora of business, accounting, and mercantile metaphors in the sacred text that add up to its characteristically "business atmosphere" (p. 3).

13. Posting to an Islamic banking and finance Internet Listserv, May 28, 2003. All spellings as in the original.

14. Not to mention ritual invocation of the Freudian scatological interpretation of money and folkloristic literature on interest.

15. I have often thought of these moments like aphasia disorders, especially through Freud's interpretation of them as the breakdown of all the complementary mechanisms bolstering speech, or as a failure of speech's overdetermination (a concept Freud first used in this context). Aphasia, then, could be seen as a condition of racial underdetermination, and an aphasiac analytical strategy as obviating the ontological determinations—realities and facts and such—that much of social inquiry-talk performs. See Freud [1891] 1953.

16. Discourses of financial deviance proliferated after September 11, 2001. See de Goede 2003 for an excellent discussion and analysis of the media and regulatory debates over *hawala*.

17. "What are HOURS?" in *Hometown Money: How to Enrich your Community with Local Currency*, Glover (n.d.).

18. U.S. Census Bureau, Census 2000.

19. These statements are culled from interlocutors' comments about their town. The last is to the tune of the Cornell alma mater which rings out every day from the McGraw Tower overlooking the campus.

20. While there has been some excellent scholarly writing on Local Exchange and Trading Systems (LETS), relatively little has been written about local scrip currencies like the HOUR. On LETS, see Lee 1996; O'Doherty, Dürrschmidt, Jowers, and Purdue 1999; North 1999; Thorne 1996; Williams 1996. On local scrip currencies, see Cohen 1999; Hart 2000; Helleiner 1999, Zelizer 2000; in each of these works local scrip currencies get a brief mention. Although it is controversial within LETS/LETSystems circles, I will use "LETS" rather than "LETSystems" for the sake of orthographic ease. LETS is frequently used to refer to "schemes" rather than "systems," as discussed below.

21. Quotations are from Michael Linton, "Frequently Asked Questions about LETSystems," available at < http://www.gmlets.u-net.com/faq.html>, last accessed June 8, 2003. I am in debt to Roger Lee for discussions on the topic. See Lee 1996.

22. Jennings's research on LETS and HOURS grew from her interest in American populism, Depression-era local currencies, and territorial currencies and stamps in the nineteenth century.

23. Their more recent work tries to activate such differences by "releasing economic identity from the 'law' of the (capitalist) Economy and generating new economic identities that reflect the diversity of economic relations" (Gibson 2001:639).

24. Ferguson is also like an Islamic banker here, using *qiyas* or reasoning by analogy rather than comparison, a technique this book adopts as well.

CHAPTER 2
OF LAW AND BELIEF

1. paulmac, *3000 feet high* (music CD). Eleven: A Music Company, and Virgin Records. Fibromajestic Studio, the Blue Mountains, Australia (2001).

2. These quotations are from interlocutors' comments over e-mail or in person.

3. These sentiments are also expressed in print. Martin (2000:112) writes that "cynicism is a real problem at the moment." He refers to the poor returns of some Islamic banks in the Middle East, as well as the Bank of Credit and Commerce International, in which some prominent Middle Eastern Islamic banks had interest-earning deposits before it fell in scandal. Regarding the idea that Islamic banking is "just a bunch of meetings and conferences," *New Horizon*, a periodical publication of the IIBI, ran an article whose headline read, "Islamic Banking—Too Many Conferences?" (cited by Hirsch 2000:114).

4. As Haroon (2000:55) puts it, "It is imperative that Islamic banks are staffed by people who are not only competent technically but also well-versed in the Islamic financial system, believe in it and are committed to it. At present, not all Islamic bankers fall into this category; some jumped on the bandwagon for selfish reasons." As some of my interlocutors put it, some are in the business "to make big money," and there is only an "Islamic veneer" to their activities. In Indonesia, one interlocutor said that Islamic banking has only an Islamic name and flavor (*"hanya nama dan nuansa Islam saja"*)—and he worked for an organization that promotes Islamic banking!

5. U.S. Constitution, art. 1, sec. 8, cl. 5.

6. *Parade Magazine*, July 5, 1998, p.18.

7. U.S. Stats. at Large 13 (1864): 120.

8. The fractional paper currency provision appears in U.S. Code, vol. 18, sec. 491 (1995): "Whoever makes, issues, circulates, or pays out any note, check, memorandum, token, or other obligation for a sum less than $1, intended to circulate as money or to be received or used in lieu of lawful money of the United States, shall be fined . . . or imprisoned not more than six months, or both" (see Solomon 1996:141, n. 41).

9. U.S. Code, vol. 18, sec. 486 (1988), quoted in Solomon 1996:98.

10. *U.S. v. Roussopulous*, 95 F. 977 (1899).

11. *State v. Livingston Quackenbush*, 98 Minn. 515, 108 N.W. 953 (1906).

12. Citing *People v. Dimick*, 107 N.Y. 13, 14, N.E. 178.

13. *State v. Livingston Quackenbush*, 955. Citations omitted.

14. *United States v. Gellman et al.*, 44 F. Supp. 360 (1942).

15. E.g., *United States v. Charles Smith, Jr.*, 318 F. 2d 94 (1963); *Anchorage Centennial Development Co. v. Van Wormer and Rodrigues, Inc.*, 443 P. 2d 596 (Alaska 1968).

16. *United States v. Richard Falvey, aka "Dick Foley,"* 676 F. 2d 871 (US App. 1982).

17. In interviews after September 11, 2001, three interlocutors on separate occasions cited with concern the George W. Bush administration's apparent Huntingtonianism, and asked me whether I had read Huntington's book.

18. Such comments were often framed in terms of sameness (usually, an argument from self-interest or political economy) or difference (often, an argument from culture).

19. Strathern (1999:6) writes that ethnographic moments are the effect of the relationship between immersement and movement. Like Strathern, "I want to find a way of acknowledging the fact that my attention has been transfixed by certain (ethnographic) moments I have never been able—wanted—to shake off."

20. Salzman (2003) levied a similar critique against Maurer 2002a, urging me to attend more to the "real constraints of the world" rather than "indulge in epistemological conceits." Again, the opposition here between real constraints and epistemological conceits parallels so precisely Siddiqi's criticisms of Choudhury that I am compelled to ask why *this* is the way the debate gets framed, in anthropology *and* Islamic banking, and whether this framing obviates something else, and is a McGuffin that merely carries all of us along to somewhere else.

21. The following examples are drawn from conversations on the IBF Net Internet Listserv, and from informal conversations I had during my research.

22. Latour 1999:304.

23. Thus, I see Charles Taylor's (2002) emphasis on belief and William Connolly's (1999) emphasis on the visceral as a means of squaring religious experience and democratic inclusivity and tolerance as beside the point here. Islamic banking is a debate over and a practical toying with techniques and instruments that obviate questions of belief and interiority and instead themselves, in their practical workings out, casuistically perform virtue. We are not "post-Durkheimian" (Taylor 2002:111), I would argue, so much as postpluralist: the model of difference warranting democratic pluralism no longer seems to have traction for describing the kinds of worlds with which this book is concerned, nor for proscribing future worlds of (democratic) possibility. See MacIntyre 1984 on virtue and ethics.

CHAPTER 3
OF MONETARY ALTERNATIVES AND THE LIMITS OF VALUES PAST

1. From *A Thousand Plateaus: Capitalism and Schizophrenia* (Minneapolis: University of Minnesota Press, 1987), pp.188–89.

2. Although he might not recognize himself in this chapter, Frank Cancian inspired it, and I would like to thank him for that.

3. Where Jacob criticizes Poovey for writing "bad history" (2001:288), she means that Poovey gets the facts wrong and places them in a sloppy narrative that is not true to the historical record. Proponents of Ithaca HOURS and Islamic banking also write that kind of bad history, full of sloppy readings of key texts, historical inaccuracies, and derivative accounts. My point is that bad history may be good to think with, to help outthink the conventional grounds of critique.

4. A commitment to increasing your wealth at everyone's expense, as well as a commitment to altruism, for example, can both be maximized.

5. See Mirowski 1989.

6. Take "magnitude effects": people on average will not distinguish between being given $15 immediately or $60 in a year, on the one hand, and $3,000 immediately or $4,000 in a year, on the other, although the former is a much better deal than the latter. Verses 75:20–21 in the Qur'an state, "ye love the fleeting life [that which is sooner] and leave alone the hereafter." Take preference reversals, in which a person asks more for an object he owns than he is willing to pay for the same object if he doesn't own it. The Qur'an states that, even when a person possesses the "Treasures of the Mercy of God," he still "holds back for fear of spending them" (17:100). Also, "Those who, when they have to receive by measure from men, exact

full measure; but when they have to give by measure or weight to men, they give less than due" (83:2–3). See El-Gamal 1999:32–34.

7. Qureshi 1946.

8. See Maurer 2003 for a survey and discussion.

9. That is, that causes both produce and precede their effects.

10. In other words, there may be what MacIntrye (1989) calls an internal good in doing so.

11. Although it should be that, too. See, in this regard, Sohn-Rethel's (1978: 45) discussion of the difference in perceptions of an encounter at the butcher's shop between himself and his dog, which authorizes the very abstraction of the (Cartesian) human his critique seeks to deny other forms of philosophical speculation.

12. See Helleiner 2003 and Ritter 1997.

13. This is the theme of Thomas Nast's images poking fun at the virtualism of paper currencies, such as his "Milk-Tickets for Babies, in Place of Milk" of 1876. For one of the most interesting discussions of the theme of substance and sign in monetary imaginaries, see Shell 1995.

14. I.e., 1971–1973. For a general discussion, see Leyshon and Thrift 1997. Some in the global Islamic banking community explicitly seek a return to the gold itself as a medium of exchange. See chapter 5.

15. And more comfortable with contextual readings of the tale, as in Foley 2000, even though, as should become evident, I do not endorse this separation of text from context and want to resist the conscription of textual contexts into an ontologically prior real. On Bartleby, see Michaels 1987; Thomas 1984.

16. Herman Melville, "Bartleby, the Scrivener, a Story of Wall Street," in *Billy Budd, Sailor and Selected Tales*, edited by Robert Milder (Oxford: Oxford University Press, 1997), pp. 3–41.

17. *Refuse* as a noun has an archaic monetary referent, as well, referring to odd or worthless money (OED).

18. Agamben views Bartleby's formula as being "characterized . . . precisely" by the Skeptics' experience of suspension, or *epokhe* (1999, p. 256); language in the *epokhe* "becomes the pure announcement of appearance, the intimation of Being without any predicate" (p. 257).

19. The W. D. Halls translation cited in the bibliography is somewhat different.

20. Derrida thus contradicts Goux 1990. See also Brantlinger 1996: 206–7.

21. See, for example, Caruth 1991. I have discussed this issue in relation to fact making in Maurer 2001c. There, I argue that the idea of factual history is itself the product of the dynamics of trauma. The very idea of the historical fact "before" it becomes distorted or filtered by memory demands the traumatic separation of words from things, deracinated particulars from moral commitments, and the repression of that separation—or, better, the reterritorialization of that repression into the familiar (Western, bourgeois) separation of subjects from objects—the commodity form, the form of the fact, the neatly purified world of words and things to which they refer.

22. The "radical openness of the future" is from Elizabeth Grosz, as quoted by Wiegman 2000:821.

23. It also relies on a set of notions about scientific and legal facts and evidence. Here, see Poovey 1998; Shapin and Schaffer 1985; Daston and Park 1998; and Shapiro 1991.

24. Quoted in Siegel 1997:15.

25. For these etymologies, see Echols and Shadily 1997: 261.

CHAPTER 4
INNUMERATE EQUIVALENCIES: MAKING CHANGE WITH ALTERNATIVE CURRENCIES

1. From a conversation in the land of HOURS, on "direct barter" relationships.

2. Calculation and comparison entail a specific mathematical world that substitution obviates, or decomposes (Verran 2001). This decomposition, in turn, implies a different cut through the problem of number than usually at evidence in the ethnomathematical literature. See Urton 1997 for a useful discussion. The present chapter is indebted to work that operates to one side of the conventionally ethnomathematical by bringing ethnographic materials to bear on Platonic/Fregian accounts of number; see Verran 2001, Mimica 1992; Lave 1991; and Crump 1990.

3. Although they take different approaches to the problem of money as the general equivalent, all share the underlying assumption that the equivalence function is central: see, for example, Akin and Robbins 1999; Bloch and Parry 1989; Bohannan 1959; Goux 1990; Hart 2000; Leyshon and Thrift 1997; Marx [1865–66] 1997; Polanyi 1957; Simmel [1907] 1990; Taussig 1980; Zelizer 1997.

4. While Appadurai's call to reconsider the distinction between the gift and commodity is well taken, accepting the common sense of calculation risks solidifying an analytical opposition implicit in accounts of money, that between the sacred and the profane. It also allows Appadurai, as well as Zelizer and others, to maintain their awkward relationship to Simmel, for whom the profanity of money and calculation was a foregone conclusion. On the pitfalls of the Simmelian approach, see Ferguson 1988. On another, related note, Belk and Wallendorf (1990) have written a fascinating compendium of the sacred meanings of money, but do not make the analytical move of seeing the "sacred" in money's supposedly "profane" meanings, that is, of using their analysis to call into question the sacred/profane distinction.

5. In Maurer 2002c I explore the relationship between individual SSBs in different financial institutions and the creation of transnational Islamic accountancy norms. I argue that the apparent shift from religious to bureaucratic authority in Islamic accountancy is not a struggle between religion and bureaucracy but a sort of complicity. SSBs provide a transnational standards-setting body (the Accounting and Auditing Organisation for Islamic Financial Institutions, AAOIFI) the "data" it needs to devise "best practices" which then, when disseminated, gain SSB seals of approval, in a neat and self-fulfilling prophecy whose main effect is the aura of technical precision for outside observers and regulators.

6. In other words, the DJIM does *not* proceed by seeking out "Muslim corporations." It assumes that everything that does not violate Islamic norms *is* Islamic, even if not necessarily Muslim. I would like to thank Saba Mahmood for comments on earlier drafts that helped me clarify this section (and I accept all responsibility for the muddles that remain).

7. There is, however, great debate on this topic. See Kamali 1996, 1997, 1999; Maurer 2001a.

8. See, for example, DeLorenzo 2000:73, which maintains that these kinds of issues render *zakat* a process best "left to the individual Muslim investor or depositor," not the fund managers.

9. As discussed earlier, another vexing convertability issue has to do with the equation between labor-time and HOURs. In principle, one HOUR signifies one hour of labor, of any sort. This concept is absolutely central to the egalitarian and labor-theory of value ideology behind the HOURs system. Many people I talked to expressed concern that some people might "calculate backwards" in order to determine how many HOURs to charge for their labor. In other words, a contractor who "normally" charges $30–40 per hour might translate that amount into HOURs and ask for 16–20 HOURs for one hour of labor-time. Research on LETS has found similar labor-time convertability issues at stake in those systems (see especially O'Doherty et al. 1999:1645; and North 1999:79 for examples). However, since LETS systems do not use a physical object as currency, the problem of "making change" explored here never arises.

10. Exactly as they did, incidentally, in the post–World War II international financial architecture which defined the international numeraire as the national currency of the United States. See Eckes 1975; Leyshon and Thrift 1997.

11. The more standard translation preserves the sense of the original concluding reference to Goethe's *Faust*, but is not quite as melodious: "By turning his money into commodities which serve as the building materials for a new product, and as factors in the labour process, by incorporating living labour into their lifeless objectivity, the capitalist simultaneously transforms value, i.e., past labour in its objectified and lifeless form, into capital, value which can perform its own valorization process, an animated monster which begins to 'work,' 'as if its body were by love possessed' " (Marx 1976:302).

12. When I have presented versions of this chapter before different audiences, the mousetrap *concept* did not confuse so much as the *term* itself. But consider what a mousetrap does, how it functions: What is the mouse's crime? The mouse steals the cheese out of the cupboard. How do you catch the mouse? You restage the scene of the crime with an artificial "cupboard" within which you place a piece of cheese.

13. My thanks to Jim Ferguson for pointing out the importance of the parenthetical here.

14. I think my analysis here resonates with that of North (1999) and O'Doherty et al. (1999), who find in LETS a sort of microresistance that is more about engaging a new kind of critical reflexivity in social practice than overthrowing a monetary order. Where these authors are interested in the political consciousness of the actors involved, however, I am more concerned with what we might call the political unconscious, the other dimension of the "lines of flight" North discusses (1999:73), following Deleuze and Guattari (1987).

15. I get the term "social science fiction" from Diane Nelson (1999), who in turn borrows it from Pfohl (1992).

16. Lear has so carefully demarcated the shares of his kingdom that will devolve to Albany and Cornwall, his daughters' husbands, that neither will feel he has been slighted upon examination of the other's inheritance.

17. The 1831 translator, Frederic Rosen, complains that, in the last third of al-Khwarizmi's text, "[t]he solutions which the author has given of the remaining problems of this treatise, are, mathematically considered, for the most part incorrect. It is not that the problems, when once reduced and [sic] into equations, are incorrectly worked out: but that in reducing them to equations, arbitrary assumptions are made, which are foreign or contradictory to the data first enounced" (Rosen, in al-Khwarizmi 1831:133). What Rosen misses is that these "arbitrary" numbers are only arbitrary if one assumes number to be referential, which al-Khwarizmi did not.

18. Thus, contra Rotman, I am not convinced of zero's "secular effect" (Rotman 1987:5). The failures of equivalence suggest that the numerical pivot of algebra—zero—did not always deliver on what it promised: equivalence. Rather, zero's mystical associations transformed to hinge on the doubt that failure produced. Zero thus became associated with the remainders left over after attempted equivalence functions.

19. Pascal's work with magic squares points up his complicated relationship to the work of Ramon Lull, the thirteenth-century Christian mystic, and Nicolas da Cusa, the fifteenth-century German scholastic. Each, in turn, had complicated relationships with medieval Islam. I cannot explore this here, but see Burman 1991; Menocal 1990; Urvoy 1990; Adamson 1995:46 and Armour 1993:17 on Lull; and Smirnov 1993; Jaspers 1957; Hopkins 1980; and Watts 1982 on da Cusa. The mutual participation of each in one field of discourse about number and divinity relieves my own anxieties about relating contemporary Islamic banking to Renaissance and Enlightenment debates within Christendom—these worlds are not so separate as one might wish to believe. See Asad 1993.

20. The ballad tradition in seventeenth- and eighteenth-century England had always found ample material in sea serpents, ghosts and apparitions, and monstrous births (Dugaw 1998:45). During the South Sea Bubble, however, after the naturalization of the monstrous effected by the new science, monsters were considered to be creatures only fools would believe in. To the songsmiths, so, too, was paper credit, based on equivalence, the balance, and zero, an object only for the belief of the overly credulous and women (see Ingrassia 1995). In one popular balled from 1720, hapless and feminized stock-jobbers react swiftly, and, for their finances, disastrously, to news from landlocked Moscow that a gigantic whale is devouring ships. Rumor and fancy—in a word, fiction—turn the material into the immaterial and back again (Dugaw 1998:55). In their commentary on stock trading, the songsmiths did not distinguish between rumor and information. Both led people to make bad decisions. Both contributed to the demise of the old order. For a newly constituted and investing public, the distinction between fact and fiction collapsed in a frenzy of paper trading.

21. As Žižek admonishes, "It is not sufficient to reduce the form to the essence, to the hidden kernel; we must also examine the processes—homologous to the 'dream-work'—by means of which the concealed content assumes such a form" (1995:300).

22. This is a point Marx realized in his discussion of "fictitious capital" and the relationship between "money-capital and real capital" (Marx 1967:516–17).

23. I am indebted to Jim Ferguson and Liisa Malkki for the first term of this equation.

CHAPTER 5
WISEMAN'S AND FOOL'S GOLD

1. Most onshore jurisdictions place duties or Value Added Tax on gold. On Labuan as an offshore jurisdiction, see J. Abbott 1999. On gold duties and the relationship between gold and offshore financial service centers, see Naylor 1996 and World Gold Council "Gold Information Sheet: Gold Coins and Small Bars," which notes that when taxes have been introduced on gold coins, bullion has tended to flow toward Switzerland, Luxembourg, and the Channel Islands.

2. Murabitun earned the attention of Richard Douthwaite (1996) slightly earlier, appearing in his book on local currencies and community economic empowerment (a book blurbed on the back jacket by Michael Linton, the founder of LETS, as discussed in chapter 1).

3. 2 Cor. 8:12–15: "If a man is willing to give, the value of his gift is in its proportion to what he has, not to what he has not. I do not mean to be easy upon others and hard upon you, but to equalize the burden, and in the present situation to have your plenty make up for what they need, so that some day their plenty may make up for what you need, and so things may be made equal." The Greek uses ισοτης ("equality"). The term itself is fascinating. Gustav Stählin argues (in Kittel 1967, 3:343–55) that the word drew together mathematical, empirical, moral, political, and spiritual senses of equality and balance, rather than the sense of monetary equivalence, and would have appealed to readers familiar with the Greek political discourse on equality. Stählin suggests the term primarily signified that latter in Greek, and it was the Greek New Testament's specific employment of the word that gathered the other meanings into it.

4. Apologies for the gender-specific term. As will become apparent I have reasons for using it.

5. Apologies, too, for the hypostasization of the market here and its "laws" of supply and demand. Here I merely parrot the opinions of gold market–watchers, for the purpose of opening them up later on.

6. An ironic fact not least because the MUI had successfully killed a national lottery in the 1980s on religious grounds.

CHAPTER 6
MUTUAL LIFE, LIMITED: INSURANCE, MORAL VALUE, AND BUREAUCRATIC FORM

1. This important point is brushed aside in Kindleberger's encyclopedic and authoritative *Financial History of Western Europe*. His blanket statement that "financial institutions were needed to cope with risk efficiently and . . . they developed, at different times in different societies . . . largely in spurts, and in parallel with other financial institutions" (Kindleberger 1984:182) neglects the moral and cul-

tural embeddedness of insurance practices in ideas about the disruptive "passions" (Hirschman 1977; see also Baker 2000).

2. I do not wish to linger over questions of doctrine here. For the purposes of this chapter, the basic proposition is that we live in a universe of risk and uncertainty (*gharar*). Taking risks with the hope of a gain has a positive value, although one must enter into such risks with as much knowledge about the possible gain and loss as possible and must also be responsible for the losses and not off-load them onto someone else. Loaning money with interest (*riba*) shields the lender from the risks borne by the borrower, since one is guaranteed a rate of return regardless, and should the borrower default, the lender has claim on the borrower's property. Courting risks for the sheer fun of it, as in gambling, and courting risks by choice that would not otherwise impact one's life and work, is also forbidden. Siddiqi 1985, published by the Islamic Foundation in Leicester, United Kingdom, is the most commonly encountered source on Islamic insurance within IBF circles. The other sources on insurance listed are in Indonesian; of them, Lupiyoadi cites Siddiqi. Siddiqi was translated into Indonesian in 1987. In my credentializing course in Islamic banking and finance, the section on life insurance spent considerable time on the distinction between insurance and gambling.

3. Given the abolition of Indonesia's national lottery in recent memory, at the insistance of Muslim intellectuals and leaders, the casual equivocation around the topic of gambling is somewhat striking, though perhaps not surprising given the sorts of critical casuistry that characterize Islamic banking, as discussed in chapters 1 and 2.

4. The Indonesian case is particularly interesting in that Mohammad Hatta, the first vice president of Indonesia after independence, and an architect of many of the country's cooperative credit and finance systems, made a distinction between prohibited interest (*rente consumptif*) on loans for consumptive purposes and necessary, less onerous (to him) interest (*rente productif*) on loans for productive purposes. The latter constituted a form of capital and the productive *rente* was a share of the profits earned by the borrower with the lent capital. Even with productive *rente* Hatta believed the rate of interest should be reasonable—he decried a bank's charging 40 percent interest on productive loans. The effect of Hatta's drawing of distinctions between different forms of interest is that Indonesians, even devout Muslims, do not always agree on what exactly constitutes *riba* and what does not. See Rahardjo 1988 for a discussion of Hatta's writings on interest.

5. Did the film promote, or simply reflect, the gendered associations of life insurance in the West?

6. Readers have been surprised by this figure. People borrowed and rapidly paid back small loans (usually within a week of borrowing); the interest was levied at 10 or 15 percent for each loan (i.e., the interest is not calculated per annum, but per transaction!). And, other members joined during the month, adding their capital to the shared pool.

7. The pattern of using pawn shops as one of a set of credit organizations rather than as a last resort in dire need seems long-standing. Laanen (1990:263) notes that during the colonial period the use of government-created pawnshops supplemented

other forms of savings and credit and "facilitated the monetisation of the indigenous community."

8. "Melepaskan kelompok sasaran dari lintah darat; membangun perekonomian Indonesia; menciptakan lapangan kerja."

9. Virtually identical representations of *takaful* appear in two separate chapters of a book published by the University of Indonesia titled "Concepts of Islam and Economics" (Antonio 1997, fig. 5; and Husein 1997, figs. 4a and 4b).

10. Bowen notes that although many Indonesians imagine the term *gotong royong* to be Javanese, in fact it seems to be of Indonesian (i.e., national state) provenance (1986:546).

11. That several education textbooks contain guidelines on how to instill the spirit of *gotong royong* (e.g., Lie 1999) suggests that this particular nationalist project still has some pull for Indonesians as it is reimagined in the post-Suharto era.

12. Much as in Boellstorff's (2003) analysis of mass media, where a dubbed television program creates a nonoriginary performance that is never self-contained. The word *corporation* would generally be translated *perusahaan*, after *usaha* ("effort"). It might also be translated *badan hukum* (in the sense of the body corporate at law). In some situations, however, the word *koperasi* might stand in for "corporation," especially when collective enterprise or investment (as in a joint stock corporation) is being emphasized. It is unclear to me whether this would be considered a metaphorization (a joint stock corporation is like a *koperasi*) or a strict translation. On language ideologies in Indonesia and the linguistic transformation of nationalist discourse, see Boellstorff 2004.

13. I am indebted to Annelise Riles for conversations on means and ends.

14. The contingent effects of the intertwining of the sacred and the secular on the *haj* itself has received anthropological attention; see Bernal 1994; Delaney 1990; and O'Brian 1999.

CONCLUSION: RESTAGING ABSTRACTION AND ADEQUATION

1. After in the sense of directed toward and seeking to attain, and after in the sense of temporal subsequence, after Strathern 1992a.

2. Unless otherwise noted, references are to the *Collected Papers of Charles Sanders Peirce*, edited by Paul Hartshorne and Paul Weiss (Cambridge: Harvard University Press, 1932); the first number refers to volume, the second to paragraph.

3. In the *Nation* 54 (June 23, 1892), pp. 472–73; in Ketner and Cook 1975: 1:157–59.

4. Peirce explicitly invokes the science of statistics, which, as many (including some of my informants) have pointed out, emerged from post-Pascalian debates over the nature of chance in a world of divine design. For Abraham de Moivre, the eighteenth-century inventor of the bell curve (the maxima of which is central to the argument of Peirce's book review), the bell curve itself was evidence of divine plan, for "errors" seemed naturally to fall into a regular pattern. See Maurer 2002b.

5. In the *Nation* 82 (January 18, 1906), p. 61; in Ketner and Cook 1975: 3:254–56.

6. Cornel West places Peirce's conservative sentimentalism in the context of an industrializing America undergoing a period of national consolidation (including the fiscal and monetary aftermath of the Civil War, as well as the Spanish American War) and Peirce's and other intellectuals' fears about the erosion of community solidarity and upper-class privilege (West 1989:43–45). Like Bryan, whose famous "Cross of Gold" speech argued that there is no natural basis for value but rather that value is social convention to serve the greater good, "Peirce revel[ed] in the contingency and revisability promoted by the scientific method" (West 1989:47) and an "evolutionary optimism about collectivities, not individuals, in human history" (p. 50). Medieval scholasticism seems a better context in which to situate Peirce's semiotic, and serves to bind Peirce's semiotic to his ethics and evolutionary agapism.

7. As Derrida demonstrates, Benveniste and Heidegger assert that the quality of "being" has degenerated, in human language, into the copula "is," the mark of equivalence (which in some languages, Benveniste writes, is effaced altogether and made mere oral pause or lexicalized absence).

8. Peirce may very well have "wanted to avoid both the revisionary metaphysics of idealism and the promissory notes of physicalism" (Rorty 1991:130). According to Richard Rorty, however, Peirce merely replaced a proposition about correspondence or adequation with one about the progress of human inquiry. I am claiming, in contrast, that the Scotian proposition about the progress of human inquiry remains necessarily welded to the proposition about correspondence, because the former presupposes a community that is the made-flesh of the logos presupposed in the latter. Thus, contra Simmel's simile ("Money is . . . similar to the forms of logic which lend themselves equally to any particular content, regardless of that content's development or combination" (1907) [1990:441]), money is the motor of the *moral* processes of abstraction and adequation that are central to anthropological and other (post-)Baconian modes of fact making and theory building.

9. In references to this work, the numerals refer to the book number, followed by chapter and section numbers.

10. Quoted in Hart 2000:78.

11. There are two Lamechs in Genesis. The first is the last named descendent of Cain; he was the first polygamist and the second murderer (after Cain), but there is no reference to the encounter between him and Adam that Locke imagined, and the only moral lesson suggested regarding his actions is perhaps in his being contrasted with the second Lamech. The second Lamech is the father of Noah, of the line of Seth, who was Eve's third child after God sought fit to give her "issue" to replace the murdered Abel. It was after Seth's first child was born that people began to invoke the name of God, Yahweh. Genesis 4:19–28.

12. The new terms refer to new ideas that fall into Locke's "mixed mode" category; they refer to combinations of different kinds of ideas. The new ideas are also adequate to their objects, since they were produced by Adam's own unique and original combination of ideas without reference to any preexisting archetype.

13. Caffentzis notes (1989:219, n. 19) that the Lockean doctrine of substances found new life in Hilary Putnam's (1996) theory of "natural kinds" and the "baptismal events" through which they are named; Putnam's exemplar is gold.

14. One might ask of Locke, why gold or silver and not lead or iron? The answer comes in the *Second Treatise* and has to do with their scarcity, as well as their durability (they don't rust) and ductility (they're easy to mold into small, transportable items).

15. Briefly, with his first diagram, Eco argues that the name given to the general type "stone" (St) arises once our Australopithecine realizes that his particular stone S1 has a function F and that another stone S2, whether he picks it up or not, is an instance of the general model St. Similarly, when use value is transformed into exchange value, the operation is the same as when S1 and S2 were subsumed under St; here, commodity 1 and commodity 2 are subsumed under an equivalence function (Ev) which represents human labor (HL). "Money" is in the same position on Eco's second diagram as Name was in the first, here a sign of Ev. Finally, and thankfully without the aid of diagram, Eco asserts that the exchange of women operates in the same manner as the commensuration of stones and the formation of money. "The woman, the moment she becomes a 'wife,' is no longer merely a physical body: she is a *sign* which connotes a system of social obligations" (Eco 1976:26). Presumably, W1 and W2 are to S1 and S2 as Wife is to Stone, which leaves unasked the vitally important question of how, if we accept the circulating connubium model, people come to have objectified rights in others in the first place (Collier 1988). This is how we know Eco's hypothetical Australopithecine is a male. Happily, an anonymous reader inscribed the words "Oh Dear . . . " in the margins of the copy of the book that I borrowed from the Australian National University library. For an unraveling of the supposed homology between the exchange of women and the exchange of commodities, see Maurer 2000; see also Strathern 1988; Collier 1988.

16. Compare Brock's comments on Heidegger's neologisms: "Heidegger chooses his concepts, especially if he has to coin them afresh, not arbitrarily and only after long searching reflection and . . . it is the phenomena and the problems themselves which he envisages that compel him to do so" (Brock 1949:145). This, in a commentary on Heidegger's "On the Essence of Truth" that is preoccupied with coins, gold, money, and counterfeiting.

17. Compare Boyle; see chapter 4.

18. Hence, the classic criticisms of Saussure's doctrine of "arbitrariness" in Hjelmslev (1961) and Benveniste (1966), not to mention Jakobson (e.g., 1956; 1990).

19. Available at <http:www.deceptiondollar.com/mission.htm>, last accessed May 19, 2003.

20. Once again, I am grateful for conversations with Annelise Riles on these issues.

References Cited

Abbott, Jason P. 1999. Mahathir, Malaysia and the Labuan International Offshore Financial Centre: Treasure island, pet project, or ghost town? In *Offshore Finance Centres and Tax Havens: The Rise of Global Capital*, edited by Mark P. Hampton and Jason P. Abbott, pp.192–211. London: Macmillan Business.

Abbott, Nabia. 1972. *Studies in Arabic Literary Papyri*. Vol. 3: *Language and Literature*. Chicago: University of Chicago Press.

Abdul-Rahman, Yahia. 1994. LARIBA Bank: Islamic Banking. Pasadena, Calif.: Cedar Graphic.

Abdul-Rahman, Yahia, and Mike Abdelaaty. 2000. The capitalization of Islamic (lariba) finance institutions in America. Paper presented at the Fourth International Harvard Islamic Finance Information Program Conference, Sept. 30.

Abdul-Rahman, Yahia, and Abdullah Tug. 1999. Towards Lariba (Islamic) mortgage financing in the U.S.: Providing an alternative to traditional mortgages. *International Journal of Islamic Financial Services* 1 (2) (July–Sept.). Available on-line at <http://www.islamic-finance.net/journal>, last accessed September 29, 2000.

Adamson, Donald 1995. *Blaise Pascal: Mathematician, Physicist and Thinker about God*. New York: St. Martin's Press.

Agamben, Giorgio. 1993. The *Coming Community*. Translated by Michael Hardt. Minneapolis: University of Minnesota Press.

———. 1999. "Bartleby, or On Contingency," in *Potentialities: Collected Essays in Philosophy*, edited and translated by Daniel Heller-Roazen, pp. 243–71. Stanford, Calif.: Stanford University Press.

Ahmed, Kurshid. 2000. Islamic economics based on human values. In *Anthology of Islamic Banking*, edited by Asma Siddiqi, pp. 32–37. London: Institute of Islamic Banking and Economics.

Akin, David and Joel Robbins. 1999. *Money and Modernity: State and Local Currencies in Melanesia*. Pittsburgh: University of Pittsburgh Press.

Alexander, Jennifer. 1987. *Trade, Traders and Trading in Rural Java*. Singapore: Oxford University Press.

Ali, Muazzam. 2000. Equality and morality in Islamic banking. In *Anthology of Islamic Banking*, edited by Asma Siddiqi, pp. 62–65. London: Institute of Islamic Banking and Finance.

Allen, John, and Michael Pryke. 1999. Money cultures after Georg Simmel: Mobility, movement, and identity. *Environment and Planning D: Society and Space* 17:51–68.

Altmann, A., and S. M. Stern. 1958. *Isaac Israeli: A Neoplatonic Philosopher of the Early Tenth Century, His Works Translated with Comments and an Outline of His Philosophy*. Oxford: Oxford University Press.

Anderson, Benedict. 1972. The idea of power in Javanese culture. In *Culture and Politics in Indonesia*, edited by Claire Holt, pp. 1–69. Ithaca: Cornell University Press.

Antonio, Muhammad Syafi'i. 1997. Asuransi dalam perspektif Islam. In *Wawasan Islam dan Ekonomi: Sebua Bunga Rampai*, edited by Mustafa Kamal, pp. 253–63. Jakarta: Lambaga Penerbit Fakultas Ekonomi, Universitas Indonesia.

Appadurai, Arjun. 1986. Introduction: Commodities and the Politics of Value. In *The Social Life of Things: Commodities in Cultural Perspective*, edited by Arjun Appadurai, pp. 3–63. Cambridge: Cambridge University Press.

———. 1996. *Modernity at Large*. Minneapolis: University of Minnsota Press.

Armour, Leslie. 1993. *"Infini Rien": Pascal's Wager and the Human Paradox*. Carbondale: Southern University of Illinois Press.

Asad, Talal. 1993. *Genealogies of Religion: Discipline and Reasons of Power in Christianity and Islam*. Baltimore: Johns Hopkins University Press.

———. 2003. *Formations of the Secular: Christianity, Islam, Modernity*. Stanford, Calif.: Stanford University Press.

Baker, Tom. 2000. Insuring morality. *Economy and Society* 29 (4): 559–77.

Barnes, T. J. 1989. Rhetoric, metaphor, and mathematical modelling. *Environment and Planning A* 21 (10):1281–1422.

Baudrillard, Jean. 1981. *For a Critique of the Political Economy of the Sign*. St. Louis, Mo.: Telos Press.

Beck, Ulrich. 1992. *Risk Society: Towards a New Modernity*. London: Sage.

Beito, D. T. 1999. To advance the "practice of thrift and economy": Fraternal societies and social capital, 1890–1920. *Journal of Interdisciplinary History* 29 (4):585–612.

Belk, Russell W., and Melanie Wallendorf. 1990. The sacred meanings of money. *Journal of Economic Psychology* 11:35–67.

Bennett, P. 1999. Governing environmental risk: Regulation, insurance and moral economy. *Progress in Human Geography* 23 (2):189–208.

———. 2000. Mutuality at a distance? Risk and regulation in marine insurance clubs. *Environment and Planning A* 32 (1):147–63.

Benthall, Jonathan. 2001. Comment: Speculations on Islamic financial alternatives. *Anthropology Today* 17 (3):28–29.

Benveniste, Emile. 1966. *Problems in General Linguistics*. Translated by Mary Elizabeth Meek. Coral Gables, Fla.: University of Miami Press, 1971.

Bergson, Henri. 1911. *Matter and Memory*. Translated by Nancy Margaret Paul and W. Scott Palmer. London: George Allen and Unwin.

Bernal, Victoria. 1994. Gender, culture, and capital: Women and the remaking of Islamic tradition in a Sudanese village. *Comparative Studies in Society and History* 36 (1): 36–67.

Bhabha, Homi. 1994. *The Location of Culture*. New York: Routledge.

Blair, Sheila, and Jonathan Bloom 1999. Art and architecture: Themes and variations. In *The Oxford History of Islam*, edited by John Esposito, pp. 215–67. Oxford: Oxford University Press.

Bloch, Maurice, and Jonathan Parry. 1989. Introduction: Money and the morality of exchange. In *Money and the Morality of Exchange*, edited by J. Parry and M. Bloch, pp. 1–93. Cambridge: Cambridge University Press.

Bloomfield, Brian, and Theo Vurdubakis. 1997. Visions of organization and organizations of vision: The representational practices of information systems development. *Accounting, Organizations, and Society* 22 (7): 639–68.

Boellstorff, Tom. 2003. Dubbing culture: Mass media and lesbi/gay subjectivities in Indonesia. *American Ethnologist* 30 (2): 225–42.

———. 2004. Gay language and Indonesia: Registering belonging. *Journal of Linguistic Anthropology* 14 (2): 248–68.

Bohannan, Paul. 1959. The impact of money on an African subsistence economy. *Journal of Economic History* 19 (4): 491–503.

Boundas, Constantin. 1991. Translator's introduction: Deleuze, empiricism, and the struggle for subjectivity. In *Empiricism and Subjectivity: An Essay on Hume's Theory of Human Nature*, edited by Gilles Deleuze, translated by C. Boundas, pp. 1–19. New York: Columbia University Press.

Bourdieu, Pierre. 1977. *Outline of a Theory of Practice*. Cambridge: Cambridge University Press.

Bowen, John. 1986. On the political construction of tradition: Gotong royong in Indonesia. *Journal of Asian Studies* 45 (3): 545–61.

Brantlinger, Patrick. 1996. *Fictions of State: Culture and Credit in Britain, 1694–1994.* Ithaca: Cornell University Press.

Braudel, Fernand. [1949] 1995. *The Mediterranean and the Mediterranean World in the Age of Philip II.* Berkeley and Los Angeles: University of California Press.

Brock, Werner. 1949. An account of "the four essays." In *Existence and Being*, by Martin Heidegger, pp. 117–231. Chicago: Henry Regnery.

Browne, Mark J., and Kihong Kim. 1993. An international analysis of life insurance demand. *Journal of Risk and Insurance* 60 (4): 616–34.

Buckmaster, Daphne. 2000. The principles of Islamic economics. In *Anthology of Islamic Banking*, edited by Asma Siddiqi, pp. 38–40. London: Institute for Islamic Banking and Insurance.

Buck-Morss, Susan. 1995. Envisioning capital: Political economy on display. *Critical Inquiry* 21: 434–67.

Burman, Thomas E. 1991. The influence of the *Apology of Al-Kindi* and *Contrarietas Alfolica* on Ramon Lull's late religious polemics, 1305–1313. *Mediaeval Studies* 53:197–228.

Business Week. 2001. Western Union: Where the money is—in small bills. November 26, pp. 40–41.

Butler, Judith. 1987. *Subjects of Desire: Hegelian Reflections in Twentieth-Century France.* New York: Columbia University Press.

Caffentzis, Constantine. 1989. *Clipped Coins, Abused Words and Civil Government: John Locke's Philosophy of Money.* Brooklyn: Autonomedia.

Callon, Michel. 1998. Introduction: The embeddedness of economic markets in economics. In *The Laws of the Markets*, edited by Michel Callon, pp. 1–57. Oxford: Blackwell.

Cancian, Frank. 1966. Maximization as norm, strategy, and theory. *American Anthropologist* 68 (2): 465–70.

———. 1974. Economic man and economic development. In *Rethinking Modernization: Anthropological Perspectives*, edited by John J. Poggie, Jr. and Robert N. Lynch, pp. 141–56. Westport, Conn. and London: Greenwood Press.

Carruthers, Bruce, and Wendy Espeland. 1998. Money, meaning, and morality. *American Behavioral Scientist* 41 (10): 1384–1408.

Cartwright, Nancy. 1999. *The Dappled World: A Study of the Boundaries of Science.* Cambridge: Cambridge University Press.

Caruth, Cathy. 1991. Unclaimed experience: Trauma and the possibility of history. *Yale French Studies* 79:181–92.

Castree, Noel. 1999. Envisioning capitalism: Geography and the renewal of Marxian political economy. *Transactions of the Institute of British Geographers* 24 (2): 137–58.

Chambers, Bruce W. 1988. *Old Money: American Trompe L'Oeil Images of Currency.* New York: Berry Hill Galleries.

Chapra, M. Umer. 1992. *Towards a Just Monetary System.* Leicester: Islamic Foundation.

Choudhury, Masudul Alam. 1997. *Money in Islam: A Study in Islamic Political Economy.* London: Routledge.

Cohen, Benjamin. 1999. The new geography of money. In *Nation-States and Money: The Past, Present and Future of National Currencies,* edited by E. Gilbert and E. Helleiner, pp. 121–38. London: Routledge.

Collier, Jane F. 1988. *Marriage and Inequality in Classless Societies.* Stanford, Calif.: Stanford University Press.

Connolly, William. 1999. *Why I Am Not a Secularist.* Minneapolis: University of Minnesota Press.

Crosby, Alfred. 1997. *The Measure of Reality: Quantification and Western Society, 1250–1600.* Cambridge: Cambridge University Press.

Crump, Thomas. 1990. *The Anthropology of Numbers.* Cambridge: Cambridge University Press.

Darriulat, Jacques. 1994. L'arithmétique de la grâce: Pascal et les carrés magiques. Paris: Les Belles Lettres.

Daston, Lorraine 1988. *Classical Probability in the Enlightenment.* Princeton: Princeton University Press.

———. 1994. Marvelous facts and miraculous evidence in early modern Europe. In *Questions of Evidence: Proof, Practice and Persuasion across the Disciplines,* edited by James Chandler, Arnold Davidson, and Harry Harootunian, pp. 243–74. Chicago: University of Chicago Press.

Daston, Lorraine, and Katharine Park. 1998. *Wonders and the Order of Nature, 1150–1750.* New York: Zone Books.

Davidson, Donald. [1987] 2000. Knowing one's own mind. In *Subjective, Intersubjective, Objective,* pp. 15–38. Oxford: Oxford University Press, 2000.

Debord, Guy. 1958. Theory of the dérive. *Internationale Situationniste* #2. Archived at <http://www.cddt.vt.edu/sionline/si/theory.html>, last accessed July 26, 2004.

Defert, Daniel. 1991. "Popular life" and insurance technology. In *The Foucault Effect: Studies in Governmentality,* edited by Graham Burchell, Colin Gordon, and Peter Miller, pp. 211–33. London: Harvester Wheatsheaf.

de Goede, Marieke. 2003. Hawala discourses and the war on terrorist finance. *Environment and Planning D: Society and Space* 21 (5): 513–32.

Delaney, Carol. 1990. The haj: Sacred and secular. *American Ethnologist* 17 (3): 513–30.

Deleuze, Gilles. 1988. *Bergsonism*. Translated by Hugh Tomlinson and Barbara Habberjam. New York: Zone Books.

———. 1991. *Empiricism and Subjectivity: An Essay on Hume's Theory of Human Nature*. Translated by Constantin V. Boundas. New York: Columbia University Press.

———. 1997. "Bartleby; or, the Formula," in *Essays Critical and Clinical*, translated by Daniel W. Smith and Michael A. Greco, pp. 68–90. Minneapolis: University of Minnesota Press, 1997.

Deleuze, Gilles, and Felix Guattari. 1987. *A Thousand Plateaus*. Minneapolis: University of Minnesota Press.

DeLorenzo, Yusuf Talal. 2000. Shari'a supervision of Islamic mutual funds. In *Proceedings of the Fourth Harvard University Symposium on Islamic Finance*, pp. 67–75. Cambridge: Harvard Islamic Finance Information Program.

Derrida, Jacques. 1976. *Of Grammatology*. Translated by Gayatri Spivak. Baltimore: Johns Hopkins University Press.

———. 1979. The supplement of copula: Philosophy before linguistics. In *Textual Strategies: Perspectives in Post-Structuralist Criticism*, edited by Josué V. Harari, pp. 28–120. London: Methuen.

———. 1992. *Given Time I: Counterfeit Money*. Chicago: University of Chicago Press.

Doran, Alan. 1998. *Trends in Gold Banking*. World Gold Council Research Study no.19. Copy in author's possession.

Douthwaite, Richard. 1996. *Short Circuit: Strengthening Local Economies for Security in an Unstable World*. Devon, England: Resurgence Books.

Dow Jones. 1999. *The Dow Jones Islamic Market Index*. New York: Dow Jones Company. Booklet, 17 pp. Copy in possession of the author.

Doyle, Richard. 2003. *Wetwares: Experiments in Postvital Living*. Minneapolis: University of Minnesota Press.

Dreyfus, Hubert, and Paul Rabinow. 1982. *Michel Foucault: Beyond Structuralism and Hermeneutics*. Chicago: University of Chicago Press.

Dugaw, Dianne. 1998. "High change in 'Change Alley' ": Popular ballads and emergent capitalism in the eighteenth century. *Eighteenth-Century Life* 22 (2): 43–58.

Ebrahim, Muhammed Shahid, and Zafar Hasan. 1993. Mortgage financing for Muslim-Americans, *American Journal of Islamic Social Sciences* 10 (1): 72–87.

Echols, John, and Hasan Shadily. 1997. *Kamus Indonesia-Inggris*. Jakarta: Penerbit Gramedia.

Eckes, Alfred E., Jr. 1975. *A Search for Solvency: Bretton Woods and the International Monetary System 1941–1971*. Austin: University of Texas Press.

Eco, Umberto. 1976. *A Theory of Semiotics*. Bloomington: Indiana University Press.

El-Gamal, Mahmoud. 1998. Introduction. In *Proceedings of the Second Harvard University Forum on Islamic Finance*, pp. 3–6. Cambridge: Harvard Islamic Finance Information Program.

———. 1999. An economic explication of the prohibition of *riba* in classical Islamic jurisprudence. *Proceedings of the Third Harvard University Forum on Islamic Finance*, pp. 29–40. Cambridge: Harvard Islamic Finance Information Program.

El-Gamal, Mahmoud. 2000a. An introduction to modern Islamic economics and finance. *Proceedings of the Fourth Harvard University Forum on Islamic Finance*, pp. 145–50. Cambridge: Harvard Islamic Finance Information Program.

———. 2000b. The economics of 21st century Islamic jurisprudence. In *Proceedings of the Fourth Harvard University Forum on Islamic Finance*, pp. 7–12. Cambridge: Harvard Islamic Finance Information Program.

Elgari, Mohamed Ali. 2000. Purification of Islamic equity funds: Methodology and shari'a foundation. In *Proceedings of the Fourth Harvard University Forum on Islamic Finance*. Cambridge: Harvard Islamic Finance Information Program, pp.77–80.

Errington, Shelly. 1983. Embodied sumange' in Luwu. *Journal of Asian Studies* 42 (3): 545–70.

———. 1989. *Meaning and Power in a Southeast Asian Realm*. Princeton: Princeton University Press.

Espeland, Wendy Nelson, and Mitchell L. Stevens. 1998. Commensuration as a social process. *American Review of Sociology* 24:313–43.

Ewald, François. 1991. Insurance and risk. In *The Foucault Effect: Studies in Governmentality*, edited by Graham Burchell, Colin Gordon, and Peter Miller, pp. 197–210. London: Harvester Wheatsheaf.

Fachruddin, Fuad Mohammad. 1993. *Riba dalam bank, koperasi, perseroan dan assuransi*. Bandung: PT Alma'arif Penerbit.

Ferguson, James G. 1988. Cultural exchange: New developments in the anthropology of commodities. *Cultural Anthropology* 3:488–513.

———. 1999. *Expectations of Modernity: Myths and Meanings of Urban Life on the Zambian Copperbelt*. Berkeley and Los Angeles: University of California Press.

Fine, Ben, and Costas Lapavitsas. 2000. Markets and money in social theory: What role for economics? *Economy and Society* 29 (3): 357–82.

Fischer, Michael M. J. 2004. *Emergent Forms of Life and the Anthropological Voice*. Durham, N.C.: Duke University Press.

Fitchen, Janet. 1991. *Endangered Spaces, Enduring Places: Change, Identity, and Survival in Rural America*. Boulder, Colo.: Westview Press.

Foley, Barbara. 2000. From Wall Street to Astor Place: Historicizing Melville's "Bartleby." *American Literature* 71 (1): 87–116.

Fortun, Kim. 2001. *Advocacy after Bhopal: Environmentalism, Disaster, New Global Orders*. Chicago: University of Chicago Press.

Foster, Robert J. 1998. Your money, our money, the government's money: Finance and fetishism in Melanesia. In *Border Fetishisms: Material Objects in Unstable Spaces*, edited by Patricia Spyer, pp. 60–90. London: Routledge.

———. 1999. The legitimacy of Melanesian currencies. In *Money and Modernity: State and Local Currencies in Melanesia*, edited by David Akin and Joel Robbins, pp. 214–31. Pittsburgh: University of Pittsburgh Press.

Foucault, Michel. 1991. Governmentality. In *The Foucault Effect: Studies in Governmentality*, edited by Graham Burchell, Colin Gordon, and Peter Miller, pp. 87–104. London: Harvester Wheatsheaf.

Franklin, James 2001. *The Science of Conjecture: Evidence and Probability before Pascal*. Baltimore: Johns Hopkins University Press.

Frege, Gottlob. [1892] 1996. On sense and reference. In *Translations from the Philosophical Writings of Gottlob Frege*, edited by Peter Geach and Max Black, translated by Max Black, pp. 56–78. Oxford: Basil Blackwell.

Freud, Sigmund. [1891] 1953. *On Aphasia: A Critical Study*. Translated by E. Stengel. New York: International Universities Press.

———. [1919] 1955. The 'uncanny.' In *The Standard Edition of the Complete Psychological Works*, translated by James Strachey et al., 17:217–56. New York: W.W. Norton.

Friedman, Milton. 1987. Quantity theory of money. In *The New Palgrave: A Dictionary of Economics*, edited by J. Eatwell, M. Milgate, and P. Newman. London: Macmillan.

Fukuda, Haruko. 1999. Keynote speech. The Denver Gold Group, Mining Investment Forum, Westin Hotel Tabor Center, Denver, Colo. October 18, 1999. Copy in author's possession.

Furnivall, J. S. 1934a. *State and Private Money-Lending in Netherlands India: Studies in the Social and Economic Development of the Netherlands East Indies IIIb*. Rangoon: Burma Book Club.

———. 1934b. *State Pawnshops in Netherlands India: Studies in the Social and Economic Development of the Netherlands East Indies IIIc*. Rangoon: Burma Book Club.

———. 1939. *Netherlands India: A Study of Plural Economy*. Cambridge: Cambridge University Press.

Gambling, Trevor, and R. A. Karim. 1991. *Business and Accounting Ethics in Islam*. London: Mansell.

Ganguly, M. 2001. A banking system built for terrorism. *Time Magazine*, October 5.

Geertz, Clifford. 1973. The *Interpretation of Cultures*. New York: Basic Books.

———. 2000. *Available Light: Anthropological Reflections on Philosophical Topics*. Princeton: Princeton University Press.

Geertz, Hildred, and Clifford Geertz. 1975. *Kinship in Bali*. Chicago: University of Chicago Press.

Gell, Alfred. 1998. *Art and Agency: An Anthropological Theory*. Oxford: Clarendon.

Giblett, Rod. 1996. *Postmodern Wetlands: Culture, History, Ecology*. Edinburgh: Edinburgh University Press.

Gibson, Katherine. 2001. Regional subjection and becoming. *Environment and Planning D: Society and Space* 19 (6): 639–67.

Gibson-Graham, J. K. 1995. The economy, stupid! Metaphors of totality and development in economic discourse. *Socialist Review* 25 (3 and 4): 27–63.

———. 1996. *The End of Capitalism (As We Knew It): A Feminist Critique of Political Economy*. Oxford: Blackwell.

Giddens, Anthony. 1990. *The Consequences of Modernity*. Cambridge: Polity Press.

Glover, Paul. N.d. *Hometown Money: How to Enrich Your Community with Local Currency*. Ithaca, N.Y. Copy in author's possession.

Goux, Jean-Joseph. 1973. *Freud, Marx: Economie et symbolique*. Paris: Editions du Seuil.

———. 1990. *Symbolic Economies: After Marx and Freud*. Translated by Jennifer Curtiss Gage. Ithaca: Cornell University Press.

Graeber, David. 2001. *Toward an Anthropological Theory of Value: The False Coin of Our Own Dreams.* New York: Palgrave.

Granovetter, Mark. 1985. Economic action and social structure: The problem of embeddedness. *American Journal of Sociology* 91:481–510.

Gregory, C. A. 1997. *Savage Money: The Anthropology and Politics of Commodity Exchange.* Amsterdam: Harwood Academic Publishers.

Greider, William. 1997. *One World, Ready or Not: The Manic Logic of Global Capitalism.* New York: Simon and Schuster.

Grosz, Elizabeth. 2000. Deleuze's Bergson: Duration, the virtual, and a politics of the future. In *Deleuze and Feminist Theory,* edited by Ian Buchanan and Claire Colebrook, pp. 214–34. Edinburgh: Edinburgh University Press.

Gunardi, Harry Seldadyo. 1994. *Kredit untuk rakyat: dari mekanisms arisan hingga BPR.* Bandung: Akatiga.

Gupta, Akhil, and James G. Ferguson, eds. 1997. *Culture, Power, Place: Explorations in Critical Anthropology.* Durham, N.C.: Duke University Press.

Hacking, Ian. 1977. *The Emergence of Probability.* Cambridge: Cambridge University Press.

———. 1990. *The Taming of Chance.* Cambridge: Cambridge University Press.

Hafidhuddin, K. H. Didin. 1998. *Tentang zakat, infak, sedekah.* Jakarta: Gema Insani.

Hallaq, Wael. 1997. *A History of Islamic Legal Theories.* Cambridge: Cambridge University Press.

Haneef, Mohamed Aslam. 1995. *Contemporary Islamic Economic Thought.* Kuala Lumpur: Ikraq.

Haraway, Donna. 2003. *The Companion Species Manifesto: Dogs, Humans, and Significant Otherness.* Chicago: Prickly Paradigm Press.

Hardt, Michael, and Antonio Negri. 2001. *Empire.* Cambridge: Harvard University Press.

Haroon, Sudin. 2000. The philosophy of Islamic banking. In *Anthology of Islamic Banking,* edited by Asma Siddiqi, pp. 55–58. London: Institute for Islamic Banking and Insurance.

Hart, Keith. 1986. Heads or tails? Two sides of the coin. *Man* n.s., 21:637–56.

———. 2000. *The Memory Bank: Money in an Unequal World.* London: Profile Books.

———. 2001. *Money in an Unequal World.* New York: Texere.

Harvey, David. 1989. *The Condition of Postmodernity.* Oxford: Blackwell.

Hasan, M. Ali. 1996. *Zakat, pajak, asuransi dan lembaga keuangan.* Jakarta: PT Raja-Grafindo Persada.

Hayek, Friedrich. 1976. *Denationalisation of Money.* London: Institute of Economic Affairs.

Hefner, Robert. 1996. Islamizing capitalism: On the founding of Indonesia's first Islamic bank. In *Toward a New Paradigm: Recent Developments in Indonesian Islamic Thought,* edited by Mark Woodward and James Rush, pp. 291–322. Tempe: Center for Southeast Asian Studies, Arizona State University.

———. 1998. Markets and justice for Muslim Indonesians. In *Market Cultures: Society and Values in the New Asian Capitalisms,* edited by Robert Hefner, pp. 224–50. Boulder, Colo.: Westview Press.

Heidegger, Martin. 1949. On the Essence of Truth. In *Existence and Being,* edited by Werner Brock, pp. 292–324. Chicago: Henry Regnery Co.

Helleiner, Eric. 1994. *States and the Reemergence of Global Finance: From Bretton Woods to the 1990s*. Ithaca: Cornell University Press.

———. 1999. Conclusion: The future of national currencies? In *Nation-States and Money: The Past, Present, and Future of National Currencies*, edited by E. Gilbert and E. Helleiner, pp. 215–29. London: Routledge.

———. 2003. *The Making of National Money: Territorial Currencies in Historical Perspective*. Ithaca: Cornell University Press.

Hentzi, Gary. 1993. "An itch of gaming": The South Sea Bubble and the novels of Daniel Defoe. *Eighteenth-Century Life* 17:32–45.

Hershey, Robert. 1996. Nintendo capitalism: Zapping the markets. *New York Times*, May 28, pp.C1, C8.

Herzfeld, Michael. 1992. *The Social Production of Indifference: Exploring the Symbolic Roots of Western Bureaucracy*. New York: St. Martin's Press.

Hirsch, Eric. 2000. Cooperation between Islamic and conventional banks. In *Anthology of Islamic Banking*, edited by Asma Siddiqi, pp. 114–17. London: Institute for Islamic Banking and Insurance.

Hirschkind, Charles. 2001. Religious reason and civic virtue: An Islamic counterpublic. *Cultural Anthropology* 16 (1): 3–34.

Hirschman, A. O. 1977. *The Passions and the Interests*. Princeton: Princeton University Press.

Hopkins, Jasper. 1980. *A Concise Introduction to the Philosophy of Nicholas of Cusa*. Minneapolis: University of Minnesota Press.

Huntington, Samuel. 1996. *The Clash of Civilizations and the Remaking of the World Order*. New York: Simon and Schuster.

Husein, Rachmat. 1997. Asuransi takaful selayang pandang. In *Wawasan Islam dan ekonomi: sebua bunga rampai*, edited by Mustafa Kamal, pp. 235–41. Jakarta: Lambaga Penerbit Fakultas Ekonomi, Universitas Indonesia.

Ingrassia, Catherine. 1995. The pleasure of business and the business of pleasure: Gender, credit, and the South Sea Bubble. *Studies in Eighteenth-Century Culture* 24:191–210.

Izutsu, Toshihiko. 2002. *Ethico-Religious Concepts in the Qur'an*. Montreal: McGill-Queen's University Press.

Jacob, Margaret C. 2001. Factoring Mary Poovey's *A History of the Modern Fact*. *History and Theory* 40: 280–89.

Jakobson, Roman. 1956. Two aspects of language and two types of aphasic disturbances. *In Fundamentals of Language*, by Roman Jakobson and Morris Halle, pp. 55–82. The Hague: Mouton.

———. 1990. *On Language*. Edited by Linda R. Waugh and Monique Monville-Burston. Cambridge: Harvard University Press.

Jaspers, Karl. 1957. *Anselm and Nicholas of Cusa*. New York: Harcourt Brace Jovanovich.

Jennings, Patrice. 1992. *Barter Networks, Local Currencies, and Community Development: Ithaca, NY, a Case Study*. Plainfield, Vt.: Goddard College. Copy in author's possession.

Jonsen, Albert, and Stephen Toulmin. 1988. *The Abuse of Casuistry: A History of Moral Reasoning*. Berkeley and Los Angeles: University of California Press.

Jureidini, R., and K. White. 2000. Life insurance, the medical examination and cultural values. *Journal of Historical Sociology* 13 (2): 190–214.

Kamal, Mustafa, ed. 1997. *Wawasan Islam dan Ekonomi: Sebua Bunga Rampai*. Jakarta: Lambaga Penerbit Fakultas Ekonomi, Universitas Indonesia.

Kamali, Mohammad Hashim. 1996. Islamic commercial law: An analysis of futures. *American Journal of Islamic Social Sciences* 13 (2): 197–225.

————.1997. Islamic commercial law: An analysis of options. *American Journal of Islamic Social Sciences* 14 (3): 17–39.

————.1999. Prospects for an Islamic derivatives market in Malaysia. *Thunderbird International Business Review* 41 (4 and 5): 523–40.

Kant, Immanuel. 2003. *Critique of Pure Reason*. Edited and translated by Norman Kemp Smith. London: Palgrave Macmillan.

Karpenko, Vladimir. 1993. Between magic and science: Numerical magic squares. *Ambix* 40 (3): 121–28.

Keane, Webb. 1996. Money as matter and sign. *Etnofoor* 9 (1): 71–81.

————. 1997. *Signs of Recognition: Power and Hazards of Representation in an Indonesian Society*. Berkeley and Los Angeles: University of California Press.

————. 2003a. Semiotics and the social analysis of material things. *Language and Communication* 23: 409–25.

————. 2003b. Self-interpretation, agency, and the objects of anthropology: Reflections on a genealogy. *Comparative Studies in Society and History* 45: 222–48.

Keenan, James. 1996. The return of casuistry. *Theological Studies* 57: 123–39.

Keenan, Thomas. 1993. The point is to (ex)change it: Reading *Capital*, rhetorically. In *Fetishism as Cultural Discourse*, edited by Emily Apter and William Pietz, pp. 152–85. Ithaca: Cornell University Press.

Kennedy, Margrit. 1995. *Interest and Inflation Free Money*. East Lansing, Mich.: Seva International.

Ketner, Kenneth Laine, and James Edward Cook, eds. 1975. *Charles Sanders Peirce: Contributions to "The Nation."* Lubbock: Texas Tech Press.

Keynes, John Maynard. [1935] 1964. *The General Theory of Employment, Interest, and Money*. New York: Harcourt, Brace and Co.

Khalidi, Tarif. 1994. *Arabic Historical Thought in the Classical Period*. Cambridge: Cambridge University Press.

Khan, Muhammad Akram. 1999. *An Introduction to Islamic Economics*. New Delhi: Kitab Bhavan.

al-Khwarizmi, Muhammad ibn Musa. 1831. *The Algebra of Mohammed ben Musa (Compendium on Calculating by Completion and Reduction)*. Translated by Frederic Rosen. London: Oriental Translation Fund.

Kindleberger, Charles P. 1984. *A Financial History of Western Europe*. London: Allen and Unwin.

Kittel, Gerhard, ed. 1967. *Theological Dictionary of the New Testament*. Translated and edited by Geoffrey W. Bromiley. Grand Rapids, Mich.: William B. Eerdmans Publishing Co.

Knight, Frank. 1933. *Risk, Uncertainty, and Profit*. New York: Kelley and Millman.

Knights, D., and T. Vurdubakis. 1993. Calculations of risk: Towards an understanding of insurance as a moral and political technology. *Accounting, Organizations and Society* 18 (7 and 8): 729–64.

The Koran, with Parallel Arabic Text. 2000. Translated by N. J. Dawood. London: Penguin Books.

Kuran, Timur. 1986. The economic system in contemporary Islamic thought: Interpretation and assessment. *International Journal of Middle East Studies* 18: 135–64.

———. 1995. Islamic economics and the Islamic subeconomy. *Journal of Economic Perspectives* 9:155–73.

———. 1996. The discontents of Islamic economic morality. *American Economic Review* 86:438–42.

———. 1997. The genesis of Islamic economics: A chapter in the politics of Muslim identity. *Social Research* 64 (2): 301–37.

———. 2001. Comment: Speculations on Islamic financial alternatives. *Anthropology Today* 17 (3): 28–29.

Laanen, Jan T. M van. 1990. Between the Java bank and the Chinese moneylender: Banking and credit in colonial Indonesia. In *Indonesian Economic History in the Dutch Colonial Era*, edited by Anne Booth, W. J. O'Malley, and Anna Weidemann. Yale University Southeast Asia Studies monograph 35. New Haven: Yale Center for International Area Studies.

Lash, S. 1994. Reflexivity and doubles: Structure, aesthetics, community. In *Reflexive Modernization: Politics, Tradition and Aesthetics in the Modern Social Order*, edited by U. Beck, A. Giddens, S. Lash, pp. 110–73. Cambridge: Polity Press.

Latour, Bruno. 1992. *We Have Never Been Modern*. Cambridge: Harvard University Press.

———. 1999. *Pandora's Hope: Essays on the Reality of Science Studies*. Cambridge: Harvard University Press.

Lave, Jean. 1991. *Cognition in Practice: Mind, Mathematics, and Culture in Everyday Life*. Cambridge: Cambridge University Press.

Lee, Benjamin, and Edward LiPuma. 2002. Cultures of circulation: The imaginations of modernity. *Public Culture* 14 (1): 191–213.

Lee, R. 1996. Moral money? LETS and the social construction of local economic geographies in Southeast England. *Environment and Planning* A 28: 1377–94.

Leenhardt, Maurice. 1947. *Do Kamo: La personne et le mythe dans le monde Mélanésien*. Paris: Gallimard.

———. 1979. *Do Kamo: Person and Myth in the Melanesian World*. Translated by Basia Miller Gulati, Chicago: University of Chicago Press.

Lévi-Strauss, Claude. 1963. *Totemism*. Translated by Rodney Needham. Boston: Beacon Press.

———. 1969. *Elementary Structures of Kinship*. Translated by James Harle Bell, John Richard von Sturmer, and Rodney Needham. Boston: Beacon Press.

Lewis, Mervyn K. 2001. Islam and accounting. *Accounting Forum* 25 (2): 103–27.

Leyshon, Andrew, and Nigel Thrift. 1997. *Money/Space: Geographies of Monetary Transformation*. London: Routledge.

Lie, Anita. 1999. *Metode pembelajaran gotong-royong*. Surabaya: Citra Media.

Locke, John. 1975. *An Essay Concerning Human Understanding*. Oxford: Clarendon.

Loe, Leo Hadi. 1997. Country case study: Indonesia. Paper presented at the World Gold Council annual conference, Prague. Available at <http://www.gold.org/Wgc/Sp/Y97/LHL.htm>, last accessed August 6, 2001.

Lubiano, Wahneema. 1999. Yeah, and I'm scared too. *Boundary* 2 26 (3): 13–17.

Lukács, Georg 1971 *History and Class Consciousness: Studies in Marxist Dialectics.* Translated by Rodney Livingstone. London: Merlin Press.

Lupiyoadi, Rambat. 1997. Konsep asuransi: Wacana Islam dan kapitalis. In *Wawasan Islam dan Ekonomi: Sebua Bunga Rampai*, edited by Mustafa Kamal, pp. 243–52. Jakarta: Lambaga Penerbit Fakultas Ekonomi, Universitas Indonesia.

Lynch, Michael. 1993. *Scientific Practice and Ordinary Action: Ethnomethodology and Social Studies of Science.* Cambridge: Cambridge University Press.

MacIntyre, Alasdair. 1984. *After Virtue: A Study in Moral Theory.* Notre Dame, Ind.: University of Notre Dame Press.

———. 1989. *Whose Justice? Which Rationality?* Notre Dame, Ind.: University of Notre Dame Press.

Mahmood, Saba. 2001. Feminist theory, embodiment, and the docile agent: Some reflections on the Egyptian Islamic revival. *Cultural Anthropology* 16(2): 202–36.

Marcus, George. 1998. *Ethnography through Thick and Thin.* Princeton: Princeton University Press.

———. 1999. The uses of complicity in the changing mise-en-scène of anthropological fieldwork. In *The Fate of "Culture": Geertz and Beyond*, edited by Sherry Ortner, pp. 86–109. Berkeley and Los Angeles: University of California Press.

Martin, Jeremy. 2000. Enhancing the competitiveness of Islamic banks. In *Anthology of Islamic Banking*, edited by Asma Siddiqi, pp. 111–13. London: Institute for Islamic Banking and Insurance.

Marx, Karl. [1844]. 1977. *Economic and Philosophic Manuscripts.* In *Karl Marx, Selected Writings*, edited by David McLellan, pp. 75–112. Oxford: Oxford University Press.

———. [1865–66]. 1997. *Capital*, selections from vols. 1 and 3. In *Karl Marx, Selected Writings*, edited by David McLellan, pp. 414–507. Oxford: Oxford University Press.

———. 1967. *Capital.* Vol. 3. New York: International Publishers.

———. 1976. *Capital.* Vol. 1. London: Penguin Books.

Maududi, Maulana. 1975. *The Economic Problem of Man and Its Islamic Solution.* Lahore: Islamic Publications.

Maurer, Bill. 1995. Complex subjects: Offshore finance, complexity theory and the dispersion of the modern. *Socialist Review* 25 (3 and 4): 113–45.

———. 1997. *Recharting the Caribbean: Land, Law and Citizenship in the British Virgin Islands.* Ann Arbor: University of Michigan Press.

———. 2000. A fish story: Rethinking globalization on Virgin Gorda, British Virgin Islands. *American Ethnologist* 27 (3): 670–701.

———. 2001a. Engineering an Islamic future: Speculations on Islamic financial alternatives. *Anthropology Today* 17 (1): 8–11.

———. 2001b. Comment:. Speculations on Islamic financial alternatives. *Anthropology Today* 17 (3): 28–29.

———. 2001c. Visions of fact, languages of evidence: History, memory and the trauma of legal research. *Law and Social Inquiry* 26 (4): 893–909.

———. 2002a. Section news. *Association for Political and Legal Anthropology. Anthropology News* 43 (7) (October).

———. 2002b. Repressed futures: Financial derivatives' theological unconscious. *Economy and Society* 31(1): 15–16.

———. 2002c. Anthropological and accounting knowledge in Islamic banking and finance: Rethinking critical accounts. *Journal of the Royal Anthropological Institute*, n.s., 8 (4): 645–67.

———. 2003. Redecorating the international economy: Keynes, Grant, and the queering of Bretton Woods. In *Queer Globalizations: Citizenship and the Afterlife of Colonialism*, edited by A. Cruz-Malave and M. Manalansan, pp. 100–33. New York: New York University Press.

———. 2004a. Finance. In *Handbook of Economic Anthropology*, edited by James Carrier. London: Edward Elgar, in press.

———. 2004b. On divine markets and the problem of justice: *Empire as Theodicy*, in Empire's New Clothes, edited by Paul Passavant and Jodi Dean, pp. 57–72. New York: Routledge.

Mauss, Marcel. 1990. *The Gift: The Form and Reason for Exchange in Archaic Societies*. Translated by W. D. Halls. New York: W. W. Norton.

McCloskey, Deirdre N. 1998. *The Rhetoric of Economics*. 2d edition. Madison: University of Wisconsin Press.

Melville, Herman. 1997. Bartleby, the Scrivener, a Story of Wall Street. In *Billy Budd, Sailor, and Selected Tales*, edited by Robert Milder, pp. 3–41. Oxford: Oxford University Press.

Menocal, Maria Rosa. 1990. Love and mercy at the edge of madness: Ramon Llull's *Book of the Lover and the Beloved* and Ibn 'Arabi's "O doves of the arâk and the bân trees . . . ". *Catalan Review* 4 (1 and 2):155–78.

Michaels, Walter Benn. 1987. *The Gold Standard and the Logic of Naturalism*. Berkeley and Los Angeles: University of California Press.

Miller, Daniel. 1998. Conclusion: A theory of virtualism. In *Virtualism: A New Political Economy*, edited by James G. Carrier and Daniel Miller, pp. 187–215. Oxford: Berg.

Mills, Paul S., and John R. Presley. 1999. *Islamic Finance: Theory and Practice*. New York: Palgrave.

Mimica, Jadran. 1988. *Intimations of Infinity: The Mythopoeia of the Iqwaye Counting System and Number*. Oxford: Berg.

Mirowski, Philip. 1987. Shall I compare thee to a Minkowski-Ricardo-Leontief-Metzler matrix of the Mosaks-Hicks type? Or, rhetoric, mathematics, and the nature of neoclassical economic theory. *Economics and Philosophy* 3:67–96.

———. 1989. The probabilistic counter-revolution, or how stochastic concepts came to neoclassical economic theory. *Oxford Economic Papers* 41:217–35.

Mitchell, Timothy. 1998. Fixing the economy. *Cultural Studies* 12 (1): 82–101.

———. 2002. *Rule of Experts: Egypt, Techno-Politics, Modernity*. Berkeley and Los Angeles: University of California Press.

Miyazaki, Hirokazu. 2003. The temporalities of the market. *American Anthropologist* 105 (2): 255–65.

———. 2004. *The Method of Hope*. Stanford, Calif.: Stanford University Press.

Moehammad, Goenawan. 1997. *Metodologi ilmu ekonomi islam*. Yogyakarta: UII Press.

Mourant, John A. 1964. *Introduction to the Philosophy of Saint Augustine: Selected Readings and Commentaries*. University Park: Pennsylvania State University.

Muamalat Institute. 1999. *Perbankan syriah: perspektif praktisi*. Jakarta: Muamalat Institute.

Muhamad. 2000. *Prinsip-prinsip akuntansi dalam Alquran*. Yogyakarta: UII Press.

Muhammad, Cedric. 1998. Toward an Islamic gold standard. *Final Call*, January 6 and 20.

Munn, Nancy. 1986. *The Fame of Gawa: A Symbolic Study of Value Transformation in a Massim (Papua New Guinea) Society*. Cambridge: Cambridge University Press.

Muslehuddin, Mohammad. 1995. *Asuransi dalam Islam*. Translated by Wardana. Jakarta: Bumi Aksara, originally published by the Islamic Foundation, Leicester.

Naylor, R. T. 1996. The underworld of gold. *Crime, Law and Social Change* 25 (3): 191–241.

Nelson, Benjamin. 1969. *The Idea of Usury: From Tribal Brotherhood to Universal Otherhood*. Chicago: University of Chicago Press.

Nelson, Diane. 1999. *A Finger in the Wound: Body Politics in Quincentennial Guatemala*. Berkeley and Los Angeles: University of California Press.

North, Peter. 1999. Explorations in heterotopia: Local exchange and trading schemes (LETS) and the micropolitics of money and livelihood. *Environment and Planning D: Society and Space* 17:69–86.

Obaidullah, Mohammed. 2000. Introduction to Part III: Islamic Finance. *Proceedings of the Fourth Harvard University Forum on Islamic Finance*, pp. 131–33.

O'Brian, S. 1999. Pilgrimage, power and identity: The role of the haj in the lives of Nigerian hausi bori adepts. *Africa Today* 46(3 and 4): 11–40.

O'Doherty, R.K., J. Dürrschmidt, P. Jowers, and D. A. Purdue. 1999. Local exchange and trading schemes: A useful strand of community economic development policy? *Environment and Planning A* 31:1639–53.

Olsson, Gunnar. 1980. *Birds in Egg/Eggs in Bird*. London: Pion.

O'Malley, Pat. 1999. Imagining insurance: Risk, thrift and industrial life insurance in Britain. *Connecticut Insurance Law Journal* 5: 675–706.

———. 2000. Uncertain subjects: Risks, liberalism and contract. *Economy and Society* 29 (4): 460–84.

Pandolfo, Stefania. 1997. *Impasse of the Angels*. Chicago: University of Chicago Press.

Park, Katharine, and Lorraine Daston. 1981. Unnatural conceptions: The study of monsters in sixteenth- and seventeenth-century France and England. *Past and Present* 92:20–54.

Patton, Paul. 2000. *Deleuze and the Political*. London: Routledge.

Peirce, Charles S. 1932. *Collected Papers of Charles Sanders Peirce*. Edited by Paul Hartshorne and Paul Weiss. Cambridge: Harvard University Press.

Pfohl, Stephen. 1992. *Death at the Parasite Café: Social Science (Fictions) and the Postmodern*. New York: St. Martin's Press.

Pietz, William. 1985. The problem of the fetish, I. Res 9:5–17.

Polanyi, Karl. 1957. *The Great Transformation: Origins of Our Time*. Boston: Beacon Press.

Pomeranz, Felix. 1997. The accounting and auditing organization for Islamic financial institutions: An important regulatory debut. *Journal of International Accounting, Auditing and Taxation* 6 (1): 123–30.

Ponzio, Augusto. 1993. *Signs, Dialogue and Ideology.* Edited and translated by Susan Petrilli. Amsterdam and Philadelphia: J. Benjamins.

Poovey, Mary. 1998. *A History of the Modern Fact: Problems of Knowledge in the Sciences of Wealth and Society.* Chicago: University of Chicago Press.

———. 2001. The twenty-first-century university and the market: What price economic viability? *differences* 12 (1): 1–16.

Posner, Richard. 1977. *The Economic Analysis of Law.* Boston: Little, Brown.

Postone, Moishe. 1993. *Time, Labor, and Social Domination: A Reinterpretation of Marx's Critical Theory.* Cambridge: Cambridge University Press.

Prawiranegara, Sjafruddin. 1988. *Ekonomi dan keuangan makna ekonomi Islam.* Jakarta: CV Haji Masagung.

Presley, John, and John Sessions. 2000. Islamic economics: The emergence of a new paradigm. In *Anthology of Islamic Banking,* edited by Asma Siddiqi, pp. 131–33. London: Institute for Islamic Banking and Insurance.

Putnam, Hilary. 1983. *How Not to Solve Ethical Problems.* The Lindley Lecture. Lawrence: Department of Philosophy, University of Kansas.

———. 1996. The meaning of "meaning." In *The Twin Earth Chronicles,* edited by Andrew Pessin and Sanford Goldberg, pp. 3–52. Armonk, N.Y.: M. E. Sharpe.

Qayum, Khaled. 2000. Islamic banking: Scope and challenges. In *Anthology of Islamic Banking,* edited by Asma Siddiqi, pp. 77–82. London: Institute for Islamic Banking and Insurance.

Qureshi, Anwar Iqbal. 1946. *Islam and the Theory of Interest.* Lahore: Shaikh Muhammad Ashraf.

Radin, Margaret Jane. 1993. *Reinterpreting Property.* Chicago: University of Chicago Press.

Rahardjo, M. Dawam. 1988. The question of Islamic banking in Indonesia. In *Islamic Banking in Southeast Asia,* edited by Mohamed Ariff, pp. 137–63. Singapore: Institute of Southeast Asian Studies.

Rahman, Fazlur. 1982. *Islam and Modernity.* Chicago: University of Chicago Press.

Ricardo, David. [1817] 1975. *On the Principles of Political Economy and Taxation.* Cambridge: Cambridge University Press.

RI Departemen Agama. 2000. *Laporan dan evaluasi penyelenggaraan ibadah haji embarkasi/debarkasi Hasanuddin Makassar tahun 1420H/2000M.* Makassar.

Riles, Annelise. 2000. *The Network Inside-Out.* Ann Arbor: University of Michigan Press.

———. 2004. Real time: Unwinding technocratic and anthropological knowledge. *American Ethnologist* 31 (3): 392–405.

Ritter, Gretchen. 1997. *Goldbugs and Greenbacks: The Antimonopoly Tradition and the Politics of Finance, 1865–1896.* New York: Cambridge University Press.

Rorty, Richard. 1991. Essays on Heidegger and Others. *In Philosophical Papers,* vol. 2. Cambridge: Cambridge University Press.

Rose, Nikolas. 1996. The death of the social? Reconfiguring the territory of government. *Economy and Society* 25 (3): 327–56.

Rossi-Landi, Ferruccio. 1977. *Linguistics and Economics.* The Hague: Mouton.

Rotman, Bryan. 1987. *Signifying Nothing.* Stanford, Calif.: Stanford University Press.

Rutherford, Danilyn. 2001. Intimacy and alienation: Money and the foreign in Biak. *Public Culture* 13 (2): 299–324.

Saeed, Abdullah. 1999. *Islamic Banking and Interest: A Study of the Prohibition of Riba and Its Contemporary Interpretation*. Leiden: Brill.

Saleh, Nabil A. 1986. *Unlawful Gain and Legitimate Profit in Islamic Law*. Cambridge: Cambridge University Press.

Salzman, Philip Carl. 2003. Fact and value in Islamic banking and anthropology. *Anthropology News* 44 (1) (January).

Al-Saud, HRH Prince Mohammed Al-Faisal. 2000. A state of trusteeship. In *Anthology of Islamic Banking*, edited by Asma Siddiqi, pp. 3–5. London: Institute for Islamic Banking and Insurance

Saussure, Ferdinand de. 1966. *Course in General Linguistics*. Edited by Charles Bally and Albert Sechelhaye in collaboration with Albert Riedlinger, translated by Wade Baskin. New York: McGraw Hill.

Schlecker, Markus, and Eric Hirsch. 2000. Incomplete knowledge: Ethnography and the crisis of context in studies of media, science and technology. *History of the Human Sciences* 14 (1): 69–87.

Schwartz, Hillel. 1996. *The Culture of the Copy: Striking Likenesses, Unreasonable Facsimiles*. New York: Zone Books.

Shapin, Steven, and Simon Schaffer. 1985. *Leviathan and the Air Pump: Hobbes, Boyle and the Experimental Life*. Princeton: Princeton University Press.

Shapiro, Barbara. 1991. *"Beyond Reasonable Doubt" and "Probable Cause": Historical Perspectives on the Anglo-American Law of Evidence*. Berkeley and Los Angeles: University of California Press.

Shell, Marc. 1978. *The Economy of Literature*. Baltimore: Johns Hopkins University Press.

———. 1982. *Money, Language and Thought*. Berkeley and Los Angeles: University of California Press.

———. 1995. *Art and Money*. Chicago: University of Chicago Press.

Sherman, Sandra. 1996. *Finance and Fictionality in the Early-Eighteenth Century: Accounting for Defoe*. Cambridge: Cambridge University Press.

Shore, Cris, and Susan Wright. 1999. Audit culture and anthropology: Neo-liberalism in British higher education. *Journal of the Royal Anthropological Institute* 5 (4): 557–75.

Siddiqi, Asma, ed. 2000. *Anthology of Islamic Banking*. London: Institute of Islamic Banking and Insurance.

Siddiqi, Muhammad Nejatullah. 1983. *Issues in Islamic Banking*. Leicester: Islamic Foundation.

———. 1985. *Insurance in an Islamic Economy*. Leicester, U.K.: Islamic Foundation.

———. 1999. Introduction. In *Proceedings of the Third Harvard University Forum on Islamic Finance: Local Challenges, Global Opportunities*, pp. 3–5. Cambridge: Harvard Islamic Finance Information Program.

Siegel, James T. 1998. *A New Criminal Type in Jakarta: Counter-revolution Today*. Durham, N.C.: Duke University Press.

———. 1997. *Fetish, Recognition, Revolution*. Princeton: Princeton University Press.

Silverstein, Michael. 1976. Shifters, linguistic categories, and cultural description. In *Meaning in Anthropology*, edited by Keith Basso and Henry Selby. Albuquerque: University of New Mexico Press.

———. 1998. The uses and utility of ideology: A commentary. In *Language Ideology: Practice and Theory*. Edited by Bambi Schieffelin, Kathryn Woolard, and Paul Kroskrity, pp. 123–45. Oxford: Oxford University Press.

Simmel, Georg. [1907] 1990. *The Philosophy of Money*. Edited by David Frisby, 2d ed. London: Routledge.

Simon, Jonathan. 1988. The ideological effects of actuarial practices. *Law and Society Review* 22: 771–800.

Smirnov, Andrey V. 1993. Nicholas of Cusa and Ibn 'Arabi: Two philosophies of mysticism. *Philosophy East and West* 43 (1): 65–85.

Smith, Adam. [1776] 1976. *An Inquiry into the Nature and Causes of the Wealth of Nations*. New York: Penguin.

Smith, Duncan. 2000. Islamic finance—past, present and future. In *Anthology of Islamic Banking*, edited by Asma Siddiqi, pp. 97–101. London: Institute for Islamic Banking and Insurance

Sohn-Rethel, Alfred. 1978. *Intellectual and Manual Labor: A Critique of Epistemology*. Atlantic Highlands, N.J.: Humanities Press.

Solomon, Lewis D. 1996. *Rethinking Our Centralized Money System: The Case for a System of Local Currencies*. Westport, Conn.: Praeger.

Soros, George. 1998. *The Crisis of Global Capitalism: Open Society Endangered*. New York: BBS/Public Affairs.

Sperber, Dan. 1975. *Rethinking Symbolism*. Translated by A. L. Morton. Cambridge: Cambridge University Press.

Stark, David. 2002. The economic sociology of value. Paper presented at the conference "Empire of Economics," New York University, May 22–24.

Stern, Gustav. 1931. *Meaning and Change of Meaning*. Bloomington: Indiana University Press.

Strange, Susan. 1986. *Casino Capitalism*. Oxford: Blackwell.

Strathern, Marilyn. 1984. Marriage exchanges: A Melanesian comment. *Annual Review of Anthropology* 13:41–73.

———. 1988. *The Gender of the Gift: Problems with Women and Problems with Society in Melanesia*. Berkeley and Los Angeles: University of California Press.

———. 1991. *Partial Connections*. Savage, Md.: Rowman and Littlefield, Publishers.

———. 1992a. *After Nature: English Kinship in the Late-Twentieth Century*. London: Routledge.

———. 1992b. Qualified value: The perspective of gift exchange. In *Barter, Exchange and Value: An Anthropological Approach*, edited by Caroline Humphrey and Stephen Hugh-Jones, pp. 169–91. Cambridge: Cambridge University Press.

———. 1999. *Property, Substance and Effect: Anthropological Essays on Persons and Things*. London: Althone Press.

Sullivan, Norma. 1994. *Masters and Managers: A Study of Gender Relations in Urban Java*. St. Leonard's, N.S.W.: Allen and Unwin.

Sumitro, Warkum. 1996. *Asas-asas perbankan Islam dan lembaga-lembaga terkait (bamui dan takaful) di Indonesia*. Jakarta: PT RajaGrafindo Persada.

Sykes, Karen. 2003. My aim is true: Postnostalgic reflections on the future of anthropological science. *American Ethnologist* 30 (1): 156–68.

Taussig, Michael. 1980. *The Devil and Commodity Fetishism in South America*. Chapel Hill: University of North Carolina Press.

Taylor, Charles. 1987. Interpretation and the sciences of man. In *Interpretative Social Science: A Second Look*, edited by Paul Rabinow and William Sullivan, pp. 33–81. Berkeley and Los Angeles: University of California Press.

———. 2002. *Varieties of Religion Today: William James Revisited.* Cambridge: Harvard University Press.

Taylor, Jay. 1998. The Islamic (gold) dinar. *Gold Eagle*, November 30. Available at <http://www.gold-eagle.com/editorials_98/taylor112598.html>, last accessed August 5, 2001.

Thibault, Paul J. 1997. *Re-Reading Saussure: The Dynamics of Signs in Social Life.* London: Routledge.

Thomas, Abdulkader. N.d. Methods of Islamic home finance in the United States: Beneficial breakthroughs. Ms. copy in possession of the author.

Thomas, Brook. 1984. The Legal Fictions of Herman Melville and Lemuel Shaw. *Critical Inquiry* 11:24–51.

Thorne, L. 1996. Local exchange and trading systems in the United Kingdom: A case of re-embedding? *Environment and Planning* A 28: 1361–76.

Thrift, Nigel. 1996. Shut up and dance, or, is the world economy knowable? In *The Global Economy in Transition*, edited by P. Daniels and W. Lever, pp. 11–23. London: Longman.

———. 2000. Afterwords. *Environment and Planning D: Society and Space* 18:213–55.

Torrey, Charles C. 1892. *The Commercial-Theological Terms in the Koran.* Leiden: E. J. Brill.

Tsing, Anna. 2000. Inside the economy of appearances. *Public Culture* 12 (1): 115–44.

Turner, Bryan. 1986. Simmel, rationalisation and the sociology of money. *Sociological Review* 34 (1): 93–114.

Urton, Gary. 1997. *The Social Life of Numbers: A Quecha Ontology of Numbers and Philosophy of Arithmetic.* Austin: University of Texas Press.

Urvoy, Dominique 1990. La place de Ramon Llull dans la pensée arabe. *Catalan Review* 4 (1 and 2):201–20.

Useem, Jerry. 2002. Banking on Allah. *Fortune*, Monday, June 10.

Usmani, Muhammad Taqi. 2002. *An Introduction to Islamic Finance.* The Hague: Kluwer Law International.

Verran, Helen. 2001. *Science and an African Logic.* Chicago: University of Chicago Press.

Vogel, Frank, and Samuel L. Hayes III. 1998. *Islamic Law and Finance: Religion, Risk, and Return.* The Hague: Kluwer Law International.

Wagner, Roy. 1975. *The Invention of Culture.* Englewood Cliffs, N.J.: Prentice Hall.

———. 1978. *Lethal Speech: Daribi Myth as Symbolic Obviation.* Ithaca: Cornell University Press.

———. 1986. *Symbols that Stand for Themselves.* Chicago: University of Chicago Press.

———. 2001. *An Anthropology of the Subject: Holographic Worldview in New Guinea and Its Meaning and Significance for the World of Anthropology.* Berkeley and Los Angeles: University of California Press.

Wallace, Mark. 2001. HOUR town. *Harper's Magazine* no. 303, 1818 (November): p. 54.

Warde, Ibrahim. 2000. *Islamic Finance in the Global Economy.* Edinburgh: Edinburgh University Press.

Watt, W. Montgomery. 1974. *The Majesty that Was Islam: The Islamic World, 661–1100.* New York: Praeger.

———. 1990. God's caliph: Qur'anic interpretations and Umayyad claims. In *Early Islam: Collected Articles,* by W. Montgomery Watt, pp. 57–63. Edinburgh: Edinburgh University Press

Watts, Pauline Moffitt. 1992. *Nicolaus Cusanus: A Fifteenth-Century Vision of Man.* Leiden: E. J. Brill.

West, Cornel. 1989. *The American Evasion of Philosophy: A Genealogy of Pragmatism.* Madison: University of Wisconsin Press.

WGC. 1999. Emas ONH: "Go Haj with Gold": A Safer Solution to Fulfill Pilgrimage. World Gold Council working proposal. Typescript, copy in the author's possession.

Whaples, R., and D. Buffum. 1991. Fraternalism, paternalism, the family and the market: Insurance a century ago. *Social Science History* 15 (1): 97–122.

Wiegman, Robyn. 2000. Feminism's apocalyptic futures. *New Literary History* 31 (4): 805–25.

Williams, C. C. 1996. Local exchange and trading systems: A new source of work and credit for the poor and unemployed? *Environment and Planning A* 28: 1395–1415.

Willman, John. 2001. Trail of terrorist dollars that spans the world. *Financial Times,* November 29.

Wilson, Rodney, ed. 1990. *Islamic Financial Markets.* London: Routledge.

Winch, Peter. 1958. *The Idea of a Social Science.* New York: Humanities Press.

Wittgenstein, Ludwig. 1983. *Remarks on the Foundations of Mathematics.* Edited by G. H. von Wright, R. Rhees, and G.E.M. Anscombe. Cambridge: MIT Press.

Woolard, Kathryn. 1998. Introduction: Language ideology as a field of inquiry. In *Language Ideology: Practice and Theory,* edited by Bambi Schieffelin, Kathryn Woolard and Paul Kroskrity, pp. 3–47.

Yusanto, Ismail, Cecep Maskanul Hakim, Zaim Saidi, Abdur-Razzaq Lubis, Umar Ibrahim Vadillo, Mulya Siregar, and Sigit Purnawan Jati. 2001. *Dinar emas: solusi krisis moneter.* Jakarta: SEM Institute, INFID, and Pirac.

Zelizer, Viviana. 1978. Human values and the market: The case of life insurance and death in nineteenth-century America. *American Journal of Sociology* 84 (3): 591–610.

———. 1979. *Morals and Markets: The Development of Life Insurance in the United States.* New York: Columbia University Press.

———. 1997. *The Social Meaning of Money: Pin Money, Paychecks, Poor Relief and Other Currencies.* Princeton: Princeton University Press.

———. 1998. Introduction: How people talk about money. *American Behavioral Scientist* 41 (10): 1373–83.

———. 2000. Fine tuning the Zelizer view. *Economy and Society* 29 (3): 383–89.

Zhan, Mei. 2001. Does it take a miracle? Negotiating knowledges, identities, and communities of traditional Chinese medicine. *Cultural Anthropology* 16 (4): 453–80.

Žižek, Slavoj. 1989. *The Sublime Object of Ideology.* London: Verso.

Žižek, Slavoj. 1995. How did Marx invent the symptom? In *Mapping Ideology*, edited by Slavoj Žižek, pp. 296–331. London: Verso.

————. 2000. Class struggle or postmodernism? Yes, please! In *Contingency, Hegemony, Universality: Contemporary Dialogues on the Left*, by Judith Butler, Ernesto Laclau and Slavoj Žižek, pp. 90–135. London: Verso.

Znoj, Heinzpeter. 1998. Hot money and war debts: Transactional regimes in southwestern Sumatra. *Comparative Studies in Society and History* 40 (2): 193–222.

Zuhri, Muhammad. 1996. *Riba dalam al Qur'an dan masalah perbankan*. Jakarta: PT RajaGrafindo Persada.

Zupančič, Alenka. 1992. A perfect place to die: Theatre in Hitchcock's films. In *Everything You Always Wanted to Know about Lacan but were Afraid to Ask Hitchcock*, edited by Slavoj Žižek, pp. 73–105. London: Verso.

Index

Page references in *italics* indicate an illustration or table.

haji (pilgrimage savings account), 127,
140; *takaful* and, 138
scheme, economic, 46
Schlecker, Markus, 98
Schwartz, Hillel, 104
Second Treatise (Locke), 184n.14
self-referentialism, 123, 132
semangat berkoperasi, 149, 150–51
semiotics, 158–63. *See also* obviation
sentimentalism, conservative, 157, 183n.6
September 11, 2001, events of, 134
Sessions, John, 57
1774 Life Assurance Act, 137
Shafi school of *fiqh*, 73
Shakespeare, William, 112, 115–16, 136,
179n.16
shari'a (law): IBF and, 20, 25, 31, 32, 57, 58,
61–62, 72; sociopolitical origin story of
IBF, 38; supply and demand, law of, 68
Shari'a Supervisory Board (SSB), 105
Shell, Marc: on chrysography, 122, 134;
coins and, 15; and greenbacks, U.S., 129;
monetary information of thought and,
21, 155; on money materializing problem
of adequation, xiii; on sacred/profane dis-
tinctions of Koin Emas ONH, 133; truth
and, xiv
Sherman, Sandra, 118
Shore, Cris, 142
*Short Circuit: Strengthening Local Economies
for Security in an Unstable World* (Douth-
waite), 26
Siddiqi, Asma, 172n.5
Siddiqi, Muhammad Nejatullah, 29, 30, 71,
138, 181n.2
Siegel, James T., 33, 96, 97, 132, 133
Silverstein, Michael, 156
Simmel, George, 6, 134
Simon, Jonathan, 136
SISKOHAT (*Sistem Komputer Haji Terpadu*,
Integrated Pilgrim Computer System),
140
social change, and capitalism, 105
social reality, and anthropology, 7
social science fictions, xiv, 111–15
society, class, 84–85
Socrates, 169n.1
Sohn-Rethel, Alfred, 85, 86–87
solipsism, 85–87, 176n.10
Solomon, Lewis D., 45, 62–63, 67
Soros, George, 3, 170n.3

South Korea, 124
South Sea Company, 116–17, 118, 179n.20
South Sulawesi province, 139–40
Sperber, Dan, 75
SPROUTS!, 47
SSB (Shari'a Supervisory Board), 105
Stählin, Gustav, 180n.3
state governance: currencies and, 4; debts
and, 4; *gotong royong*, 145, 146, 147, 182
nn. 10 and 11; IBF and, 4, 37, 38, 71,
175n.20; *koperasi* (cooperatives) and, 145,
146; paradoxical nature of relation to,
149; political legitimacy issues, 71,
175n.20; sociopolitical origin story of
IBF, 37, 38; *tolong-menolong* (mutual assistance), 145, 146, 149
State v. Livingston Quakenbush, 64
statistics, science of, 182n.4
Stern, Gustav, xiv
Stevens, Mitchell L., 152
stock market, 106, 116–17, 118, 138,
179n.20
Strange, Susan, 6
Strathern, Marilyn: analysis of data and, 6;
bureaucratic forms and, 142; commodification of women and, 184n.15; on equivalencies in barter economy, 101–2; on ethnographic moments, 174n.19;
merography and, 98; models of choice
and, 170n.7; oscillation in alternative currencies and, 75; perspectivalism and, 80,
170n.4; and relationships, Melanesian,
19; temporal prepositions and, 171n.14;
transaction and, 169n.6
Suara Merdeka (periodical), 127, 131
substance, and money, 89–90
substitution, and barter economy, 102,
177n.2
Sukarno, 146, 147
Sullivan, Norma, 127
Summa Theologica (Aquinas), xiv
sunnah, 31, 32
supply and demand, law of, 68
Surabaya Post (periodical), 127, 133
swindling pilgrim case, 131, 134
Sykes, Karen, 16
symbols, 60, 130. *See also* Wagner, Roy
systems, economic, 46. *See also* finance

tabungan haji (pilgrimage savings account),
127, 140